# British Empiricism and Early Political Economy

Gregory King appears on the right in this illustration from *The History of the Coronation of James II and of His Royal Consort Queen Mary*. King wrote most of the book, which was published by T. Newcomb in 1687, but allowed Francis Sandford to identify himself as the author. This is the only known depiction of Gregory King. Courtesy of Washington University Libraries, Department of Special Collections.

# British Empiricism and Early Political Economy

## Gregory King's 1696 Estimates of National Wealth and Population

John A. Taylor

Contributions to the Study of World History, Number 109

PRAEGER

Westport, Connecticut
London

**Library of Congress Cataloging-in-Publication Data**

Taylor, John A., 1942–
British empiricism and early political economy : Gregory King's 1696 estimates of national wealth and population / John A. Taylor.
p. cm.— (Contributions to the study of world history, ISSN 0885–9159 ; no. 109)
Includes bibliographical references and index.
ISBN 0–313–31306–7 (alk. paper)
1. England—Population—History—17th century. 2. Wealth—England—History—17th century. 3. Demography—England—History—17th century. 4. King, Gregory, 1648–1712. I. Title. II. Series.
HB3585.T39 2005
304.6′0942′09032—dc22 2004028057

British Library Cataloguing in Publication Data is available.



Library of Congress Catalog Card Number: 2004028057
ISBN: 0–313–31306–7
ISSN: 0885–9159

First published in 2005

Praeger Publishers, 88 Post Road West, Westport, CT 06881
An imprint of Greenwood Publishing Group, Inc.
www.praeger.com

Printed in the United States of America

The paper used in this book complies with the Permanent Paper Standard issued by the National Information Standards Organization (Z39.48–1984).

10 9 8 7 6 5 4 3 2 1

**Copyright Acknowledgments**

For Masato

# Contents

*Acknowledgments* ix

Chapter 1 Preliminary Remarks 1

Chapter 2 Mathematical Probability and Demographic Prediction 5

Chapter 3 Gregory King: Man of Projects 15

Chapter 4 British Empiricism and Shop Arithmetic 23

Chapter 5 Higher Mathematics and Seventeenth-Century Political Economy 37

Chapter 6 Shop Arithmetic, Conversation, and Projects 49

Chapter 7 Queen Anne's Bounty 61

Chapter 8 Gregory King's Methods of Calculation 67

Chapter 9 What Was Political Arithmetic, Really? 75

Chapter 10 George Chalmers and the Stagnation of Political Arithmetic 83

Chapter 11 Wobbles and Perturbations 91

APPENDICES: REPRINTED DOCUMENTS BY OR ABOUT GREGORY KING 97

*Appendix 1. King's Autobiography* 97

*Appendix 2. King on the Naval Trade of England* 113
*Appendix 3. King's Natural and Political Observations 1696* 125
*Appendix 4. Gregory King's Letter about Queen Anne's Bounty* 157
*Appendix 5. The Life of Gregory King by George Chalmers* 161
*Notes* 169
*Select Bibliography* 181
*Index* 189

# Acknowledgments

Writing this book has been a joy. First of all, it has been a joy to have the assistance and advice of many colleagues. Without them, I could have done nothing. Robert Coulter introduced me to many of the mathematical concepts in this book, undertook the task to tutor me in mathematical probability, encouraged me at every stage, read and reread the chapters, helping especially with Chapters 8 and 11, and made many corrections and improvements throughout. Adam Fox read the manuscript for the publisher just before publication. The book benefited from especially skillful copyediting by Amy Freitag. Deirdre Johnson obtained many rare and obscure materials from distant libraries. Reading this book carefully, Jeremy Rowan contributed valuable revisions. John Simon read this manuscript at various stages, helped me with writing grant proposals, wrote many letters of recommendation for me, fed me delicious lunches, and offered general encouragement and academic advice. Margaret Spufford read the manuscript in 2002, gave me very valuable insights, suggested important sources, and was very kind and supportive. Heather Staines, the History Editor at Greenwood Publishing Group, is the best editor anyone could have—encouraging, interested, patient, and supportive. Ezio Vailati read the manuscript at different stages, carefully corrected grant proposals, and helped me with the prospectus that I sent to the publisher. I thank everyone from the bottom of my heart.

Second, it is a joy to thank the J. William Fulbright Foreign Scholarship Board, the U.S. Department of State, and the Council for International Exchange of Scholars for two Fulbright awards. The first allowed me to lecture in Japan for the academic year from autumn 1999 until spring 2000. I especially thank my splendid colleagues at International Christian University, Tokyo; the University of Tokyo; and Waseda University for the interest they took in this book. Thanks, too, to the University of Tokyo Library for the many Xerox copies that they made from materials in their collections. A second Fulbright award now sends me to lecture and research at Smolny College of Saint Petersburg State University in Russia for the academic year from autumn 2004 until summer 2005. My Russian colleagues have extended a very warm welcome to me.

Third, it has been a joy to read so many wonderful books about the history of seventeenth-century natural philosophy and mathematics. I list them in the bibliography. Many students and even some senior historians have told me that they dislike mathematics. I beg everyone who has such thoughts to give these books a chance. I especially recommend the study of any elementary textbook on mathematical probability.

Finally, I want to say a few words about possibilities for further research on Gregory King. First, scholars should keep an eye out for any papers whatsoever left by George Chalmers. Anyone who finds such papers should look among them carefully for King documents. I continue to believe that Chalmers used King materials that have since disappeared. Second, King was a surveyor, and someone might seek surveying plans and records from his hand. Third, we know that King was connected to Queen Anne's Bounty on one specific occasion. A search of other records might yield information about more connections of that sort.

I have loved writing this book. I hope readers enjoy it, too.

# CHAPTER 1

# Preliminary Remarks

Gregory King (1648–1712) was an engraver, herald, surveyor, and Secretary to the Commissioners for the Public Accounts, but he is best known for two quantitative contributions to political economy. First, he compiled renowned and valuable estimates of the wealth and population of England. Writing in 1696 but calculating for the year 1688, he estimated the population to be approximately five and one-half million. Second, economists associate King with the so-called Law of King or Law of Demand—a significant early insight into the correlation between supply and demand. King's colleague Charles Davenant (1656–1714) published the Law, and some people called it the King-Davenant Law. The Law sounds grand, but it was a simple table that showed how grain prices rose when a harvest fell below expectations.[1]

In this book, I interpret King's 1696 estimates and King's Law in light of the history of statistical science. Statistics is the collection, classification, and interpretation of large amounts of data. For instance, if we look at *Domesday Book*, compiled by servants of King William I after 1085, we see the importance of statistics very clearly. Masses of undigested facts were available to the medieval English government. *Domesday* contained data on approximately 45,000 holdings in about 14,000 identified sites.[2] How to analyze and summarize such data?

King and his contemporaries met the challenge in new ways. Anyone who compares *Domesday* with King's 1696 estimates or King's Law will see that King was clever in his analysis and summary of data. Moreover, the work of some of King's predecessors, in particular, led directly to the development of mathematical probability and inferential statistics. Mathematical probability, the calculation of chances, is among the most valuable techniques that statisticians can employ. They use it to design experiments and, in particular, to do random sampling as accurately and reliably as possible.

The next chapter will argue that the mathematical probability of our own time provides the best context for beginning our interpretation of King's 1696 estimates. Having thus begun a discussion of King's place in the history of statistics, we will then in Chapters 3, 4, 6, and 7 discuss King's career, associates, and analytical work for Queen Anne's Bounty. The Bounty was a royal program to increase the income of poor clergy, and King provided the governors of the Bounty with analysis of their quantitative data. Chapter 6 makes one of this book's most important points: King's participation in a circle of conversation was key to his quantitative methods. Davenant was also a member of the same conversational circle, and King's Law was a casual empirical observation put forth in the conversation of that circle. The Law was similar to tables in a merchants' handbook dedicated to Davenant, I argue. Chapter 8 adds new detail about King's empirical background and simple mathematics. As Chapters 5 and 9 show, King nevertheless also interacted with the higher mathematics of his age. Chapter 10 deals with the nineteenth-century biographer of King and champion of the 1696 estimates, George Chalmers (1742–1825). Chapter 11 argues that King's Law dealt with analytical challenges that were a magnitude greater than those King faced in compiling his 1696 estimates.

Even though previous historians produced a collection of excellent work on King's contributions to political economy, all their opinions need to be reviewed, and some need to be amended. This book largely reaffirms the views of three skillful twentieth-century historians, P. E. Jones, A. V. Judges, and D. V. Glass.[3] They were moderate, careful, admirable scholars, all three, and it will be very hard for anyone who follows them in the twenty-first century to do better work on King's 1696 estimates than they did. Chapter 11 also praises the late Roy Porter's use of King's 1696 data. On the other hand, I contradict some of the conclusions of two other historians, Peter Laslett and Geoffrey Holmes, both of whom are still well known as students of King's 1696 estimates.

Of course, the work of Holmes and Laslett on the 1696 estimates had many good points, no doubt. Laslett was King's great champion in the middle of the twentieth century, recognizing the crucial importance of King's 1696 estimates, bringing them to wide notice, situating them clearly in the bureaucratic and political history of the age, and testing them by comparison with twentieth-century calculations.[4] Holmes also did important research, uncovering, in particular, valuable details of King's biography, research from which my next two chapters have especially benefitted.[5]

Even so, both Laslett's and Holmes's analyses of King's 1696 estimates had defects. I will deal with these defects more at length in the next two chapters; meanwhile, here is a brief summary. Laslett, seeing King as a precursor of subsequent scientific demography, paid too little heed to King's actual methods and presuppositions. Researching these same methods and presuppositions, Holmes recognized that they were not those of twentieth-century economists and demographers, and he therefore dismissed King's data as not scientific, not rigorous. His view of King's data was Laslett's argument inside out. Laslett accepted King's methods with too little caution, and pronounced them modern and scientific, and Holmes denounced them with too great ardor. While Laslett clearly stated King's importance, and while Holmes shed light on King's biography, therefore, neither Holmes nor Laslett shed much light on King's 1696 estimates.

Because of these defects, the work of Holmes and Laslett yielded a stereotype of the 1696 estimates that became commonplace among historians. By this stereotype, King was a mere creature, a paid servant of powerful Tory politicians. The 1696 estimates cannot be viewed as objective, on this interpretation. Instead they were hackwork, endorsing the Tory views, sometimes called the country party views, that England needed peace abroad and strict economy at home; King's estimates gave those views the appearance of quantitative plausibility. This stereotype was damaging for several reasons.

The stereotype was conjecture, not fact. It was never set forth in any great detail for the excellent reason that the sources would not support it. Books like Mario Biagioli's *Galileo Courtier* made fashionable the writing of histories about the social and political careers of leading seventeenth-century contributors to natural science and philosophy; however, the papers available in archives would not support an effort to write a similar book called *Gregory King Courtier.* I carefully read through papers about King in the British Library, and a strong sense of King's personality arose from those papers.[6] In the Public Record Office, I found King's astrological diary and some of his recipes for cooking. Jones, Judges, Glass, Laslett, Holmes, and others had thoroughly researched all that material, nevertheless, and little new remained in either place to be discovered about King. I did discover in Lichfield, King's birthplace, materials that had not been noticed by Glass, Holmes, or the other scholars, and I report on those new materials in Chapter 7. However, nothing in any archive clearly linked King to any fudge of data for a party purpose.

The stereotype also obscured the volume and character of the calculations that King undertook for his 1696 estimates. Not included in the final copy of the 1696 estimates, the calculations were nevertheless extensive. If the 1696 estimates had been hackwork, King would have known his numbers in advance. He would not have needed such lengthy and elaborate calculations as these. Chapter 8 follows some of the calculations in detail, noting their eccentricities, and concludes that King did not tailor his calculations to produce figures known to him in advance.

Above all, the stereotype also obscured the inherent difficulty of King's task as a demographer. Jones, Judges, and Glass clearly laid out these difficulties. They said that King was an honest compiler who worked hard to get the numbers right but whose methods were idiosyncratic, obscure, and at times faulty. Making this basic interpretation of King's estimates myself, I returned to the work of Jones, Judges, and Glass, adding the new King manuscript material that I discovered, and also adding the advances made by very recent historians of seventeenth-century natural philosophy and mathematics. Excellent as the work by Jones, Judges, and Glass was, this new research nevertheless compels reconsideration of some their views.

The stereotype was wrong, in short, and King did the best he could. As I asserted before, the discipline of mathematical probability is the best context for beginning our discussion. We can understand the strengths—and weaknesses—in King's 1696 data by comparing them with demographic estimates produced using the mathematical probability of our own day. Furthermore, these very techniques of mathematical probability are now in a state of crisis. Reviewing the crisis, we will see that the inherent difficulty of their task must warp and twist the estimates of all demographers, not just King's estimates, and we can begin this book with the understanding that King, in his time, struggled honorably and well with limitations that his successors still face.

# CHAPTER 2

# Mathematical Probability and Demographic Prediction

Because world human population has long been rapidly increasing, many policymakers feel considerable alarm at the prospect of yet further increases, but, according to projections by demographers Wolfgang Lutz, Warren Sanderson, and Sergei Scherbov, such alarm is needless, and leaders can now safely base public policy on the assumption that the pace of world population increase will abate in the twenty-first century. Publishing their "welcome news" in the journal *Nature*, the three scholars outlined these population projections:

> Improving on earlier methods of probabilistic forecasting, here we show that there is around an 85 per cent chance that the world's population will stop growing before the end of the century. There is a 60 per cent probability that the world's population will not exceed 10 billion people before 2100, and around a 15 per cent probability that the world's population at the end of the century will be lower than it is today. For different regions, the date and size of the peak population will vary considerably.[7]

This might be good news, but it is not gospel. Writing in the same issue of *Nature*, demographer Nico Keilman drew awkward conclusions about the value and method of these predictions by contrasting them with the starkly different predictions in a study by the National Research Council. "Lutz *et al.*" said Keilman, "estimate that there is a 95% chance that the world population will reach 6.6 billion to 11.4 billion in 2050," but "the US National Research Council (NRC) uses a different method and has calculated that there is a 95% chance that the 2050 world population will be between 7.9 billion and 10.9 billion."[8]

This exchange in *Nature* gives us a glimpse of the evolving science of demographic prediction in its current state. It is still an imperfect science, a point to which Chapter 11 will return. This current discussion illuminates the work of Gregory King. Demographic controversy was much the same in his day. Three arguments from *Nature* in particular provide a context for the discussion of King's seventeenth-century estimates of English population and wealth.

First, demographic prediction in the twenty-first century has an intimate connection with public policy. *Nature*'s demographers are often tenured academics, but they nevertheless feel political pressure. Government is both a source of grants for research and also the principal consumer of demographic predictions. The data cited by Keilman were from the National Research Council, and the Lutz article was directed to policymakers.

Second, *Nature*'s demographers take pride in using advanced mathematics, the more advanced the better, and, in particular, these authors gave a central role to theory. In the two papers cited from *Nature*, "probability" was the key word. The first graph of the Lutz article offered to the reader "forecasted probability that population will start to decline at or before the indicated date." For several of the different regions of the world, they graphed or charted probability against time. Keilman's rebuttal also discussed theory.

Third, note again that use of advanced mathematics did not create consensus about the accuracy of demographic predictions. Having made their claim to improve probability techniques, Lutz and his colleagues packed the body of their paper with detailed evidence to support their probability predictions. Despite the claims of Lutz and his colleagues that they have improved mathematical probability and presented abundant evidence, Keilman just as energetically denied the accuracy of their predictions. Methodologically, the use of higher mathematics in demographic predictions became the norm, necessary for success among demographers, but that fashionable usage neither yielded reliable accuracy nor ensured consensus in the profession.

This third point is most important because we learn from it how demographers face the quandary inherent in applications of current mathematics to social analysis. In a sentence, the prediction of human behavior by mathematical probability is so difficult because, using current probability theory, we must presume that innumerable variables interact with one another, rendering future results inherently uncertain. The approach of current mathematicians contrasts with that of their seventeenth-century predecessors. For examples from the seventeenth century, let us search in books by two current historians of seventeenth-century statistics, Stephen M. Stigler and David Salsburg. When I said in the Acknowledgments at the beginning of this book that people who do not like mathematics should give new books a chance, these by Stigler and Salsburg were two that I had in mind. The books are both brilliant, and I found them very helpful in my understanding of Gregory King's seventeenth-century context.

A practicing statistician, Stigler wrote a history of statistical science before 1900. He said that seventeenth-century theorists assumed that each natural material event was entirely determined by prior material events, and therefore in theory every future event was exactly predictable in advance, indefinitely, but this proved difficult because human observation and understanding of nature were clouded, hindering accurate prediction. For instance, when astronomers looked through a telescope, shimmering clouded their vision and made it impossible to establish the exact location of an object in the heavens. Stigler found the key areas of progress in astronomy and geodesy, the application of mathematics that determined the exact location of points on large areas of the earth's surface. Even when astronomers made observations under identical conditions, they found that small discrepancies hindered recognition of patterns in their data. Astronomers feared at first to take too many observations because they feared that more observations would multiply error. However, at last they learned from students of games of chance to consider the question of equally likely cases.

The point about determinism and statistics was vital to understanding why mathematical probability is important to our understanding of Gregory King's 1696 estimates. Salsburg stipulated that the "determinist view" or model was used by statisticians before 1900. Salsburg said that,

> Newtonian physics had effectively described the motion of planets, moons, asteroids, and comets—all of it based on a few well-defined laws of motion and gravity. . . . Attempts were even made to extend the search for scientific laws into the realms of sociology, political science, and psychology. It was believed at the time that the major problem with finding these laws lay in the imprecision of the measurements.[9]

Stigler's further discussion was also valuable for our purpose. Originating in studies of gambling, seventeenth-century mathematical probability allowed a way around clouded understanding and observation in astronomy, he said. Estimates of probable values could be made when the actual and precise values themselves were not available. After beginning with a study of gambling, seventeenth-century mathematical probability's "two main themes [were] the combination of observations and uses of probability models in inference."[10]

In creating mathematical probability from the study of gambling, Blaise Pascal (1623–1662) and Pierre de Fermat (1601–1665), French mathematicians, were the leading figures. Both wandered into the field from other areas of study. Pascal was a philosopher of religion, and Fermat, a lawyer, was only a part-time mathematician. Swiss mathematician Jacob Bernoulli (1654–1705) was also very important, contributing the Law of Large Numbers. He had learned to calculate the odds in gambling or games of chance, but he did not at first know how to apply what he had learned there to instances outside or beyond games of chance, especially to the study of probability proportions in natural philosophy. He recognized at last that "by multiplying observations, 'moral certainty' about the unknown proportion could be approached arbitrarily closely. . . . Bernoulli recognized that we could not count on determining the ratio exactly but would have to content ourselves with an approximation to the true ratio."[11]

As for the early twentieth-century, Salsburg said that statisticians then recognized that seventeenth-century and eighteenth-century mathematical probability was not a system but instead a collection of "ad hoc methods" that often produced valuable insights but that nevertheless led to "difficult paradoxes" and theoretical contradictions.[12] That recognition led to early twentieth century improvements in mathematical probability, especially the work of British mathematician Karl Pearson, and the main result was that scientists used probability theory to construct their experiments. The tasting of tea was an example: Sir Ronald Fisher used mathematical probability to construct an experiment to tell when someone could unfailingly detect whether tea or milk had been poured into a cup first. This type of experiment was second nature for someone in the twentieth century but very unlikely or unknown in the seventeenth century. The challenge was to decide when a result was due to mastery rather than mere chance. However, twentieth-century mathematicians treated probability and statistics as something of "lesser value" until the Russian mathematician A. N. Kolmogorov identified "a small set of axioms upon which he could construct the entire body of probability theory."[13]

In turn, the new system of mathematical probability was undermined at the end of the twentieth century, as the seventeenth-century system had been undermined after 1900. As Salsburg put it, "new philosophical problems . . . emerged as statistical methods . . . [were] extended into more and more areas of human endeavor."[14] When the determinist approach to science collapsed in the early twentieth century, Karl Pearson had suggested ways forward. Now, at the beginning of the twenty-first century, probability theory and statistics are again in great theoretical difficulties, and the new way forward has yet to appear. Perhaps now in the twenty-first century, statistics will need to be replaced by an entirely new discipline. An analogous situation occurred at the end of the eighteenth century and the beginning of the nineteenth century when political arithmetic was replaced. It broke down, and a new way forward, economics, appeared. We will take up that point in Chapters 10 and 11.

An example will state the current quandary of mathematical probability more clearly and simply than would further abstract discussion. I take the example from statistician Peter Stalker's new book on international migration.[15] If we want to study migration, he says, we might go to the French side of the Channel Tunnel and there interview, let us say, an Iraqi who wishes to pass into Britain. The migrant may cite several factors such as family and economic circumstances, and these might make us seem capable of quantifying such circumstances and then predicting future migration. However, if we look at the mass of migrants, not at one or two individuals, then we see overwhelming complexity. As more migrants reach Britain, they influence the climate there for future migrants. As migrants leave Iraq, they influence the situation there. The same is true for France and other countries through which migrants transit. And so it goes. Quickly, there are so many interacting variables that exact prediction seems impossible.

No doubt the techniques of probability analysis at use in the *Nature* pieces are still rudimentary. Accumulated piecemeal, as Salsburg said, and many of them invented only late in the twentieth century, the techniques may yet reveal greater potential. Nevertheless, few demographers hope for a perfected mathematics that will enable someone to raise predictions about human behavior from art to science. Even future and brilliant advances in probability theory are unlikely to enable demographers to reach reliable results that would be above controversy.

The problem goes beyond demography and the science of statistics, and it concerns the absence of discernable laws by which one could use statistics to predict behavior in human society. When seventeenth-century natural philosophers predicted outcomes in physics, they relied upon a series of laws to describe the action of the material universe. The rise of various systems of perceived laws of nature, and alterations in those systems, dominated the history of physics since the seventeenth century. Physicists sometimes hoped that an analogous approach could be used for social analysis.[16]

These hopes have not been fulfilled. Since the eighteenth century, writers have tried to fulfill them, hoping to discover laws for human society similar to the laws that Newton perceived in the material world. They saw Newton as a "hard" scientist, a view that Voltaire (1694–1778) did much to establish.[17] Historians have since extensively revised these eighteenth-century and nineteenth-century views of Newton, discovering long-forgotten material about his work at the mint, in alchemy, Biblical prophecy, and in other areas. Discoveries such as these have made it very difficult to continue to classify him as a "hard" scientist.[18] We will see in Chapter 11 that the nineteenth-century economist W. S. Jevons (1835–1882) hoped to make economics into a "hard" science by finding laws like those of physics.[19] Jevons viewed King's Law of Demand in that way, and therefore he made attempts that King and Davenant never made. As readers of *Nature* know, Jevons did not succeed in establishing such laws. We are farther than ever from doing so now, and it would be bold and perhaps foolhardy ever to reiterate Newton's or Jevons's hope of finding them.

The point is so important because demagogues and polemicists go boldly where mathematicians fear to tread. Pat Buchanan's *The Death of the West*, for instance, portrays immigrants as terribly dangerous.[20] Buchanan says that the decline of the Christian religion and the rise of abortion and homosexuality caused birth rates in Western countries to decline, allowing nonwhites with higher birth rates to dominate not only the non-Western parts of the world from which they come, but also, through immigration, the populations of Western countries themselves. Buchanan assumes that the decline, as he sees it, in Western moral values caused the shift in Western social structure and opened the door for an influx of non-Western migrants.

No doubt readers will have many objections to Buchanan's book. I have said Buchanan was polemical, and I said it because he did not discuss his quantitative techniques, much less did he calculate probabilities, and his argument rested more upon an appearance of quantification than upon any substantial analysis of data. Specific objections to one book are not at issue here, however. Instead, we should recognize that Buchanan's book is typical of a popular argument from statistics, and we should ask the general question: Why has no science of exact statistical prediction arisen to shield us from polemical discussion that masks as statistical analysis? Buchanan's work exploits an opportunity arising from the failure of scientific statisticians to agree about laws for statistical prediction in complex social analysis, or even about rules for collection of evidence, a quandary that we see in papers such as those in *Nature*, a quandary whose historical background Stigler and Salsburg clearly identified as due to the failure of the seventeenth-century determinist model when the science of statistics was applied to social analysis.

This range of twenty-first-century work establishes the context for historical analysis and judgment about the estimates of Gregory King. As a technical adviser, King supplied government with statistical analysis including comprehensive data on wealth and population. To quote King's own words, he said that he sought to "apprize" statesmen of " . . . the true state, and condition" of England, "especially in the two main articles, of its people, and wealth." These words appeared at the beginning of his most important paper, the 1696 estimates of national wealth and population, *Natural and Political Observations and Conclusions on the State and Condition of England.* The paper is reprinted at the back of this book. In the middle of the twentieth century, scholarly controversy surrounded the question of King's accuracy, and Geoffrey Holmes was the leading historian then to disparage the accuracy of some of King's wealth estimates. Holmes said that King's methods were primitive in the 1696 estimates, although Holmes thought King's estimate of English population for 1688, five and one-half million, was more or less right. Holmes called it "golden."[21] However, he thought King was deliberately too pessimistic and his numbers too low in general, and Holmes thought the wealth estimates had been deliberately understated. He regarded King's fault as a deliberately low statement, in contrast to Sir William Petty's (1623–1687) deliberately inflated figures. "Highly dubious," Holmes said of King's wealth estimates. If I might make my own paraphrase of what Holmes meant, I would say that he thought Gregory King was a cook who prepared demographic broth in the kitchen of public policy; King felt political heat, and Holmes thought that the heat in this kitchen had burned the broth and spoiled it.

Holmes, note, was cautious in some conclusions, and he did not make a blanket condemnation of all King's numbers. This became the standard view. "King," said historian Colin Brooks, "has traditionally been held in high regard. But recently his conclusions, presuppositions and techniques have come under devastating critical scrutiny from Geoffrey Holmes."[22]

Following Jones, Judges, and Glass, not Holmes or Laslett, I argue that it is an injustice to blame King for inaccuracies, and his achievement as a demographer was praiseworthy, his accuracy considerable. I do not think that King anticipated the methods of many later economists and demographers. To get a balanced view of his achievement, we should place his estimates alongside others, both those of twenty-first-century scientific demographers and also those of King's own contemporaries. In serving state policymakers, in bringing about controversy over his accuracy, and in using fashionable mathematics, King did resemble current demographers. Above all, King was in advance of his contemporaries. He avoided polemic, for instance, much of which was religious in his day. This was no small thing; Sir Isaac Newton himself wasted 40 years in unwise alchemical research and in fruitless efforts to predict the Second Coming of Christ.

In sum, I believe that Holmes and Laslett both had a view of demography based upon the superseded model of statistics, the model from before 1900. They thought that demographers ought to be "hard" scientists like Newton, and that demographers should discover clear laws and calculate precise values. Holmes judged King according to his having discovered, or not discovered, such laws and precise values, and, chronicling King's failure to discover clear laws, he rebuked King. On the same grounds, Laslett praised him. However, this was the sort of praise and blame that Stigler, Salsburg, and others, say is now obsolete. At the beginning of the twenty-first century, it is time to free King's writings on political economy from obsolete condemnation or approval and to place King's shortcomings as a statistician within the context of the whole ongoing failure of statisticians to construct a method of exact prediction about human society. While recognizing the continuing value and importance of Holmes's work for the study of King's biography, and especially King's political career, I will nevertheless disregard Holmes's condemnation of King's motives, methods, and conclusions as a statistician. I will instead lay great emphasis on King's place in the history of mathematics and will conclude that King made mistakes in his calculations, of course, but they were honest mistakes. King did not retail deliberate falsehoods in political economy.

To reach this conclusion, I have borrowed three notions from current scholarship about the history of mathematical probability and inferential statistics in particular and the history of science in general, new notions that were not available when Holmes wrote in the middle twentieth century. We have already encountered the first notion: Seventeenth-century, eighteenth-century, and nineteenth-century mathematical probability rested on assumptions that the material universe was determined, and current theorists of mathematical probability work on assumptions that innumerable factors interact, making uncertainty an inherent part of the fabric of events. I will return to seventeenth-century determinism again in Chapter 9. Here are the other two notions.

First, we will see in Chapter 5 that ancient Greek higher mathematics would not have assisted King in his work. Instead, other writers who used ancient higher mathematics for social analysis wandered into difficulties, for instance Archbishop James Ussher (1581–1656). One of King's great merits was precisely that he avoided these difficulties.

Second, I argue in Chapter 6 and elsewhere that the use of seventeenth-century English statistical science in affairs of state was governed in part by a social convention that had little place for higher mathematics and that instead gave priority to shop arithmetic. By *higher mathematics* I mean algebra and geometry, both available to King, and eventually calculus and mathematical probability. Ancient higher mathematics, still used by Galileo and Kepler, had been heavily based on geometry. Shop arithmetic, by contrast, was very simple mathematics: addition, subtraction, multiplication, and division. King used shop arithmetic and not higher mathematics, neither ancient geometry nor contemporary mathematical probability or calculus. There is no evidence that he even used the slide rule, although that device was available to him and used in his circle, we will see. Neither was King ever comfortable with decimal fractions, a discomfort entirely in keeping with shop arithmetic's basic literature.[23]

King's shop arithmetic should be judged within the conventions of his seventeenth-century English social circle. Arguing in this way about bureaucracy and social convention, I borrow methods developed by historians John Brewer, Ian Hacking, Steven Shapin, and others.

Brewer, summarizing the work of many other historians, has taught us to see early eighteenth-century Britain as an emerging military and naval power, one whose success in war depended on a fiscal system administered by skillful bureaucrats.[24] Brewer's description of the social milieu, the social context in which King presented his estimates, gives us great insight into the social conventions that governed his career. My contention is that shop arithmetic was conventional within this growing bureaucratic state.

King's predecessors, John Graunt (1620–1674) and Sir William Petty, established this convention, and, as we will see in Chapter 9, the philosophy of Thomas Hobbes (1588–1679) reinforced it. Since the convention allowed practitioners of quantitative political analysis to present data to ministers of state while using shop arithmetic, persons in high office found it easy to criticize and understand the data. Men in high position often had experience with the management of landed estates, and they understood political economy by reference to that standard, the management of landed estates. King's avoidance of higher mathematics was therefore both deliberate and fashionable, even necessary, because it followed contemporary social convention and common usage or practice.

King was on the *Nature* side of the line that separates demography from polemic. He made valuable contributions because he applied mathematics to social analysis, reaped many benefits, avoided many pitfalls, and was about as accurate in his estimates and predictions as we might reasonably expect him to have been, given the inherent difficulties of the task. King's failure to use higher mathematics or to develop new methods of statistical inference should be placed within the tradition that led from John Graunt and Sir William Petty to the demographers in *Nature*. King's work should be placed in that large context, and we should remember that demographers of our own day still fail to obtain precision in prediction or to create consensus. King achieved a remarkable degree of accuracy, greatly surpassing that of his English predecessors, and current demographers have been hard pressed to double or triple it.

We now turn, in the next chapter, to King's biography. Holmes used biographical facts about Gregory King's life and as the basis, the "*point d'appui*" as Holmes himself said, of his analysis of King's work. Holmes was a master of those facts, but, writing more recently, we will see, Margaret Spufford suggested plausible alternative particulars of King's turn to demography from heraldry in 1694. Moreover, Holmes used his knowledge of King's biography to condemn King's motives. King's explanation of his switch from the service of King James II to that of King William III was a bit suspicious, as we will also see.

# Chapter 3

# Gregory King: Man of Projects

"Then farewell to popery in England," King recalled his saying, boldly, "being that instant in company," when King James II sent seven bishops to the Tower of London for refusing an Order in Council requiring that all churches read the second declaration of indulgence. King feared James would undo himself because imprisonment of the seven bishops would bring Protestant anger to a head. It "would inflame the people of England against the Roman Catholics," said King. (These quotes are from King's autobiography, which is reprinted in the document section at the end of this book.) Such prescience was possible, of course. James should have foreseen the danger that resulted from his declarations, and King may have done so. However, James did not foresee it, and he issued the second declaration on April 27, 1688, designing by it to besiege the Church of England. King was therefore astute to say that he had always believed James would undo himself: King recalled his early loss of faith in James only when William and Mary were firmly on their thrones.

Besieging Troy, ancient Grecks withdrew their ships from the city because their leaders adopted that ruse in order to end the long war. Not only did they feign withdrawal, but they also, famously, left a wooden horse filled with Greek soldiers whom the Trojans admitted unwittingly, and James attempted much the same with his declarations. When issuing the first declaration in 1687, James had said that he "heartily wish[ed], as it will be easily be believed, that all the people of our dominions were members of the Catholic Church." To that end, he seemed to withdraw from his object. He insinuated a Roman horse into the Church of England, toleration. He intended the established Protestant church to admit or tolerate a range of Christian sects, mostly dissenting Protestants but among them also Roman Catholics. James had the guile of the Greek king, Agamemnon, but neither his courage nor skill, and the ruse failed.

Protestants reacted with the anger that Gregory King said he predicted. Imprisoned in June 1687 and tried at the end of that month on charges of seditious libel, all seven bishops were acquitted among much public jubilation, and then a Dutch army came into England with the Protestant prince of Orange, William, at its head. Protestant opinion turned decisively against King James. As Gregory King recalled himself also to have said at that time, Prince William came not into England without expectation of the crown. When James fled abroad, English peers declared him to have abdicated by reason of his flight, and they ordered William and his wife Princess Mary to be proclaimed king and queen in 1688.

In this change, Gregory King chose to prosper. King's exclamation, "Farewell to popery in England," was bold because it was written when he had accepted a new course for himself. Peers had invited William and Mary, and peers called their coming a Revolution. Acting on orders of the House of Lords, King was among the heralds who proclaimed William to be king and Mary queen. King helped to prepare their coronation as he recently had lavished many pains on the 1686 coronation of King James.

By contrast, King would not have been astute actually to have said an early and public farewell to popery while James was still on the throne because strong ties bound King. One tie was financial investment. Hoping to prosper, King said in his autobiography, he took several risks. For instance, he purchased a lease of 33 years for 60 houses, a very large investment. While King reckoned himself worth eight hundred pounds in 1688, these investments plunged him deeply into debt. He related these things in the same autobiographical breath, as it were, that told of his reaction to the second declaration of indulgence. As King no doubt feared when he heard about the second declaration, his lease on houses proved less valuable than he had hoped when he bought it. The Revolution unsettled not only the state of the realm but also the estate or property market.

Despite these investments, King's chief bond to James in 1688, and his chief hope for prosperity, was through the College of Arms where he was a herald, and, when James fell from power, King suffered most from the loss of prospects at the College. King was not principally a speculator in houses, nor was he a Roman Catholic. He was a herald, and his loss at the College made a crisis for him. Sir John Vanbrugh (1664–1726), the architect and playwright, eventually became Clarenceux King of Arms, a post for which King was much better prepared. To quote the College of Arms itself, Vanbrugh "is said to have known nothing of heraldry and genealogy and to have ridiculed both." King protested, and he persuaded other heralds to join in the protest, but in vain. The College of Arms lists King among those heralds who have had keen insight into their craft while distinguishing themselves in other fields as well.[25]

The fall of King James meant that Gregory King lost his prospects for advancement in a heraldic career.

At the time of King James's coronation in 1686, King's prospects in the College seemed bright. The College operated in this time, as it still does today, under a charter of Queen Mary I. The sovereign appointed 13 members of the royal household to be officers of arms-in-ordinary, further divided the 13 into kings, heralds, and pursuivants of arms, and gave them special responsibility for armorial, ceremonial, and other related functions. The garter king took precedence over others in the College. Heralds were members of the royal household, the sovereign's personal staff, and as rouge dragon pursuivant, a sort of assistant professor, Gregory King worked directly and extensively on coronations, for instance, preparing many of the official books and papers used during the ceremonies by their royal participants.

King's most immediate colleague and long-time associate there, Francis Sandford (1630–1694), suggested a scheme that provided a measure of King's ways of working and hopes for advancement in 1686. Sandford suggested that he and King should prepare a printed book, *The History of the Coronation of James II and of His Royal Consort Queen Mary*, as a permanent heraldic memorial. The book was sumptuous, costing six hundred pounds to print when Sandford published it in 1687, and its preparation exemplified the tasks done by a herald, tasks that made a herald's road to prosperity. Although Sandford did not put King's name on the title page as an author of the 1687 book, King had written most of the text and hoped to receive one-third of any profits. By the end of 1688, however, it was clear there would be no profits. Sandford had managed to sell only enough copies of the book barely to clear the six hundred pounds of expenses, and the remaining copies had become unsalable after William and Mary came to power. It was loss of this potential prosperity, in part, that King must have anticipated when he heard about the seven bishops. If he did anticipate trouble, he was prescient in that matter, too, because he became Lancaster Herald in 1688 at the retirement of his colleague, Sandford, but he obtained little further significant advance in rank or title at the College of Arms thereafter, and instead he had many troubles and disappointments.

By the way, this 1687 folio volume of the coronation contained 30 beautiful engravings that showed many of the persons who took part in the coronation procession, among them Gregory King himself. That picture of him in the coronation procession is reproduced as the frontispiece of this present book.

What the 1687 folio tells us clearly is that King was very ambitious, and his ambition depended on patronage, so he changed sides. He accepted James's fall from power and willingly proclaimed the prince of Orange king of England. We began this chapter with what Gregory King constructed as his reaction to the second declaration of indulgence, and we may very easily measure how different it was from what must have been King's real views at the time. We can imagine what King's actual views must have been early in

1688 because we can extrapolate what Sir William Dugdale's would have been had he lived to that year. Dugdale (1605–1686) would have supported King James in 1688 no matter what. Not only had Dugdale been devoted to King Charles during the Civil War, and made much of this loyalty in his autobiography, but Dugdale also remained of the same loyal mind during the previous great crisis of King James II's reign, Monmouth's rebellion in 1685. The duke of Monmouth was an illegitimate son of Charles II. James had the duke executed together with many others accused of the rebellion. Dugdale wrote all this to Gregory King on the occasion of the rebellion. Dugdale told King that Monmouth's supporters were fanatics who deserved to fail.

Until Dugdale died, he was King's patron at the College of Arms. Dugdale was an especially distinguished herald and therefore a good role model for both King and Sandford. King and Dugdale made heraldic visitations of English counties together, with King using his skill at drawing to make the pictures of coats of arms. Dugdale was never truly powerful enough to be an ideal patron for King, but Dugdale could do something and did do something. King's connection to Sandford was an example of the benefit to King of Dugdale's patronage because King and Sandford had both served Dugdale. In his autobiography, King called Dugdale "that great antiquary and indefatigable writer," and Dugdale published many famous books of mixed antiquarian and heraldic cast, especially his history of English monasteries, perhaps the most famous of all his books, and also several others, among them his history of old Saint Paul's Cathedral in London, his history of Warwickshire, and a history of the draining of the fens.

The downfall of King James greatly complicated King's task of finding another patron to replace Dugdale. King probably had a genuine and unfeigned loyalty to James, and such views were necessary for patronage before 1688 but were afterward liabilities. Of course King could prosper only if he kept loyalty to William and Mary on public display after 1688. King helped to prepare for their coronation. We know how he tried to shift allegiance because we have his autobiography, and it is basically a testimony of the shift. "Farewell to popery," with its hostility to Roman Catholicism, was King's way of announcing that he had always been loyal to the new regime. The autobiography served no other purpose than to announce this, and it was a poor account of any other aspect of his life. After the Revolution of 1688, King still hoped to advance his career along lines clearly laid out by Dugdale and others at the College of Arms. Between King's early farewell to popery in 1688 and his estimates of wealth and population in 1696, however, stood a further shift in his career prospects or a shift in his method of fulfilling his hopes for success.

King may have done an imperfect job of shifting allegiance. Significantly, although King helped prepare William's coronation, King made no printed book such as the one made for James. Chalmers tells us that King got into big trouble in the College of Arms. Whatever the cause, the upshot was clear, and King lost his career prospects in heraldry after Dugdale's death and especially after the Revolution of 1688. By 1694, he was looking elsewhere.

When King's heraldic career had its crisis and when he failed in his efforts to obtain further great advance in the College, he faced a choice. He turned from heraldry to demography, seeking patronage, finally assisting Robert Harley (1661–1724) in a number of capacities in the middle 1690s. In 1696, King produced the now famous *Natural and Political Observations on the State and Condition of England.* King did not publish his work, but Charles Davenant did publish some of it. Davenant published bits of King's data together with extended discussions and analysis.[26] As we will see in Chapter 10, George Chalmers published the entire text of King's *Natural and Political Observations* at the beginning of the nineteenth century. The text has since been republished and is very well known to historians, as are many of King's papers from the 1690s.[27]

King could have become bitter. He could have stayed on as a failed herald and written acid but witty condemnations of the College of Arms and the royal court. These might have earned him literary notice, but they would not have made his career a success. Instead, King transferred his ambition elsewhere and sought powerful patrons from whom or through whom he might earn place and income outside the College.

While King ended up an advisor to Harley, I think it is wrong to imagine that King had sold his soul and become a paid Tory party hack when he made the 1696 estimates. Instead, King began his work at the calculation of wealth and population after his crisis in 1694, and he then passed the results around. The historian Margaret Spufford thought that King first turned to Lord Danby (1631–1712), President of the Privy Council in late 1695 and from December of that year Commissioner of the new Committee on Trade.[28] The point is crucial because it meant that King did not draw up his 1696 estimates at the direction of Harley. Instead, King attracted Harley as a patron because of his skill and accuracy, and Harley was not the first patron to be attracted. King certainly obtained notice from Harley, at that time an opposition member of parliament. Harley and other high officials employed King thereafter, and King became a success. King obtained a state position and salary as Secretary to the Commissioners of Account in April 1702. He later advised on interpretation of the data that officials collected for Queen Anne's Bounty.

King's professional course after 1694 reflected his birth and his background in mathematics. Born in Staffordshire, King died in London, but he remained in many ways a Staffordshire man all his life. King learned shop arithmetic from his father, also named Gregory, an accomplished surveyor and maker of dials.[29] King mentioned in his autobiography that he did not make the progress as a boy in school that he should have made because his father kept him out of school and at work in measuring land during the years when the son was from 12 to 14 years of age. "However, the knowledge he had gained in the mathematics did very well recompense it, and hath been of good advantage to him in the further course of his affairs." King became himself a surveyor who laid out London's Soho district. Soho Square was once King's Square. The present Greek Street was Grig Street, *Grig* perhaps for Gregory. Perhaps his purchase of house leases was an extension of his surveying of landed property.

King, showing great aptitude in study, hoped to matriculate at one of the universities, but he was apprenticed to Dugdale instead, and King served as page and assistant in the 1660s, moving out of Staffordshire. King eventually moved to London and entered the College of Arms as a herald himself, becoming Rouge Dragon Poursuivant in 1677, and rose to be Registrar of the College in 1684 and Lancaster Herald in 1688.

Since King ceased writing his autobiography in 1694, we cannot know his view of his later career in demography. However, the autobiography does clarify King's motives for us, and we may safely conclude that he did his demographic work as a speculation with a view to profit. King undertook speculations throughout his life, and I call them speculations because others have already used that word, and not only for the dabbles in the real estate market but also for Sandford's and King's book on the 1686 coronation. William Hamper, the nineteenth-century editor of Dugdale's diary, for instance, called King's and Sandford's history of the coronation, "a very unprofitable speculation," ruined he said by the arrival of the prince of Orange. Hamper wrote in the notes that he added at the back of his published edition of Dugdale's diary. Chalmers also used the word "speculation" in connection with King.

Aside from his house leases, King's speculations before 1694 were often publishing efforts and were more often heraldic, and he directed them toward obtaining for himself both immediate money profit and also an increased reputation in the College of Arms. Heralds often published with a view to profit. Like twenty-first-century academics, seventeen-century heralds published books not only to earn money royalties but also to advance themselves in their professional reputation, thus to obtain increased salary and also sometimes fees as consultants. Had James stayed on the throne, and had King continued to follow Dugdale's model, King would have hoped to become Garter King himself. The book about the coronation exemplified his speculations before 1688.

Dugdale's heraldic projects were models for King's projects. That was true even after 1688. Dugdale's diary, for instance, must have been the model for King's own autobiography written in 1694, and King listed the same sort of accomplishments as Dugdale had, steps necessary to a fully successful heraldic career. Heralds visited counties and recorded these visitations, sometimes in published books. Heralds also acted as ambassadors to foreign princes, and King went abroad for that purpose himself and recorded his visits in his autobiography and in published books about his visits. King never entirely abandoned Dugdale's models for speculations, but King molded and formed them into different and new shapes. Heralds operated in a political and policy context—they were after all members of the royal household—so the change from seeking patronage as a herald to seeking it as a demographer was not an absolute one.

We might think that King's being a speculator or projector impugned the honesty of his 1696 estimates. A 1950s Charles Addams cartoon in *The New Yorker* showed a ghoul at work in an office with a sign above his desk that read "Scheme!" The word *project* was a bit like that when the seventeenth century ended. The word was cognate with a French word in general use, and both were widely used to designate a preliminary plan or rough draft. The English word *project* had a sinister connotation, however. Jonathan Swift's (1667–1745) satires "An Argument against Abolishing Christianity," "A Modest Proposal," and above all his brutal caricature of the Royal Society in Book III of *Gulliver's Travels*, all come to mind in connection with the sinister connotations of the English word, *project*.

That King was a projector and speculator does not mean that he fudged his numbers, however. The difference, Davenant said, was that King was so superior that he had transcended the projector category. Davenant said other projectors, wretched men, were "always buzzing about the ministers." King was a "jewel" by comparison.[30] Davenant's statements were backhanded admissions that King's 1696 estimates were projects, but Davenant thought them much more admirable than the general run of projects. All seventeenth-century European countries had educated men who wanted to give advice to rulers, and, as the historian Joan Thirsk has shown, England had its share. Many of them suggested ways by which England could substitute articles of domestic production for imported goods, for instance. Even at the best of times, however, such projects disrupted English production and consumption in ways that English projectors and government servants neither understood nor predicted, said Thirsk.

King must have leaned something from the model for projects that he found in Dugdale's history of the fens. It had some suggestive points. The draining of the fens was an example of a "giddy project" that required shop arithmetic.[31] The point is that the draining of the fens and the 1696 estimates were projects that depended on *accurate* quantification. By this standard, King *was* better.

I suggest that specific details about bureaucratic projects and political contacts are not the only proper sources for a study of King's turn to demography. They do tell us a lot, of course, and perhaps somewhere a letter to King from another great lord will turn up, or a stray autobiographical fragment in King's hand will emerge from an archive center. I myself have searched for those things. If we wish to learn why King did his demography as he did, and how he began that work, however, we might remember that many frustrated middle-aged people return to their youthful dreams. King was not the first middle-aged man to come prematurely against career-ending obstacles in his place of employment. King remembered especially the simple mathematics that he had learned as a boy. This early mathematics reappeared as the shop arithmetic of his 1696 estimates. True, King had meanwhile acquired great polish in pleasing men like Harley and Davenant. Both the quantitative skills and the polish King could have learned by example from Francis Bacon (1561–1626) or Petty. Dugdale must also have been an example for the polish as, I believe, he was a model for King's accuracy and integrity. Adding his father's mathematics to Francis Bacon's empirical method, which was then fashionable among the great men he served, King did honest and important demographic work.

# Chapter 4

# British Empiricism and Shop Arithmetic

In 1719, John Woodward (1665–1728), professor of medicine at Gresham College in London, wrote an account of his having quarreled with a medical colleague, Richard Mead (1673–1754). The quarrel was so violent that the two men drew swords, Woodward said, and he acknowledged that he lost his own sword in the fracas. Mead then made him beg for his life. Refusing, Woodward said proudly, he instead coolly replied that Mead was much more dangerous as a physician than as a swordsman. Woodward added that he would not beg Mead to spare his life unless he were Mead's patient and Mead opened a bottle of medicine.[32] This was sour grapes, by the way. Mead was the more distinguished of the two, with the better practice.

What Woodward said of Mead's patients, nevertheless, was true of seventeenth-century and eighteenth-century invalids in general: They were more likely to die when attended by a doctor, however qualified and distinguished, than when nursed by a lay person who used no invasive treatment. When attended by physicians, for instance, women died in childbirth in greater numbers than when attended by midwives. The more professional medical attention you got, the worse off you were. The higher mortality of those who could afford lots of doctors may account for the decline of aristocratic families.[33]

Empiricism could have provided a way out of this sorry state of affairs in medicine, but empiricism was long tried without much success. We have already encountered Stephen Stigler's account of the history of statistical science. Here is what he said about John Graunt. Quoting the famous 1692 dictum of John Arbuthnot (1667–1735), a practitioner of political arithmetic and sometime correspondent of Gregory King, that human knowledge was "small and confused" except when capable of being reduced to quantitative reasoning or expression, Stigler said that Graunt showed the very great difficulty of applying mathematical methods to empirical analysis. Stigler said that Graunt "made many wise inferences," but his work mainly showed the value of collecting empirical data, and his analysis of the data themselves had no pathmaking innovation. Empiricism became powerful only when combined with inferential statistical analysis. That inferential analysis revealed patterns in large numbers of data, patterns that were not accessible when someone studied only individual instances. Mathematical probability, in other words, allowed empiricism to rise above idiosyncrasy. Despite the shortcomings of Graunt's analysis, his work with London bills of mortality, or reports of deaths, began the application of mathematics to these sorts of data.[34]

Graunt worked closely with Sir William Petty.[35] A physician and sometime professor of anatomy, Petty gave part of his own work the title "political anatomy." This political anatomy was "curious Dissections" of national "Symmetry, Fabrick, and Proportion," and he tauntingly compared this model to the practice of "Old-women and Empryicks."[36] Petty dated his anatomy of Irish data 1672, and he also turned his attention to England. He paid close attention to mortality and morbidity. He took too little care to be accurate, although he promised to be guided by number, weight, and measure. Despite its faults, his political anatomy provided one starting point for Gregory King's calculations. Petty wrote midway in the reign of Charles II, perhaps from 1671 to 1676. Petty gave another part of his work the title "political arithmetic," perhaps inventing the phrase. Gregory King read this in the edition published in 1691.

As we will see again in later chapters, *political arithmetic* was a phrase in general use in Britain until the early nineteenth century. It was of seventeenth-century origin, but the idea that statesmen should make wise use of arithmetic was a very old commonplace. The seventeenth-century phrase *political arithmetic* did not yet denote argument carried on in public through printed books. Instead, it then denoted a conduct of policy by statesmen who took care to know the numbers of people and of wealth.[37] For many, the phrase meant the policy itself, the work of statesmen, and not the collection of data. That last part was the work of lesser hands.

Graunt made important advances. Many textbooks list his work on the bills of mortality as the beginning of scientific statistics. After him, two ways diverged. One way led to King's 1696 estimates. We will return to that way in a moment. In the other way, people developed inferential statistics and the theory of mathematical probability. When current demographers use mathematical probability to prepare articles for publication, for instance in the journal *Nature*, they infer correlations between data, using a system that goes directly back, through this second way, to Graunt.

Annuities and commercial life insurance were two important early applications for this second system. Christiaan Huygens (1629–1695) was especially important in this regard. A Dutch contemporary of Graunt's, he was an astronomer and physicist who worked on the pendulum clock. He also was a tutor of the great German mathematician G. W. Leibniz (1646–1716). Huygens studied annuities, government programs that established regular payments over time for persons who advanced a lump sum at the beginning. This practice went back to the Romans, but its theory had not been refined or improved much in the many intervening centuries. Huygens developed better estimates of the way that government agencies could assure profitability when they issued annuities.[38]

English mathematician and astronomer Edmund Halley (1656–1742) also did pioneer work in this regard, directly based on Graunt. His work led to the life tables that were needed not only for annuities but also for commercial life insurance. Almost contemporary with King's demographic work, but predating it by a bit, Halley's estimates appeared in 1693. The estimates dealt with the German city of Breslau, capital of Silesia. Halley obtained there the precise and full data that allowed him to calculate the value of annuities on lives. Halley explicitly mentioned his debt to Graunt.

Jacob Bernoulli's family of Swiss mathematicians produced 12 men who wrote on one or another branch of higher mathematics and inferential statistics, and 5 of them wrote on mathematical probability. The son of a pharmacist, Jacob himself wrote the *Ars Conjectandi*, published posthumously in 1713, the most important of the family's various works on mathematical probability.[39] Jacob's brother Johann or Jean (1667–1748) contributed many important improvements to calculus, especially calculus of variations. A French mathematician, the Marquis de l'Hôpital (1661–1704), working with the help of this Bernoulli, published the first textbook on differential calculus in 1696, the same year that King wrote his most famous paper.

Another member of the famous family, Nicholas Bernoulli (1687–1759), recognized that Graunt's analysis of mortality in particular revealed patterns in large numbers of data, patterns not apparent to those who studied only individual instances. Graunt had demonstrated the stability of ratios in the bills of mortality, and he had established analysis of such ratios as the basis of a mathematical statistical analysis, but he stuck to shop arithmetic. Nicholas Bernoulli inferred probable distributions of male and female births from the same sort of data that Graunt had collected. Nicholas Bernoulli's "investigation is the first attempt to fit a binomial to data and to test the goodness of fit."[40] The work of all these men led directly to the population estimates that we saw used in *Nature*. The trail of influence was clear. Huygens, Halley, and the Bernoulli brothers all added higher mathematics to statistics.

Instead of using mathematical probability to develop inferential statistics, as Huygens, the Bernoulli brothers, and Halley did, Graunt and Petty instead built, and King inhabited, a halfway house. Graunt and Petty added mathematics to social analysis, true, but they added only shop arithmetic, not higher mathematics.

The word *statistics* previously meant merely a verbal description of states and countries. The word came from the Italian language and meant someone who discussed states or affairs of state. The phrase "political geography" now conveys many of the points that then came under the heading of statistics. Slowly, students of statistics included quantitative data in these discussions, but the terms and methods remained unformed and irregular. We will see in Chapter 10 how the eighteenth-century Scottish writer Sir John Sinclair (1754–1835) borrowed the word *statistics* from the German and brought it into the English language in connection with quantitative study, but he still did not use inferential statistics. His colleague and contemporary was George Chalmers who reprinted King's 1696 estimates. Neither Sinclair nor Chalmers, however, improved much on King's quantitative methods. Chalmers was a successful antiquary and civil servant but not a skillful scholar of official statistics, and he was uncritical in some of his judgments about King's data.

Therefore, Petty and Graunt began, and King continued, a transformation that added mathematics to statistics, but none of these men followed this transformation to its logical conclusions, namely mathematical probability and inferential statistics. Borrowing his mathematical technique from Petty and Graunt, not from Halley, whose work was clearly available to him, King stopped at the halfway house and so did some of his British successors, such as Chalmers and Sinclair.

This halfway house of political arithmetic was an impressive but elementary structure. On the one hand, it was serviceable. Petty, Graunt, and King all deliberately avoided the worst nonsense that usually plagued the seventeenth-century addition of higher mathematics to social analysis, like predicting the exact date of the Second Coming of Christ, and they also provided valuable data to the government and others. On the other hand, they borrowed or devised no tools of the new mathematical probability such as Huygens, Halley, and the Bernoulli brothers did. Petty and Graunt constructed a halfway house between two very different systems of higher mathematics, that of the ancients and that of Huygens, Halley, the Bernoulli brothers, and others, and King remained at that halfway house.

The reason for this dogged retention of shop arithmetic was complex. We must place shop arithmetic in its complex seventeenth-century context, paying particular attention to the shortcomings of ancient higher mathematics when used for social analysis. The ancient higher mathematical methods available to Petty, Graunt, and King were unsuitable for use in statistical analysis, as the next chapter will explain. I mentioned another point in the last chapter and return to it in greater detail now: English social convention dictated the type of mathematics that Graunt, Petty, King, and others used. We may understand why by following the judgment of many current historians of science in general, and historians of mathematical probability in particular, for instance Stephen Shapin and Ian Hacking.

Shapin began a little handbook with the famous line, "There was no such thing as the Scientific Revolution, and this is a book about it." Paying tribute to colleagues, he said the book summarized a view that is now conventional among historians of science, and he therefore claimed only to express the present consensus. Having rejected the phrase "Scientific Revolution," he also said that there was no "single coherent cultural entity called 'science' in the seventeenth century."[41] Nevertheless, he acknowledged that many people in the sixteenth century and seventeenth century thought of themselves as modern, as opposed to the ancients. These moderns attempted to change beliefs and to secure new beliefs. However, they differed among themselves, some emphasizing theory, others practical action, such as collecting and experimentation.

If there is now a consensus, as Shapin said, then Ian Hacking did much to establish it. He warned that historians who survey seventeenth-century natural philosophy should struggle against the long-established but mistaken belief in "great originators of the new experimental method" who "combined [it] with a successful mechanical model of the universe." We have to recognize, Hacking said, "that this interpretation is an artefact" and now obsolete.[42]

Shapin also said there and in other books that seventeenth-century people used social status as a criterion for truth. Rank or circumstance could warrant or authenticate a gentleman's testimony and could lead people to prefer it over the testimony of others of lesser rank. "I situate," said Shapin, "the recognition of truthfulness within a traditional culture of *honor*; and I indicate how the practices of an honor culture stood in relation to alternative ways of specifying gentle identity, with special reference to Christian and humanist patterns."[43]

These notions about the importance of rank and status in natural philosophy have been especially important for historians of seventeenth-century English probability theory. Many historians have accepted rank and status as important seventeenth-century criteria of truth, and some historians apply the matter of rank and status specifically to explain the origins of probability, even mathematical probability.[44] Barbara Shapiro seems to me especially clever and wise in this matter. She said that the common law was an important source for usages and conventions about probability. The law accorded greater weight and importance to some testimonies than to others, and lawyers called "probable" that testimony that they thought plausible and persuasive. Rank and status were often decisive in this regard.

However wise Shapiro and other historians of probability and the common law were, overall, their views nevertheless became controversial, and many working scientists, in particular, rejected aspects of them, denying especially strongly the application of rank and social status to interpret the development of probability theory in seventeenth-century higher mathematics and physics.

We need not enter into these controversies here, however, because we need to make few claims about higher mathematics and physics. We need to apply notions of rank and status only to explain King's use of shop arithmetic in social analysis. There, I believe, arguments on the models of Shapin and Shapiro worked very well.

Hacking's writings were also very persuasive. In particular, we can apply his notions of rank and status in order to understand the prestige of Gregory King's shop arithmetic in his social context. We should follow in particular what Hacking did with Petty.

Petty made a clear call for the use of mathematical analysis to break previous Galenic medical theory, Hacking said, but Petty did little to follow through. He laid out the notion of applying quantitative analysis to patterns of data in an effort to discern regularities that had escaped the notice of persons who examined only individual instances. Petty asked, to cite his own words, "whether of 100 sick of acute diseases who use physicians, as many die in misery as where no art is used, or only chance."[45] This suggested the required step, surveying large runs of data to look for ratios not apparent in individual instances. (This was what Jacob Bernoulli and others did.) However, Petty did not complete his agenda. (Nor did Graunt complete it, nor did King.) Instead of condemning Petty for failing to follow through to mathematical probability and inferential statistics, Hacking described his work in patient detail.

Having borrowed this analysis of Petty, who was King's model, we should therefore not condemn King either. He patiently surveyed and analyzed data, achieving remarkable and important results, and we should extend to him the same understanding that Hacking and others extended to Petty and Graunt. We can also apply notions of Shapin and Shapiro to King. We must first recount the steps that led to the method that Petty and Graunt developed, and that King borrowed and improved, and we may then see why shop arithmetic was already established by social convention in King's day. We begin with medicine.

A vast body of teaching, much of it very ancient, long prevented the combination of medical empiricism with mathematical analysis. Galen of Pergamum left writings that were still the basis of medical theory in Britain in the days of Woodward and Mead. A Greek resident of Rome during the second century of the Christian era, Galen became court physician to the Emperor Marcus Aurelius. Educated in rhetoric and philosophy as well as medicine, Galen cited Plato and Aristotle as his chief philosophical influences. These influences led him to monotheism, and that outlook endorsed his authority after the triumph of Christianity. Although he made original discoveries, Galen relied upon and summarized previous medical theorists, especially the revered but elusive Hippocrates. He cannot now be identified with certainty, yet he was thought in ancient times to be the author of the large body of writings that bore his name. Galen expounded old doctrine when he said that a healthy human body was a balance of the four humors: earth, air, fire, and water. Disease was an imbalance of these. Only slowly did Galen's faulty teaching fall into discredit, and Woodward and Mead still retained much of it. Mead, for instance, swallowed snake venom to test Galen's claim that venom was harmful only when injected through a puncture.

However, the sixteenth century and seventeenth century were turning points. Knowledge of anatomy was growing, and the processes of diseases became better understood, thanks to systematic observation and better communication. The mechanics of the cardiovascular system were established for the first time.

Why was progress so slow? Since the old theories so often produced deadly results when used as the basis of medical practice, why swallow snake venom to test them? Why not throw them out and start over? Doctors had an alternative to theory; they could trust in observation and experience alone. Ancient and seventeenth-century doctors both had the same impulse to discard theory and trust to experience, and anyone who did so was called an *empiric* from the Greek word for *experience.* When Petty tauntingly compared himself to midwives and empirics, he, a qualified doctor, had reference to this tradition.

However, established medical theory stifled empiricism. It did so in the ancient world and still in the seventeenth century, prevailing then for two reasons among others. First, empiricism in Galenic theory had come to play somewhat the same role that equity later played in English common law: Common law absorbed equity and vitiated its original, reforming impulse. Second, Paracelsus (1493–1541) and his followers cornered much of the market for medical reform in the sixteenth century and seventeenth century, crushing the chance for empiricism to reform academic medical teaching.

Legal theory will be helpful soon in our consideration of the natural philosophy of Francis Bacon, so we will review it now. The common law was customary jurisprudence, the unwritten law of England, the common custom. *Equity* was an alternative system. At first, it meant not insisting too rigorously upon one's rights. Tempering justice with equity led to mercy. Then *equity* came to mean an appeal to natural right where the customary law or common law produced a result that seemed contrary to simple justice. A process grew up to accommodate such appeals, but the process became as rigid and hidebound as the common law, so equity became only a separate system that had separate rules and remedies. It lost its spontaneity and its appeal to mercy and simple justice. It was absorbed into the common law apparatus so that, for instance in the United States, most courts now rule according to common law and equity both, although I understand that Virginia still allows some separation between the two systems. Empirical medicine was absorbed like that. Although the empirical tradition became well established in ancient medicine, Galen and other proponents of medical theory took it into their teaching and vitiated its original impulse. It became only a separate system with its own distinct rules and remedies, its own body of writings, and sometimes its own practitioners. It lost its originality, its spontaneous application of common sense to experience.

Paracelsus did the opposite of Galen. Paracelsus grasped that ancient medicine was faulty and should be discarded, but he hindered reform, and garbled empirical theory, with fruitless new connections between medicine and alchemy. Paracelsus may or may not have studied at Padua and may or may not have had a medical degree, but he certainly was professor of medicine in Basel and certainly lost his post there because he had books of Galen's medical theories publicly burned. The very name *Paracelsus* indicated that he spurned ancient theory: The name meant *Beyond Celsus,* Aulus Cornelius Celsus being a Roman medical writer, probably himself a physician, who lived in the reign of the Emperor Tiberius. In Paracelsus' day, Celsus was especially valued for his Latin prose, and his medical writings were widely read and credited on that account. One must sympathize with a medical reformer who publicly derided the established but erroneous theories of his predecessors, especially their preference for gilded prose over the welfare of patients. Melodrama is tempting when one deals with one's academic colleagues, but Paracelsus did too little beside the melodramatic to promote improvements in medicine. As I said, he did little to advance empiricism in particular and may actually have hindered or impugned it. Even in the matter of prose style, he worked no improvement.[46] The result was to impugn the whole concept of medical reform.

Paracelsus did not advance empiricism in medicine, but Andreas Vesalius (1514–1564) of Brussels did. He made a crucial contribution when he published his *De Humani Corporis Fabrica* in 1543. It became the most famous anatomical book in history; its illustrations are still well known, even today. Vesalius contributed to another empirical advance, even more important than his book with its famous illustrations, moreover. Doctors in his day bled their patients, and Vesalius entered into a controversy concerning which vein of the patient the attending doctor was to select for his incision. The controversy influenced William Harvey (1578–1657), perhaps the most famous English physician of the seventeenth century, a man who attended both Francis Bacon and King Charles I. Educated at Padua where Vesalius had taught, Harvey took up the controversy in which Vesalius had engaged, and it led Harvey step by step to devise his novel theory of the circulation of the blood, a triumph of medical observation and a blow to Galenic theory.

Like Vesalius, whom he admired, Francis Bacon contributed to the advance of empiricism in medicine. He left a sixteenth-century legacy that allowed Petty and Graunt to combine empiricism in medicine with statistical analysis, the advance mentioned at the beginning of this chapter, but the story is a complex one, and the advance was slow, so slow that Woodward and Mead still held many of the old doctrines nearly one hundred years after Bacon's time. We may understand obstacles to advance by reverting to Ian Hacking's writing about empiricism in medicine. He pointed out that Bacon condemned it. For instance, Hacking quoted passage 67 from the first book of the *Novum Organum: Aphorisms Concerning the Interpretation of Nature and the Kingdom of Man*, published 1620. Bacon wrote:

> The empiric school produces dogmas of a more deformed and monstrous nature than the sophistic or theoretic school; not being founded in the light of common notions (which however poor and superstitious, is yet in a manner universal and of a general tendency), but in the confined obscurity of a few experiments. Hence this species of philosophy appears probable [i.e., plausible], and almost certain to those who are daily practised in such experiments, and have thus corrupted their imagination, but incredible and futile to others. We have a strong instance of this in the alchemists and their dogmas; it would be difficult to find another in this age, unless perhaps in the philosophy of Gilbert. We could not, however, neglect to caution others against this school, because we already foresee and argue, that if men be hereafter induced by our exhortations to apply seriously to experiments (bidding farewell to the sophistic doctrines), there will then be imminent danger from empirics; owing to the premature and forward haste of the understanding, and its jumping or flying to generalities and the principles of things: We ought, therefore, already, to meet the evil.[47]

In Bacon's time, medical empiricism was almost vitiated by its being ritualized and reduced to a series of futile processes. It had also become associated with alchemy. We must distinguish therefore between Bacon's own attitudes toward medical empiricism and those of his followers Petty and Graunt.

We should do the same with arithmetic. Bacon recommended it in general, and his followers combined shop arithmetic in particular with Bacon's empirical methods. Bacon did not use shop arithmetic much himself in medical writing, although he would likely have approved of his followers' doing so.

Using shop arithmetic, not mathematical probability, Graunt still made more advances than Bacon or Petty. Why did those two fail to achieve the kind of results that Graunt did? Despite recommending arithmetic, Bacon used hardly any himself. He talked about method instead. Petty did use arithmetic, but he reached conclusions about the size of English population, and especially about the geographical size of the British Isles, that made them, in light of later statistical science, too large. This inaccuracy was recognized in Gregory King's time. Charles Davenant, who oversaw imports and exports in King's day and who worked directly with King, said that Petty had little interest in accuracy but instead was deliberately in error. While allowing for the difficulty of the calculations and in the inadequacy of information, Davenant still thought that Petty wrote to please people in power and to advance his career, not to get the numbers right.[48] Petty did with political arithmetic what Bacon did with equity in legal reform, I would add. Evidence for this is to hand, if the reader will patiently suffer a detour.

For our purposes, one of the best analyses of Bacon was made some years ago by historian Julian Martin, a student of the late Tudor historian G. R. Elton.[49] Martin connected Bacon to the scheme for social reform that Elton attributed to Thomas Cromwell (1485–1540), Lord Privy Seal in the court of King Henry VIII. On Martin's analysis, Bacon obtained this connection by being the son of Sir Nicholas Bacon, Lord Keeper of the Great Seal in Queen Elizabeth's court. Nicholas Bacon inculcated in Francis the need to reform of the common law in particular. Therefore, Francis, becoming at last chancellor himself, and, by the way, also overseer of the equity process (which was controlled by the chancellor), mentioned previously, had a chance to reform the law. He tried to do so, but ambition, hunger for office and title, thwarted his desire for legal reform.

Petty was just as sincere about applying arithmetic to medicine as Bacon was about legal reform, but no more sincere. Bacon's model for social analysis, and his impulse to reform, influenced Petty, no doubt. However, Bacon's example of personal success influenced him even more. The lesson was well learned. Considering his humble origin, Petty was a success in politics and society, founder of a great family and a great fortune. Of course, he wished for greater success: after holding public office under the Commonwealth in Ireland, he did not obtain similar office again under King Charles II. However, he was successful. This may account for Petty's failure to pursue the importance of mathematics in medical analysis, even though mathematical analysis was the key part of his schemes of reform, and even though he was sincere about his schemes. Career first, reform second, abstract theory third—that is how one should see Petty. Might one say the same of Bacon himself? He turned to writing the books that made him famous only when his career languished, first when he was young and later when he had been removed from office.

Graunt by contrast was a more modest man, a merchant who was at the zenith of his fortunes when he wrote on the bills of mortality. His business was good until the great fire of London in 1666, but it petered out afterward. He then blighted his prospects when he converted to the unpopular Roman Catholic Church. Graunt's work on the bills of mortality had the accuracy that Petty's work did not have. A man of power, Petty knew that schemes of reform depended on power. Graunt, a lesser man, with no hope of power, had the patience to try to get the numbers right. Graunt did not transform medicine by adding inferential statistics and mathematical probability, but he got some of the numbers right, using shop arithmetic, and his example of accuracy was an important contribution.

Aside from Halley, the seventeenth-century English application of mathematics to social analysis, as a result of Graunt's work, was confined to shop arithmetic. King was Graunt's English successor. Like Graunt and Petty, King stuck to shop arithmetic. Perhaps for that reason, King, like Petty and Bacon, was able to find a secure post or position in Robert Harley's circle, and King had influence on policy. He made as great an effort to be accurate in his computations as Graunt did, but he sought influence as Petty and Bacon had sought it. Use of complex, new higher mathematics might have ruined his access to ministers such as Harley.

Very sophisticated mathematical tools were available to King: Seventeenth-century Britain is justly famous for developing such tools. In 1695 and 1696 virtuosi at the forefront of philosophical and mathematical progress surrounded King. Halley had just published his paper, for instance.[50] If King had thought that these advanced mathematical tools were needed, or were helpful in obtaining access to great persons in his circle, then King would have found the means to employ them. He could have had access to whatever brilliant methods that he thought were useful. He instead used by choice only the simple, commercial mathematics that his father had taught him. He was himself especially skilled as a surveyor, and shop arithmetic was the heart of surveying in the seventeenth century. Further, advisors to the customs service used much the same methods, and so did bookkeepers.

Instead of condemning King by comparing him with Huygens and the Bernoulli brothers, we should instead compare King with some of the many seventeenth-century British writers who unsuccessfully attempted to reform social analysis by using higher mathematics and advanced natural philosophy. By a contrast to two such persons, King's reputation must benefit. They were the physicians Nicholas Barbon (1640–1698) and George Cheyne (1671–1743). King's reputation must also benefit by direct comparison (not contrast) to Sébastien de Vauban (1633–1707), Marshal of France.

A medical man, Barbon borrowed from William Harvey the notion of circulation, saying that money circulated through trade and commerce much as Harvey had said blood circulated in the human body. Barbon also borrowed notions of value or price from Locke, and he also asserted the importance of arithmetic as Petty had done. Moreover, Barbon did a great deal to establish the insurance trade. Given the mixture of theory, insurance, and arithmetic, one might hope for great things, and Barbon did argue perceptively that the European population was on the increase. He simply guessed that population was increasing, however, and his written theory on population was otherwise a disappointment. King must come off well by comparison to Barbon. One could not imagine that Barbon could ever have produced a systematic, quantitative estimate in any way comparable to King's 1696 estimates.[51]

Cheyne borrowed from Newton, or rather from "Newtonianism," and applied the borrowing to medicine. Since Newton was so secretive and eccentric but also very prestigious, many people in the 1690s lost sight of Newton's own intention and produced on their own what one historian called "a complex and conflicted discourse."[52] "Newtonianism," as the discourse was called, established, among other things, a vogue or fad for mathematics in medicine. Cheyne learned the importance of mathematics during his education at the University of Leiden, and the London fashion for "Newtonianism" in the 1690s made him remember that prior university learning. Great patronage and success opened to him because he claimed to be following Newton and to be using Newton's mathematics. Cheyne relished this patronage and success, but of course his medical results were mixed. He advocated an all-lettuce diet, linked medicine to mysticism, and was himself immensely fat. King's use of shop arithmetic must seem a wiser and more sophisticated choice than Cheyne's "Newtonianism."

The contrast, then, between King and Barbon or Cheyne was clear. Shop arithmetic and empiricism were the better choices. As we will see in the next chapter about Archbishop Ussher's higher mathematics and mysticism, shop arithmetic and empiricism enabled King to avoid mistakes, here the mistake of borrowing Newtonian pretensions or else that of wandering into a discourse about trade where he might not have made as good of a choice of medical analogies as Barbon did.

Sébastien de Vauban made excellent and famous estimates of the French population, but in comparison of those, the estimates of King must tend to support my claim that King did about as well as could have been expected in his 1696 estimates, given the difficulties of his task. Vauban was King's equal but not his superior. A great military leader, Vauban felt that seventeenth-century France's inadequate and unjust tax system was a greater threat to the nation's security than were foreign enemies. To suggest reforms, he looked to the example of a great military state abroad, China. Vauban wrote a book called *The Royal Tenth* that was influenced by examples taken from China as recounted by Jesuit writers and the Italian traveler Marco Polo (1254–1324). They said that the Chinese emperor commanded the compilation of lists of people in small districts. The district lists were kept household by household. The emperor then enumerated population and wealth by combining numbers from these districts. A great military engineer, Vauban used mathematical methods similar to King's, including a rudimentary system of sampling. Like King also, Vauban avoided mathematical probability, and he invented his method independently.[53]

One parallel of King's methods with Vauban's was clear. Both used surveying. Vauban, a military engineer, built forts and designed military camps. The similarity to Gregory King's town planning was great, at least in terms of the mathematical methods involved.

There was a contrast between King and Vauban, however. Basing his suggestions for tax reform on his estimates, Vauban published a classic book while King kept silent. Vauban's calls for reform lost him his influence at the royal court. The loss greatly harmed his career. By contrast, King's silence kept him in favor with the great ministers whom he served.

We may also find another contrast favorable to King if we remember the seventeenth-century temptation to disguise or dress up as higher mathematics what were really still merely verbal arguments without any essential connection to quantification or calculation. For instance, James Harington (1611–1677), a contemporary of Petty's, put many numbers in his 1656 political work *Oceana*, but that book was really not at all dependent on the calculations that ornamented it, and *Oceana* certainly never led anywhere in the history of statistics. No one in the Bernoulli family investigated ratios or the probability of outlying values because of the data in *Oceana.*

We should not blame King for using shop arithmetic, therefore. If we say that he should have used more advanced mathematics, then we indulge in wishful thinking. We must study the role that shop arithmetic played while English statistical analysis was being developed. King was not alone, among his circle, in applying shop arithmetic to the practical problems of government. King used shop arithmetic in part because he had benefited from the precedent that Bacon and Petty provided. He also benefited from the precedent of accuracy that Graunt added. King also used shop arithmetic in part because it was the best technique for his purposes. His innovation was to be as accurate as Graunt but to set his material before great ministers as Bacon recommenced and as Petty had done.

King depended directly on Graunt who borrowed both Petty's quantitative method in medicine and also on Bacon's empirical arguments about which factors tended to prolong human life, and, further, Graunt combined these Baconian elements with accuracy. King borrowed Graunt's work but did not see in it the same things as Huygens or Bernoulli. They solved the puzzle posed by empiricism in medicine. The trick to making empiricism work, as Bacon himself said in the passage that Ian Hacking quoted, was to find the sure ground of statistical procedure so that one could generalize beyond individual observation and experiment. Without this ground of generalization, all empiricism was merely idiosyncratic, open to the complaint that Bacon leveled against it. Huygens, Halley, the Bernoulli family, and others provided that sure ground, but, again, the story had the complexity that we have seen in this chapter.

What of Woodward? An antiquary who wrote about the Flood, he enables us to understand the excellence of King's avoidance of nonsense on that point, a matter to which we now turn in the next chapter.

# CHAPTER 5

# Higher Mathematics and Seventeenth-Century Political Economy

Noah, the ark, and the rainbow—Gregory King used the Flood described in the Bible as his base point for population chronology when he compiled his 1696 estimates of population growth. Deriving dates from Archbishop James Ussher's Biblical chronology of world history, King used Ussher's date for the Flood. King presumed that world population had grown from Adam and Eve to a substantial number. Then the Flood reduced population to the few people who had survived, and population grew a second time. Using accounts in the Bible, he computed a ratio of population increase for the children of Israel prior to the Flood; he then applied that same ratio to estimate population growth after the Flood, starting from the few couples who survived. We will see all this in Chapter 8.

King applied the same ratio to his English data. Charles Davenant summarized King's method of estimating English population. Davenant did so in a chapter entitled "Of the People of England," part of a larger work on the means of giving England a favorable balance of trade. Davenant said that King,

> lays down that, if the first people of England was by a colony or colonies, consisting of a number between 100 and 1000 people (which seems probable) such colony or colonies might be brought over between the year of the world 2400 or 2600, viz. about 8 or 900 years after the flood, and 14 or 1500 years before the birth of Christ.[54]

The analogy was clear: World population had grown from a single couple and had then grown again after the Flood from a very few couples, and English population had grown similarly from a small number of original couples. King, in other words, presumed that English population increase was on the same ratio that he had previously calculated for the early increase of the children of Israel. They had grown from a single couple, Adam and Eve.

To understand King's 1696 estimates, therefore, we need first of all to place the Flood in the intellectual context of the 1690s, and we must see that King systematized English population numbers with a minimum of damage from these Biblical materials about the Flood. In calculating his ratios, of course, King did not invent or use inferential statistics as Huygens, Halley, and the Bernoulli brothers began to do, but he did very good work nevertheless, and his contribution was in part his avoiding the traps of Biblical analysis into which people like Ussher fell.

Comparing King to Ussher, we will look in particular at how Ussher used higher mathematics. Ussher's higher mathematics was a mystical system of number symbolism very different from later systems of higher mathematics, such as mathematical probability and calculus. King did not use this ancient, mystical higher mathematics. This was a major point. King did not invent mathematical probability, and could not have done so while he stuck to shop arithmetic, but he was an empiricist, and shop arithmetic and empiricism freed his demographic estimates from the occult and spiritual causes often used by those who studied Biblical chronology.

Ancient or modern, higher mathematics can be a bit difficult. Let's start with something simpler on the Flood, Thomas Burnet's *Sacred Theory of the Earth*, a book that was especially controversial in the 1690s when King was doing his work. You can read the Burnet book in an hour. It has the charm of a fantasy novel, and that charm made it a classic. Its fame endures even though its argument ceased to be plausible. Writing the introduction to a 1965 reprinted edition of *Sacred Theory*, the historian Basil Willey praised Burnet's writing style.[55] Many earlier reprintings had established Burnet's status as early as the eighteenth century when Joseph Addison (1672–1719) admired his work.

Burnet published the first installment of *Sacred Theory* in 1681, and he completed the work and published it in full in 1689, dedicating that edition to Queen Mary. He wrote and published his book first in Latin, but he then translated and published it again in English in 1689 and thereafter. He said the English version was a renewed and expanded work, and he dedicated the 1691 edition to King William III. Burnet was a very successful man in his lifetime, Master of the Charterhouse, learned in theology, and eventually a royal chaplain.

Burnet's *Sacred Theory* presented earth's history in four stages: chaos, Eden, the Fall, and the Second Coming. God created the earth out of chaos. Then, and until the Fall, the entire earth was Edenic and its surface altogether smooth, he said. In a postlapsarian stage, sin altered the earth, however, creating its present mangled form, as Burnet explained. The earth's shell was crushed, water poured forth, the Biblical deluge, and that catastrophe left the planet scarred with the mountains and valleys now on it. Christ, coming again, would bring a new earth, while the disfigured earth would pass away in fire.

Destined for later praise, Burnet's book was controversial when it appeared, and debate about it was especially hot when the English edition had just been published (and when Gregory King was writing about the Flood) in the middle 1690s. A popular ballad summed up what Burnet's opponents said about his book. They said it claimed:

> That all the books of Moses
> Were nothing but supposes.

Among the writers who assailed Burnet was John Woodward. Woodward was an amateur specialist in the Flood, showing in this avocation the same jeering scorn that outraged his medical colleagues. Burnet's book suffered the same ridicule as Richard Mead's medical skill had suffered at Woodward's hands. "How much soever it may relish of Wit and Invention," Woodward remarked of *Sacred Theory* in 1695, "it hath no real foundation either in Nature or in History."[56]

Note the distinction between nature and history. The vexed dispute about the Flood was usually the preserve of what Woodward called history, that is of those who studied written evidence, both secular and scriptural. Burnet had rebuffed them by appealing to the court of what Woodward called nature, what we would call geology. Noah, the Ark, and the rainbow were no longer the crucial evidence, according to Burnet's appeal to nature. Fossils were the crucial evidence, but they were dicey evidence, circumstantial and unreliable. They pointed toward past catastrophe, the thing Burnet needed for his theory, but they also seemed to point toward greater variety in past plant and animal species than he needed for his argument, a variety that had passed away slowly and not in a single event. Further, seashell fossils found in high mountains pointed toward a vast saltwater flood, not a freshwater one. Finally, fossil evidence seemed to point to a flood that lasted longer than the one year described by the Bible. Some people said that the Bible's story of the Flood was an allegory, others that the devil had deliberately planted fossils to lure men and women into doubt about Christianity.[57]

Of course, this dispute about the Flood was mostly nonsense on both sides, nature and history, just as Galen's medical theory was mostly nonsense. We face with Burnet and Ussher the temptation that we faced when talking about the history of medicine, the temptation to consign all these people and their books to the dust bin. The nonsense trapped much bigger game than Burnet, moreover. Sir Isaac Newton himself was among those who spoke favorably of Burnet's history, but the Flood was only a sideline for Newton. He devoted many years and much energy to predicting the exact date of the Second Coming.

Many historians have said that seventeenth-century British empiricism was an interim method.[58] Regarding Newton's physics as the goal toward which seventeenth-century natural philosophy tended, one may say that the Royal Society, whose work often reflected empirical thinking, did not develop a mature and complete system in the seventeenth century. This also held true for Petty, Graunt, and King, of course. They all three used a method that I have called a halfway house. One aspect of this halfway attribute was the use of classical and Biblical chronologies, something of course that even the very greatest did, even Newton. James Ussher's date for the Flood was an important source for Gregory King.

Ussher was Archbishop of Armagh and Primate of Ireland during the fearful early years of civil war in the middle seventeenth century. He famously dated the creation of the world and identified even the very day and hour: "From the evening ushering in the first day of the World, to that midnight which began the first day of the Christian aera, there was 4003 years, seventy days, and six temporarie howers."[59] He also reconciled classical historians with the Biblical account, thus producing a complete account of human history. Ussher was very learned, possessing one of the largest libraries in private hands. He cited Herodotus, Thucydides, Xenophon, Polybius, Julius Caesar, and Diordorus Siculus as his principal classical sources, and lamented that the malice of time had denied his access to others. Ussher constructed a notion of Biblical cycles from cyclical arguments in works of these classical writers, especially Polybius.

Ussher's book did not outlive the ability of its core argument to persuade. Burnet's book lived on despite the eclipse of its argument because its prose was lucid, allowing the book to be read in a cursory way. Ussher's book by contrast was a thousand pages long, based on immense learning, and entirely dependent on abstruse higher mathematics. No Basil Willey praised Ussher's style; no recent edition established the book as a staple item in current libraries. Not only was Ussher's book consigned to the dustbin, he himself became a figure of ridicule. Even a standard history of calendars now allots to Ussher only one or two mentions, and those derisory, of his dating of the creation of the world to 4004 B.C.[60]

Despite the subsequent eclipse of Ussher's fame, his chronology was a good, solid piece of higher mathematics, typical of its seventeenth-century English type and very respected at the time. He hoped to reconcile the Hebrew calendar, with its lunar basis, and the Julian calendar, a solar one, creating "an artificial epoch, framed out of three Cycles multiplied in themselves; for the Solar Cycle being multiplyed by the Lunar, or the number of 28, by 19, produces the great Pascal Cycle of 532 years, and that again multiplied by fifteen. . . . " The key to historical cycles, he thought, was the regression of the equinoxes, a very complex matter.[61] Their slow alteration allowed current astronomical observation to certify or settle the dating of past accounts. He used that method to correlate the secular histories that he mentioned with the sacred one. Later scholars still labored with Ussher in that vineyard east of Eden.

There was an enormous seventeenth-century debate on the authenticity of Biblical history and chronology.[62] Both Jews and Christians noted that secular sources suggested that the world was older than the Biblical narrative seemed to warrant. Marco Polo's account challenged the Biblical narrative by suggesting that Chinese civilization was of greater antiquity than the Bible made possible. Thomas Hobbes suggested points to disprove the Mosaic authorship of the first five books of the Bible. As medieval Jewish commentaries had acknowledged, for instance, Moses could not have written the account of his own death. Other questions abounded. Where did women come from for Cain and Abel to marry? Orthodox rabbinical and Christian commentators labored to rebut these challenges.

Not everyone was trapped, of course. The microscopist Robert Hooke (1635–1703) argued that fossil evidence should be accepted on its own terms, views that anticipated Sir Charles Lyell (1797–1875) and later geologists. Gregory King knew Hooke. They worked with John Ogilby (1600–1676), John Aubrey (1626–1697), Christopher Wren (1632–1723), and Sir John Hoskins or Hoskyns (1634–1735), who was later president of the Royal Society, to prepare a printed set of *Queries in Order to the Description of Britannia.*[63] Hooke was to the Flood what Huygens, Halley, the Bernoulli family, and others were to the stability of ratios in Graunt's runs of mortality data. In retrospect, the merit of Hooke's remarks seems clear, for he anticipated the best later work in geology, as Huygens and others anticipated mathematical probability. In the 1690s, however, such brilliant points were little noticed in contemporary English controversy about the Flood.

King was remarkable not for having used Ussher's chronology in his population estimates but instead because he escaped the trap that they represented. If King had used any higher mathematics, he would probably have used the sort that Ussher did, ancient number symbolism that little resembled the mathematical probability, inferential statistics, or calculus of later time. Number symbolism still had great influence in the late seventeenth century.[64] Ussher used it to know eternal truths about the mind of God and the end of time. The same trap claimed Burnet's geology.

King stuck to shop arithmetic and avoided higher mathematics. Doing so, he followed an ancient convention that divided mathematics into two branches. Higher mathematics was a study of eternal truths. When they put over the gate of Plato's academy the warning that none should enter there without knowledge of Euclid's *Elements of Geometry*, they had in mind this separation between higher mathematics, by which one knew eternal truth, and mere base counting such as that used by craftsmen and merchants. Ancient Greeks prided themselves on having taken mathematics beyond shop arithmetic, mere counting, with which, Greeks said, other peoples were content. Greek higher mathematics might also be called *logicomathematical phi-*

*losophy*,[65] while shop arithmetic returned answers to the question, *How many?*[66] Nichomachus of Gerasa, who flourished in the first century of the Christian era, for instance, writing in his *Introduction to Arithmetic*, summed up the Greek tradition with great clarity. He distinguished between two types of mathematical knowledge, one a knowledge of substance (pure number) and the second a knowledge of accident (mere multitude).[67] The second type of knowledge was inferior and the first superior, said Nichomachus. He said that *philosophy* had always meant the love of wisdom, but, he said with scorn, before philosophy was set on its proper footing, foolish people wrongly made all knowledge to be equal, so that a carpenter, or a cobbler, or a helmsman, or any other person versed in any common art or handicraft, could all alike be called *wise*. The Pythagoreans, he said, were the ones who properly restricted philosophy. They made human happiness the measure of knowledge, and wisdom became the capacity to distinguish the things conducive to happiness. Happiness came only from contemplation of that which shall abide. Distinguishing between the two types of mathematical knowledge, Nichomachus recounted with pride that Greeks had invented the mathematics in which number was a principle of eternal being. Nichomachus gave an example, the distinction between male (odd) and female (even) numbers. This was a Pythagorean attempt to know substance apart from accident. The contrast seemed clear between mathematics as craft or art, on the one hand, and another kind of mathematics, like geometry, that offered knowledge of eternal essence.

What of shop arithmetic? It was ancient, too. Despite the Greek preference for higher mathematics, nevertheless, during the ancient and medieval periods, a practical, trading, commercial, or mercantile mathematics thrived. This practical art of mathematics was conducted on a counting board or an abacus. These devices allowed speedy, accurate, and sophisticated calculation. Merchants time out of mind sent their sons, as Italians said, "to study the abacus." Before the introduction of so-called Arabic numerals, one could not, however, keep track of intermediate stages of any calculation, so use of the abacus yielded only a final tally. Roman numerals made it difficult to write down the intermediate stages of a calculation. In the ancient and medieval practice, therefore, the practical art of trading or shop arithmetic merely yielded final results.

The introduction of Arabic numerals transformed both higher mathematics and shop arithmetic, but the changes did not occur at the same rate. Combined with the new numeral, zero, Arabic numerals transformed shop arithmetic first. New mathematical tools, starting with Gerolamo Cardano (1501–1576), only later opened up the wonderful new vistas of modern higher mathematics.

Let's take the transformation of higher mathematics first. Cardano worked in the sixteenth century. Applying the new numbers to analyze problems in classical geometry, he found a great new art replete with discoveries and innovations.[68] René Descartes (1596–1650), Pascal, and Fermat contributed even more important discoveries and innovations in the seventeenth century. Descartes transformed geometry. One of the important new tools was mathematical probability. Cardano had anticipated important points in this work, also, but the Italian had not published his findings on probability. The work was published only in 1663, nearly a century after Cardano's death.[69]

We took higher mathematics first because the older system endured so long. Ancient geometry, in particular, long had great strength. Galileo and Kepler used it to study motion, and Kepler himself was a Pythagorean whose three laws of the heavens arose from mystical studies. However, ancient geometry also had weaknesses. It was best suited to a study of static ratios. Therefore, as the work of Galileo showed, study of velocity exceeded the limits of ancient geometry and provoked the rise of new techniques. We will return to this point in Chapter 11.

Calculus was a major, transforming invention. Two different men claimed it: G. W. Leibniz and Isaac Newton. Isaac Barrow (1630–1677) also played a leading early role in that great invention. Newton, who had the idea before Leibniz, kept it to himself and developed it slowly over decades. Newton used it to solve problems in physics that made him famous, but he did not reveal his mathematics. "Let Newton be, and all was light." That was written by a poet who did not know Newton except by reputation. Leibniz developed calculus independently, in a shorter period of time, and had an equal claim to the praise of poets. Newton used a complex terminology involving fluents, secondary fluents, and fluxions (see the *Opticks* and *Principia Mathematica*). Leibniz used a better terminology of functions, integrals, and differentials that we still use today. In fact, his work still looks surprisingly modern. Newton retained many of the older mathematical forms. Despite his eccentricities, Newton was a genius of the first rank. Rightly did King George I brag of having Leibniz for a subject in one kingdom, Hanover, and Newton for a subject in the other, Britain.

By contrast to the slow evolution of the new higher mathematics, and the long retention of ancient higher mathematics, a quick transformation of shop arithmetic was completed even before Cardano began his work. By the fourteenth century, reckoning schools had appeared, first in Italy, then in Germany, and then in other parts of northern Europe. The use of Arabic numerals became well established in those schools in the fifteenth century, as represented by the *Treviso Arithmetic* of 1478.[70] So did the zero. The abacus and the tools and pieces of the counting board were less used, and their manufacture thereafter declined.[71]

This soon led to an increased prestige for shop arithmetic. Statesmen of the early sixteenth century already accorded it a prestige that no ancient Greek writer would have given it. The magnificent *The Ambassadors*, a painting by Hans Holbein the younger (1497–1543) and now in the National Gallery, London, was perhaps the most beautiful of all evidence that there had been a transformation in the status of shop arithmetic. The painting was a reminder of death. Holbein contrasted ambassadors, with their many implements of human power, and a skull or death's head. A painted book *Arithmetic for Merchants* appears among the examples of scientific and musical instruments appropriate to the craft of statesmen.

The prestige was justified. Until the time of Newton and Leibniz, much of higher mathematics still retained the ancient Greek emphasis on abstract knowledge, on knowledge of essence as distinct from mere knowledge of appearance or accident. Shop arithmetic was a powerful new tool of calculation then. When Petty, Graunt, and King used it, shop arithmetic was arguably competitive with higher mathematics in many practical arenas.

Shop arithmetic also needed to be purified of mysticism, however. Searching *The Dictionary of National Biography on CD-Rom* for the word *arithmetic*, and concentrating on seventeenth-century schoolbooks, one finds several authors. Edward Cocker (1631–1675), John Dee (1527–1608), Robert Record (1510?–1558), and Richard Witt (1568–1624) were all such. Cocker and Witt both taught young men arithmetic and penmanship. Of these writers available to exemplify shop arithmetic, I selected the most famous in each category, Dee and Record. They both created mystical but new versions of shop arithmetic, and they made it a competitor with ancient higher mathematics.

Dee spent most of his life in work of this kind.[72] He was an Elizabethan magus and astrologer both, and edited many important books.[73] Dee was a magician in an age of magicians. He recorded angelic language. He summoned spirits and familiars. He cast horoscopes and spells. All these notions were in his mind when he thought of higher mathematics. His edition of Euclid's *Geometry* reflected them.[74] It was higher mathematics, on the best Greek model, and with a long introductory essay thrown in for bonus. Dee said that numbers should be pure and free from any connection to material things, a Pythagorean notion.

Dee brought the same mystical notions to shop arithmetic. Perhaps the most important English book of shop arithmetic was Dee's edition of the standard English arithmetic textbook, a book by Robert Record.[75] Record was a medical doctor whom the University of Cambridge admitted to his degree in 1545. He was the first writer in English on many mathematical topics. He introduced algebra into England, together with fractions, and discovered the means of extracting the square root of multinomial algebraic expressions. He first used the " = " (equal sign). Tragically, both Dee and Record died in great poverty; Record was actually in prison for debt. Dee mixed shop arithmetic with some elements of ancient mathematical mysticism, including a connection with magic and angels, and Record also had similar tendencies himself, but this story was complex.

Despite the mysticism, Record also anticipated Bacon in opposition to Aristotle. Record was an independent advocate of a system of empiricism, said some historians.[76] Their analysis was persuasive. No doubt Bacon was the big direct empirical influence on Petty and Graunt, and an indirect influence on King. But King may also have taken empiricism from an independent tradition of practical mathematics derived in part from Record, witnessed by King's dogged use of shop arithmetic and never a mention of angels or the Pythagorean theory of numbers. Record's independent and practical empiricist tradition may seem in abstract analysis to be very distinct from Bacon's empiricism, but King may have seem much similarity between the two.

King's shop arithmetic was free of mysticism. He even concealed his use of Ussher's dates from any casual reader of the 1696 estimates. Although Davenant gave those dates priority of place, King did not. In the fair copy that King gave to Harley, bald statements of world population and English population appeared unsupported. (Remember that this separation of conclusions from data was a traditional feature of the old, abacus shop arithmetic: It always displayed only final results.) The change to Arabic numerals made it possible to write down the intermediate stages of calculations on the abacus, but the old habit of showing only final results lingered. King retained it.

Make no mistake, though, King used Ussher's dates for the creation of the world and the Flood. Davenant understood the importance of the date for the Flood and made it the beginning of his discussion of English population history. King cited Joseph Scaliger (1540–1609), and this citation was clear evidence of influence from Ussher, who disagreed with Scaliger's dating. Ussher cited Scaliger as the foil for many points, especially the birth of Abraham. King never cited Ussher, but King's dates were Ussher's dates, not Scaliger's.

King tempered Ussher's influence with skepticism, however. The philosopher Richard Popkin found skepticism in seventeenth-century attitudes toward Biblical chronologies. King operated on this skeptical model and took only population data and dates from Ussher but showed no interest at all in the number-based mysticism that fascinated Ussher. In borrowing his methods from Bacon, Petty, and Graunt, King shielded himself from the variety of English shop arithmetic that had, from John Dee's day, been saturated with magic, astrology, and mysticism.

King was also skeptical in other matters. As he rejected the magic in Dee and Record, King was much more skeptical of his Biblical sources than Ussher. Ussher formulated supposed laws of human history, and he projected future events based on those laws, but King was more given to empiricism, and he tried to avoid the laws. He accepted Ussher's chronology only when he thought it was plainly derived from the Bible, and he entirely neglected the higher mathematics and number symbolism that Ussher associated with that chronology. They had no firm basis in Biblical texts. King put no date for the Second Coming into his population chronology, for instance. He merely described the data that he found in the Bible, accepting only those data based in explicit Biblical reference or in his own sense experience.

I suspect that King simply used the standard techniques of seventeenth-century antiquarians. His long apprenticeship to Dugdale no doubt introduced him to these techniques. Dugdale had developed a careful research method that sifted evidence.[77] English antiquarians in general were often careful researchers. In particular, the best ones usually rejected inferences from scripture that had no direct basis in the Scriptural text.

Still, King was not skeptical enough, of course. No doubt King's credence in Biblical chronologies rendered foolish some part of his results. His major errors were in his projections of population in the long future, for instance. These projections were wrong not because he used shop arithmetic when better mathematical tools were available but because his assumptions about Biblical data were wrong. Yet, even so, one should applaud King's use of Biblical materials. He avoided much of the mysticism common to seventeenth-century writers on these topics. His estimates were wrong, but not that wrong. As for the errors, so what? There was no great impact on his use of contemporary sources to estimate projected tax revenue.

We should see both the novelty and originality of transformed shop arithmetic in general and also the novelty and originality of King's particular use of shop arithmetic. The introduction of Arabic numerals had only recently transformed shop arithmetic into a powerful new tool when Graunt had added to it Bacon's empirical system. Before the use of Arabic numerals and zero, shop arithmetic was clumsy, dependent on the abacus or the counting table. Arabic numerals enabled pen and paper or chalk and board calculations. It also enabled people to make much more sophisticated calculations than before. When King applied shop arithmetic to calculate past and future population data from Biblical chronology, he was using a new technique and applying it in a new field. He was right to reject higher mathematics insofar as it meant his rejection of mysticism and magic.

King was not a precursor of the mathematical probability now used by demographers who publish in *Nature*, but he was an important figure from an interim period in the history of political economy, and he did anticipate current actuarial practice and some other aspects of statistical science. King's use of shop arithmetic showed the power of that tool, when he combined it with empiricism and skepticism.

King used simple mathematics, and he used Biblical dates, but his results were not for those reasons inherently faulty. Comparing King to other projectors, Davenant thought King was both more practical and also more honest than most. As the accomplished results of a theoretical system, King's 1696 estimates should be measured against the work of James Ussher, John Dee, and Robert Record.

By the way, King could have gotten his calendar directly from Ussher or indirectly through another, unnamed author. The dates were widely available. John Prideaux prepared a version of history as crib for students at Oxford.[78] Many such books circulated. Ussher's was, however, the most likely one for King to have used. As Davenant noted, the crucial date for population, following this logic, was the date of Noah and the Flood. Davenant accepted the dates as common knowledge. Following that catastrophe, on this argument, the world was repeopled. I deduce a dependence of King's 1696 estimates on a general tradition of which Ussher was the most famous representative. The key point, nevertheless, was not King's resemblance to Ussher, but his divergence from Ussher who was a practitioner of ancient higher mathematics, while King used the shop arithmetic and empiricism of Petty and Graunt.

# CHAPTER 6

# Shop Arithmetic, Conversation, and Projects

In the twenty-first century, with e-mail, fax, and the mobile telephone, we may forget how important face-to-face talk was in the seventeenth century. Historians have nevertheless said it is vital to imagine face-to-face conversation. Preindustrial England was a face-to-face society, said historian Peter Laslett. We must, as it were, hear the people of past ages talking, historian G. M. Young said about the Victorian age.

Face-to-face talk was especially important for seventeenth-century British shop arithmetic. Talk was an important tool in evaluating practical political schemes or projects. Were historians to limit themselves to an examination only of printed books and formal state papers in connection with Gregory King, they would then miss his conversation, and that would be to miss two things of crucial importance to an understanding both of his 1696 estimates of national wealth and strength and also to King's Law. The casual conversations were filled with money talk, and the shop arithmetic habitually involved estimates and observations that were accurate but only approximate. Some of that conversation is reconstructed in this chapter in connection with various political schemes or projects for which shop arithmetic was an important aid and support. The Scottish philosopher David Hume (1711–1776) and the English novelist Henry Fielding (1707–1754) provided analytical notions that we will presently use for this purpose.

Let us by way of prologue, however, first examine a suggested pattern or outline of philosophical circles in seventeenth-century Europe. Sociologist Randall Collins discussed how circles of conversation characterized the development of philosophy.[79] Francis Bacon, Bacon's followers (the Royal Society), and groups of seventeenth-century British mathematicians spread intellectual influence through organized circles of philosophers, he said. When people formed themselves into these circles, they debated philosophical problems or interests, and general suppositions were shared or common within the circle. A circle defined itself by shared interests and assumptions for debate, and this provided some uniformity within the circle, therefore. Yet people also disagreed within the circle, so the philosophical influences were sometimes those of intellectual borrowing but were other times also those of having casual conversation with an adversary. Conversation helped one to clarify one's own thought, therefore, either by obtaining supplementary support from those who agreed or else through interaction with others who refused to yield. In either case, one's own point of view was refined. The circles also refined thought by consolidating members' views as a whole against the views or presumed views of people in other circles. He thought circles were important not only for Britain but also for all seventeenth-century Europe.

King was part of a conversational circle, although his circle was not on the list that Collins provided. No doubt King's circle interacted with the larger and more public circles that Collins enumerated and described, ones centered on the Royal Society, natural philosophy, and higher mathematics.[80] We will discuss some of those larger circles in Chapters 9 and 10. Meanwhile, in this chapter, we try to reconstruct the conversation of Gregory King's circle.

Its focus was on discussion of practical projects presented to ministers of state. Members of the circle were deadly serious about their own careers and advancement, and they combined projects with efforts to obtain grace and favor from ministers and the monarchy. They were amateurs, "virtuosi," natural and political philosophers. They shared a common philosophical empiricism, but they were first of all practical men. Their circle facilitated their successes in obtaining grace and favor.

In this circle, King found a safe harbor. Robert Harley was the chief person to whom King turned for favor and reward, and Harley was well positioned to reward King for the rest of King's life. Harley was a truly great man, capable to bestow great patronage.[81] King benefited from his connection to Harley more than he ever had from the previous connection with Dugdale. King eventually became an adviser who was kept on retainer and given a sinecure. He was secure during Harley's rise and died before Harley's fall. Harley did fall, but before that he had a long and very successful career. During the 1690s, he took up the cry of those in parliamentary opposition in every age, economy, and thrift at home and peace abroad with other nations.

Harley had not been born to greatness. On the contrary, he was born in 1661 into a family of middle rank, Presbyterian as it happened, and he entered parliament in 1688. One might think he would take there the side of Whigs and dissenters, but he drifted slowly away from them. Distressing the Whigs, he was instead a leading opponent of the government of King William III, becoming speaker of the House of Commons in 1701. This was a shrewd course. Harley was well positioned by it to take a leading role in the government of Queen Anne when she came to the throne in 1702. Sharing by then her concern for the Church of England, he became a principal secretary of state from 1704 until 1709. He joined with the queen's other leading ministers, John Churchill, duke of Marlborough, and Lord Treasurer Sidney Godolphin, in directing her government, and this was a time of great victory against the French in the War of the Spanish Succession, 1701–1714. Harley was in and then out of office during these years, and he obtained very high honor as earl of Oxford and knight of the Garter, but he fell from power as Anne sickened and died, and when King George I, amid an effulgent Whig triumph, appeared on the political horizon, Harley's career ended.

King was part of a circle around Harley. But how did the circle function? What kinds of projects were put forward by its members? Above all, how did they use shop arithmetic? We will try to reconstruct conversation within Harley's circle, borrowing methods from Collins and supplementing his work with materials from other scholars.

In the late seventeenth century and early eighteenth, the word *conversation* did not mean merely casual talk.[82] As defined by *The Oxford English Dictionary*, the word then meant, "Circle of acquaintance, company, society." Only toward the end of the eighteenth century did the word *conversation* become limited to denote casual talk. As is so often the case, the common law retained a particular, older, otherwise obsolete usage while ordinary English speech evolved and changed. Readers of historian Lawrence Stone's voluminous writings on divorce in early modern England will recall that "criminal conversation" or "crim. con." was the legal phrase for adultery. The word *conversation* in King's day meant the circle of one's acquaintance, therefore. The word itself meant the very thing that Collins discussed and diagrammed.

How did such circles operate? The English novelist Henry Fielding and the Scottish philosopher David Hume left clear memorials concerning conversational circles. Fielding emphasized the exclusivity of circles when he wrote as follows about "People of Fashion":

> [The] use to which these People have always made of the word circle, and the Pretence to be enclosed in a certain Circle, like so many Conjurers, and by such Means to keep the Vulgar to a Distance from them. . . . [A] polite Circle, the circle of one's Acquaintance, People that live within a certain Circle.[83]

We especially need to keep exclusivity in mind when we try to understand King's 1696 estimates. We see this exclusivity vividly in Jonathan Swift's *Journal to Stella* and in his correspondence. He was in Harley's company and wrote extensively about experiences there. Swift related events in following years, of course, not 1696, but little changed in regard to exclusivity. Swift was not as successful as King was within Harley's circle. Swift was a brilliant satirist, but he was also a very bitter and twisted one. His bitterness reflected in part his failure to obtain benefits that he desired, an English clerical appointment for instance. He languished in Dublin. He also failed when he tried to get ministers to extend Queen Anne's Bounty to Ireland. Following Fielding and Swift, I believe exclusivity was the special mark of the circle around Harley. Men who had access to the circle had access to political power and to the royal court.

King was in his own way more successful than Swift. Maybe King's father was right to apprentice King to Dugdale, not to send him to university, after all. A boy from provincial Lichfield, King could surely have acquired great polish only by long experience, and the College of Arms was a good place to acquire it. Great polish would have been essential in the conversation around Harley. When King combined his herald's polish with his native brilliance and his father's shop arithmetic, he produced a project, his estimates of 1696, that could be understood and valued in Harley's cabinet councils.[84] However brilliant King's mind was, a university education might not have had the same result. To understand King's estimates, therefore, we need to imagine their reception in an exclusive circle, a specific kind of conversation, around Harley.

David Hume made another important distinction about conversational circles when he wrote as follows:

> The elegant Part of Mankind, who are not immers'd in the animal Life, but employ themselves in the Operations of the Mind, may be divided into the *learned* and the *conversible*. The Learned are such as have chosen for the Portion the higher and more difficult Operations of the Mind, which require Leisure and Solitude, and cannot be brought to Perfection, without long Preparation and severe Labour. The conversible World join to a sociable Disposition, and a Taste of Pleasure, and Inclination to the easier and more gentle Exercises of the Understanding, to obvious Reflections on human Affairs, and the Duties of common Life. . . . And this brings Mankind together in Society, where every one displays his Thoughts and Observations in the best Manner he is able, and mutually gives and receives Information, as well as Pleasure.[85]

Higher mathematics, by contrast to shop arithmetic, was a thing of the forum, of the public place, patent, open. It often developed and spread through a network similar to what Hume called "the Learned." Of course, higher mathematics was, as Collins detailed, the subject of many circles, many conversations, but an overall common practice did link together the groups that discussed higher mathematics. As Hume suggested in his notion of the Learned, there was an international community of like-minded learned persons, people whom the French called *savants*. They divided into particular groups, each with a structured etiquette and enduring connections.[86] This was the culture of higher mathematics.

Shop arithmetic was different. At least, King's was. His conversation was largely face-to-face, what Hume called the Conversible as opposed to the Learned. Collins did not make clear enough this distinction between the

Learned and the Conversible, nor did he list King's group, and we need Hume's distinction between the Learned and the Conversible to recognize King's group. I append this distinction, therefore, to my analysis, and say that King had a group or circle and that it depended mainly on face-to-face discussion.

We also need to append Fielding's point about exclusivity to our notion of King's circle. We need to see the practice of shop arithmetic in that circle as a sign of the high status of its members, too busy to understand the details of scribbling savants. The whole tradition of political arithmetic pointed them in this direction. When Francis Bacon, writing in *New Atlantis*, distinguished sharply between the policy of those who ruled and the advice of lesser men, he made the same point. The lesser men provided the quantitative data. Davenant, who no doubt considered himself a statesman of high status, echoed Bacon:

> A great statesman, by consulting all sorts of men, and by contemplating the universal posture of the nation, its power, strength, trade, wealth and revenues, in any counsel he is to offer, by summing up the difficulties on either side, and by computing upon the whole, shall be able to form a sound judgment, and to give right advice: and this is what we mean by Political Arithmetic.[87]

What was the policy? We should remember the proud words of Sir William Petty. He wrote "that a small Country and few People, by its Situation, Trade, and Policy, may be Equivalent in Wealth and Strength to a far greater People and Territory."[88] King's circle was at a distance from the savants. Only secondarily was their shop arithmetic an intellectual tradition that derived its methods from formal written books (perhaps those of Robert Record) or embodied in public documents such as the estimates that King prepared in 1696.

The "higher" in "higher mathematics" should not mislead us, therefore. Putting Fielding and Hume together, we should distinguish King's exclusive group, with its money talk and shop arithmetic, from less exclusive groups whose conversation included philosophy and higher mathematics, often communicating through printed writing. Harley's circle was a circle of Conversible persons, then, too busy and too important to publish much of the talk. They wrote in the deeds of the state rather than in books.

Chance has preserved some examples of the face-to-face exchanges in King's circle around Harley, nevertheless. To find the first of them, let us now seek beyond King and Harley for other members of the circle. Charles Davenant is the first one to come to mind. He was of good family, the eldest son of Sir William D'Avenant, a distinguished poet. Charles was highly successful in his lifetime, becoming a member of parliament and director of imports and exports, and part of his success was due to public sympathy aroused by his many published works on political economy including *Discourses on the Publick Revenues and of the Trade of England*, 1698, and *Essays upon the Ballance of Power*;

*the Right of Making War, Peace, and Alliances; Universal Monarchy. To which is added an Appendix, containing the Records referred to in the second Essay*, 1701. He also wrote *An Essay upon Ways and Means of Supplying the War*, 1695, and *An Essay on the East India Trade*, 1697. Publishing also many occasional essays as party political pieces, he appears to have invented in these the famous phrase "Old Whig," a political slogan that later echoed loudly in British America, playing an important part in the ideology that incited the American Revolution.[89] Old Whigs were exemplars of simple country virtue, in contrast with corrupt but urbane New Whigs, said Davenant. On the strength of his service in parliament, his many political connections, and his effective political writing, he was appointed in 1705 as inspector-general of exports and imports, holding this appointment until his death in 1714. He was a leading member of the circle around Harley, perhaps the leading member after Harley himself, and as I said Davenant was Harley's chosen publicist. Davenant published some of King's data, for instance. He also published King's Law of Demand.

Davenant was always very complimentary about King. He had also seen, he said, King's work in manuscript, and

> Mr King's schemes are all of them so accurately done, that we may venture to say they are not to be controverted on any point so material, as to destroy the foundation of those reasonings, which the writer of these papers, or any other person, shall form upon them.[90]

Davenant cited King's figures at great length, although Davenant may not have well understood King's interpretations. Perhaps Davenant did not represent very well, or care very much about, the technical complexity of King's estimates. King showed his work to Davenant, most probably meeting in person, but King was reticent, not insisting on technicalities, and he failed on occasion to correct Davenant's wrong conclusions. This was skillful on King's part. In return, we hear the courtesy and polish of Davenant's description of King.

More prominent in his own day than King, widely published, and better rewarded, Davenant has nevertheless not fared well since, at least not so far as his reputation as a writer in political economy is concerned. Karl Marx, a great proponent of Sir William Petty's theories and importance, called Davenant a fool in contrast to Petty. Founder of Communism, Marx believed that Petty had discovered the notion of surplus value, essential to Communist economic theory. By contrast, Marx lumped Davenant with French physiocrats, early economic thinkers who thought that land was the basic means of production, and Marx thought these views were not science, lacking the essential break with previous theory. Marx was a harsh critic of Davenant, too harsh, and we should know how to evaluate his stentorian tone, but Davenant had few defenders to counter the harsh charges.

Davenant was not a fool, but neither was he so brilliant as King. Listening to his conversation, we are doing something analogous to what museums of nineteenth-century painting now do with the masterpieces of French impressionism. Museums hang those works alongside the more conventional paintings of lesser nineteenth-century artists, works that gathered dust in storerooms throughout much of the twentieth century. Impressionist works were often little valued when they were painted, and conventional nineteenth-century paintings were then highly valued. Although their prices and reputations have now reversed, impressionist paintings and conventional nineteenth-century paintings need to be viewed side by side. They came from the same context, and one cannot understand impressionism unless one views the other paintings that formed a context for them. Just so, King's 1696 estimates were masterful but little noticed at the time. They have been since highly valued, and the theories of his contemporary, Davenant, almost forgotten. To understand King's estimates, however, it is not enough simply to point out their intrinsic interest and worth; we must also situate them in the context of work by King's contemporaries. Nor is it enough to look only to Harley, the great and powerful politician. Other men whose work seems now of lesser value than King's, but who were at the time his associates, and perhaps superiors, provided the proper context for King's estimates.

Davenant occasionally wrote his books in the form of dialogues, perhaps reflecting his background in dramatic art. His father, Sir William, did much to maintain drama in London when the theaters there were closed down during the Commonwealth, and Sir William boasted of supposed descent from William Shakespeare. Charles wrote plays in his youth. When he published his later pieces, party pieces in particular, he used drama. He imagined various characters in whose mouths he placed messages that pointed political morals and adorned party tales. If we turn to his *True Picture of a Modern Whig*, 1701 and 1702, for instance, we find a good example of his style. "Double" was one of the characters, and he said things like, "As for the soldiers and Seamen, we whigs care not a pin if they starved or rotted."[91] Perhaps these conversations were a bit staged or histrionic, but nevertheless they had points that were very suggestive. In two respects, especially, the dialogues seem accurate. Actual talk within Harley's circle must have been very similar on these two points.

First, numbers, above all sums of money, permeated the dialogues. People quoted sums in connection with various public schemes, and they always calculated their own expected gains. Second, the sums were round. The numbers were approximately, not precisely, accurate.

Davenant's conversation was associated with accuracy but only approximate accuracy, not precise accuracy. When people used shop arithmetic they would, as we say in America, eyeball an estimate or ballpark an estimate. Shop arithmetic was also especially well suited to discussion of money. No doubt money talk, shop arithmetic, and accuracy, but only approximate accuracy, were prominent in the conversations of all members of Harley's circle. When they cited sums of money, they did so to persuade by appeal to self-interest. The numbers needed to be correct but could be only approximate, as was (and is) so often the case with casual money talk. Had the numbers been entirely illusory, then they would not have been persuasive at all. However, a few shillings astray on one side or the other did not impede the argument or cause it to lose its potency, so the numbers did not need to be exact and precise.

This point about approximation was crucial to understanding King's 1696 estimates. An especially important tract well illustrated the point. The tract was Thomas Everard's *Stereometry*, first edition in 1684.[92] Everard dedicated the work to Davenant and also to Sir Denny Asburnham, Francis Parry, Robert Huntington, John Friend, Felix Calverd, and Nathaniel Horneby, all commissioners and governors of the English excise, and William Strong, one of the commissioners of the revenue in Ireland. The tract was a treatise on using slide rules. Clever devices based on logarithms, slide rules were common until handheld computer calculators replaced them in the late twentieth century. Slide rules were expensive, and they came in fancy cases. Engineers and mathematicians carried them with pride and displayed them as status symbols in the way that young people now do with cell phones.

Everard's tract dwelt especially on the benefits of using slide rules for shop arithmetic. He detailed enough about logarithms to enable someone to use a slide rule without learning much higher mathematics. In that regard, the tract bore a very telling witness to the common practice of shop arithmetic in the late 1680s. Decimal fractions were oddities, a key point. Everard had to explain them in detail, taking many pages, more than he used on logarithms, and providing tables that showed the values of digits on each side of the decimal point. This long discussion of decimal fractions well prepares the way for a point I will make in Chapter 8 that decimals were in common use but that Gregory King was not comfortable with them. Everard's tract illuminated the context of King's calculations, therefore. Decimal fractions had come into fashion, and their use added credit and plausibility to a written presentation, but they were decoration, window dressing, for King. By contrast, mastery of decimal fractions would have been essential for anyone using a slide rule. Perhaps therefore decimal fractions had become common among some users of shop arithmetic in the circle around Harley, including King, although King did not use them much himself. He also did not buy or use slide rules himself, evidently. He probably did his calculations with pen and paper or with chalk and board, not with a slide rule.

Everard thought the methods in his book were especially good in connection with practical projects connected to the excise tax and the tariff. He demonstrated ways that one might estimate the volume of content in casks or barrels, for instance. Thrown in at the back of his book and easy to access were tables to allow one to estimate interest payments and the value of annuities. However, *estimate* was the key word. Of course, with the slide rule you had to be content with approximation. You moved a sliding ruler, as the name implied, and read off the result as best you could.

In every case, Everard tried to be accurate in general, but only in general, and he showed little concern either for exact precision or high theory. Let us take a single instance, the squaring of the circle, from Everard's fifth chapter. The problem was an ancient puzzle, famous to all students of Greek geometry. Thomas Hobbes had spent years on this problem, and solved it to his own satisfaction, but merely revealed thereby the weakness of his ability in mathematics. I will argue in Chapter 9 that Hobbes's blunders in higher mathematics strengthened the reputation of shop arithmetic in the analytical tradition that King inherited from Graunt and Petty. The puzzle of squaring the circle is not solvable in higher mathematics because the value of pi runs out to infinity, but Everard had no concern for these higher mathematical difficulties, much less for any philosophical controversy. He was content to estimate pi at a value of 3.141592, and he then set out a method for estimating the square of any circle. Of course, once you have a square for the circle, you can estimate the volume of a cylinder. Once you can estimate a cylinder's volume, you can then estimate the volume of a cask by allowing for its variation in form from that of a cylinder. Close enough for government work, to use another common American expression.

The trick of estimating the volume of containers was a standard problem in shop arithmetic, often posed in previous texts. The art historian Michael Baxandall pointed out that twentieth-century people grew so accustomed to standardized containers, spaces, and commodities, that they forgot that earlier people always and at every turn had to gauge or estimate size and quantity. Shop arithmetic provided many handy tricks for these tasks of estimation, and artists knew and employed them all. Guesswork based on skill was usually assumed to be at work in these estimates, and the results were only approximate.[93]

Since *Stereometry* was a formal, printed tract, it may seem a detour from our study of the Conversable as opposed to the Learned, but not such a big detour. The tract was chatty and easy and light, allowing one to hear people talking in it, as G. M. Young would say. As in Davenant's Whig dialogues, so in *Stereometry* they talked about shop arithmetic, round and approximate estimates, and above all about money. Money, estimation, and shop arithmetic were closely allied. *Stereometry* laid much emphasis on the use of shop arithmetic for calculation of excise tax. It may be worthwhile to note in this connection a point that Chalmers made. He reported that Gregory King's brother Thomas worked in the excise office.

Let us turn to another example of conversation in King's circle. We have Harley's own "Notes and Inquiries (touching Mr K[ing]'s Observations)." They were transcribed on a fair copy of King's estimates and dated April 26, 1697, and King's responses were also transcribed. Called the "Kashnor" manuscript, this fair copy is now in the possession of the National Library of Australia, Canberra. I have not been able to consult the original. Instead, I have used a copy printed from a microfilm tape. Glass used this manuscript extensively.

Remember our conclusions so far: Money talk, shop arithmetic, and approximate accuracy or round numbers were all characteristic of King's conversation in the circle around Harley. These conclusions summarize also the exchange between Harley and King in these notes. Harley expected King to be accurate but only approximately so. Harley asked over and over whether King had calculated this number or that, or only guessed it. Was the sum of empty houses taken directly from the hearth tax books or only guessed? If estimated, then by what rule was the proportion? What about the number of sheep slaughtered? What about prices? The method questions were the key questions, of course. Above all, by what rule was the proportion? We will return to these matters in Chapter 8, but please note Harley's calm acceptance of estimation and round numbers. He would have had little patience for long-winded disquisitions about higher mathematics, but he fully understood the methods, and the imprecision, of shop arithmetic, and although he made a careful distinction between mere guesswork and calculated estimates that depended on method, he accepted both. No doubt King employed both calculated method and guesswork. When he guessed, he did so as a great expert who used his superior judgment and experience.

Many historians view the English common law as a source for early ideas about probability, maybe even as a source for an impulse toward the development of mathematical probability. They should focus on the importance of surveying since the common law was mostly about landed property. Surveying's notions of calculation based on skilled guesswork must have been widely understood among propertied people. Remember that Vauban, King's French counterpart, knew surveying very well. As a soldier and designer of fortifications, he was a surveyor by trade. Surveyors were accustomed to producing calculations that depended on skilled guesswork and common sense.[94] King's work in surveying was no doubt an important background for the skilled guesswork that he did in his 1696 estimates. Surveying was also an important background for the easy acceptance, within Harley's circle of conversation, of estimates based on shop arithmetic.

Historians should also look to drawing and art as sources for early ideas about probability. King was also a skilled artist who produced both engravings and also heraldic pictures. Here again, shop arithmetic and skilled approximation had long been established as essential for persons skilled in drawing. It was even common for artists to use shop arithmetic when they drew up contracts and other business papers in connection with the production of works of art, so shop arithmetic was a standard and important part of an artist's skill both in artistic works themselves and also in the conduct of art as a business.[95]

I believe that King's Law was a piece of empirical observation that King communicated to Davenant by word of mouth, casually, and that Davenant borrowed and placed in his printed book among the discussion of King's calculations just cited. Here was how Davenant printed the Law:

**Defect in Supply of Wheat Above the Common Rate**

| | |
|---|---|
| 1 tenth | raises the price 3 tenths |
| 2 tenths | raises the price 8 tenths |
| 3 tenths | raises the price 16 tenths |
| 4 tenths | raises the price 28 tenths |
| 5 tenths | raises the price 45 tenths |

The Law was very similar to the various tables in Everard's tract. It was handy information bereft of theoretical context, much like Everard's instructions for squaring the circle. King did not work the Law up as a formal piece, in the way he did his 1696 estimates, and Davenant did not ask him to do so. I suggest that King's Law appeared in this way, in casual conversation, and in a printed work that reproduced conversation, because it was a bit of empirical guesswork, useful information for landowners and tax collectors, nothing more.

So much for King's face-to-face conversation, his place in a circle of the Conversible around Harley. What of King's interaction with the Learned? King and Davenant both sometimes participated in a conversation of the Learned as a natural outgrowth of the face-to-face conversation of Harley's circle. Davenant did so more than King, but we know that King did so on at least three occasions because we have the evidence. In the next chapter, on Queen Anne's Bounty, we will find King in communication with John Chamberlayne (1666–1723), an official of the Bounty and also publisher of an almanac or yearly book, begun by his father, that was an excellent and celebrated printed source of information about England and English government. Chamberlayne's name continued to appear on the popular almanac long after his death. A fellow of the Royal Society, Chamberlayne was also well known to the public as a participant in learned conversation. The *Bibliothèque Angloise* commended Chamberlayne as "known to a great number of Foreigners for the obliging manner with which he has received them at this house. He still continues to welcome kindly Savants who to travel in *England*, and he is always ready to do them all sorts of good offices."[96] He received authors and acted as a go-between by sending messages and learned queries.

Chamberlayne provided three occasions when King interacted with the Learned as opposed to the Conversible. Chamberlayne read in manuscript some of King's estimates of population and wealth, and he printed a bit of them in the margin of one of his yearbooks or almanacs, as follows:

It appears from the Observations and Calculations of *Gregory King, Esq;* lately publisht by Dr *Davenant*, that the Rents of the Lands by the Produce of the late Taxes, seem

> to be near 10 Millions *per annum:* And that the Houses (not to be let with the Lands) amount to 2 Millions *per annum:* And all other Hereditaments to about 2 Millions more; in all about 14 Millions: So that the People and Territories of the Queen of *England* alone, may be valued for Wealth and Strength at above one half of those of *France.* And since the whole Annual Expense of the Queen of *Englands* subjects is above 50 Millions, it will require but an 8th part thereof to maintain 100000 Foot, 30000 Horse, 40000 Seamen, and to defray all other Charges of the Government Ordinary and Extraordinary.[97]

King wrote to protest. Since from these data someone could infer the wealth of the nation and the number of its men capable of bearing arms, King said that he regretted the publication of these data and hoped nobody would notice them.

Chamberlayne also sent King a query from John Arbuthnot, the companion of Jonathan Swift and physician to Prince George of Denmark during the prince's lifetime. Arbuthnot was writing on the distribution of male and female births, a famous problem for probability theorists since it posed a puzzle involving equally likely chances. Arbuthnot did not take the route that led to mathematical probability, however. He instead said that the near equality of male and female births was evidence of divine providence. He inquired of King through Chamberlayne, and King replied. King was polite and reticent, just as he had been with Davenant and Chamberlayne. In spite of Arbuthnot's importance, and the importance of the balance of male and female births, this was another small inquiry.

King's larger work on the Bounty was a response to a similar request to him from Chamberlayne, and it was altogether a more important matter. Fittingly, King's reply was long and detailed, as the next chapter will demonstrate. King produced an analysis of the value of clerical livings in England and Wales, dating it November 15, 1710. The document was of considerable value for the light that it threw upon the affairs of the Bounty in 1710. The document was also of value as a very late and choice example of King's shop arithmetic.

# CHAPTER 7

# Queen Anne's Bounty

Where Gregory King was born, in Lichfield in Staffordshire, there is a collection of his papers in the archive of the Dr. Johnson Birthplace Museum. The museum honors Samuel Johnson (1709–1784), the lexicographer, who was also born in Lichfield. The King documents at the Dr. Johnson Museum comprise 20 items of various sizes, and all were purchased from Meyers and Co., Ltd.,[98] in 1952. They were skillfully cataloged in 1972 by K. K. Yung, curator of the Dr. Johnson Museum from 1968 until 1972. The collection contains papers from the last years of King's life.

The Lichfield papers indicate that King was in sustained correspondence with John Chamberlayne. Chamberlayne was secretary to the governors of the Queen's Bounty. Established in 1704, the Bounty ended when it was combined with the Ecclesiastical Commission in 1948. Queen Anne intended to relieve poor Church of England clergy, and she allocated first fruits and tenths or annates for this purpose. This money was a tax to the pope before the Reformation and was thereafter paid to the crown. Much of it had been alienated by the crown over the years, however, and had fallen into private hands from which it had to be recovered.

Through Chamberlayne, King advised the governors of the Bounty of Queen Anne, and through him also, as we have just seen, King was in indirect correspondence with John Arbuthnot who was then writing a work on the equality of male and female births and who had consulted Chamberlayne and King on that question.[99] Chamberlayne may also have known the documents that King prepared for his *Natural and Political Observations* in the 1690s.

Charles Davenant said that he saw these unpublished manuscripts, and Chamberlayne knew and used these earlier King figures.

The provenance of the King papers in Lichfield was as follows. The financial data of the Bounty were in a muddle in 1710. Despite considerable efforts by the governors, the liabilities of the Bounty to poor clergy remained unclear. Perhaps King and Chamberlayne already shared membership in the small circle or conversation, as I suggested in the last chapter. If so, we have more evidence here of the operation of that circle. Davenant was included but Arbuthnot was excluded. (Arbuthnot was known directly to Chamberlayne but had to be introduced to King, evidently.) Robert Harley was one of the governors of the Bounty, and it may be that he urged Chamberlayne to recognize King's skill in matters of fiscal computation. In any event, on the Bounty, King was already in correspondence with Chamberlayne, and Chamberlayne consulted King about the data obtained by Bounty surveys. King analyzed them for him. Only King's side of the correspondence survived in Lichfield, for King returned to Chamberlayne the official documents that King used to prepare his analysis of clerical incomes.

King's work on clerical incomes was a project from which government servants had constructed policy (or, as they would have called policy, *political arithmetic*). The distinction between policy, on the one hand, and the collection of data, on the other, was important to Gregory King, and it was reflected in his remark in the present document that policy was not his province, but the distinction was seldom made by later writers. Twentieth-century writers did not usually retain the distinction between policy and discourse. *Political arithmetic* named then the whole tradition of those in the seventeenth and eighteenth centuries who either collected and analyzed, or else used in policy, data on wealth and population. Policies based on or informed by quantitative data were especially plentiful after King William III and Queen Mary came to their thrones.

The Bounty is a particularly interesting case of policy that required to be informed by arithmetic. The policy behind the Bounty was clearly stated by the first charter at its institution. Queen Anne intended to correct the poverty of the minor clergy of the Church of England. Their poverty opened them to hostile comment by their enemies, especially dissenting Protestants and deists. Partisans of the established church customarily made great claims for the sanctity of its doctrine and the purity of its ecclesiastical polity or church government. They said the Church of England was the best ordered of the Christian churches since the apostles' time. On the other hand, as the Bounty's first charter said, the deep poverty of many clergy, and their scandalous dependence upon the philanthropy, benevolence, and compassion of their flocks, marred these happy claims.

The role of arithmetic as servant of policy was also clearly stated in the charter. The queen's first charter for the Bounty "commanded and authorized" the governors,

> to inquire, find out, and inform themselves, by all lawful ways and means, of the true yearly value of the maintenance of every Parson, Vicar, Curate, and Minister, officiating in any Church or Chapel within such counties and cities where the liturgy and the rites of the Church of England . . . shall be used and observed.[100]

The chief aim of these inquiries was to discover which incomes were under the value of £80 per year.[101]

The governors conducted surveys as directed by the charter. Two such had been done by the time that King prepared his document for Chamberlayne. In February 1705 the governors undertook their first effort to establish the number of clergy with incomes under the value of £80 per year. The charter empowered the governors to place men under oath for these inquiries, but the governors were reluctant to use that power. The governors chose to conduct their survey through the good offices of the several bishops, and considerable care was taken to command the bishops that the results should be accurate. Of course, since the task was complex, and the skills for it wanting, the results were not as desired.

The second effort was undertaken in 1707. These data must have been in King's hands in 1710. By the time of this second survey the governors had decided to remit first fruits and tenths from all incomes of £50 or less, and the sum of £50, rather than £80 per year, became the new line of demarcation. Other sums had been suggested, but £50 became the point below which the governors would use the Bounty money to augment the maintenance of the poor clergy. The 1707 survey was better conducted than the one before, though even the 1707 data were not perfect or complete. The data revealed that the condition of the clergy was bleak: Perhaps half of them were in poverty.

In 1710 the governors needed to reach consensus on the question of the numbers of poor English clergy. At this point Chamberlayne consulted King. King was given access to some or much of this official data, and he also obviously knew the various suggestions that had been made concerning the proper conduct of the Bounty. He offered comment both upon the quality of the data and also upon the analysis of those data, suggestions that Chamberlayne was then to lay before the governors.

King thought that the data were faulty because men had deliberately understated the value of their incomes. He specifically commented on the likelihood that men would lie or had lied under oath. The impulse to lie was so strong that oaths could not curb it, he said. Oaths did not and would not increase the degree to which correct values were returned. While we do not know what verbal remarks King made in conversation with Harley concerning the tendency of the 1696 estimates to underestimate income, we may extrapolate something from these suggestions from King to Chamberlayne. Low estimates were inevitable when the state surveyed incomes, but such defects did not prevent the state from making accurate judgments concerning its revenues and expenses. King was no hack. He was polite and polished, but he intended his estimates to be accurate.

Nor did King suggest that Chamberlayne undertake a new survey. King had collected his 1696 data by personal observations as well as by careful study of state documents, but King was a bureaucrat of long experience. The governors were not about to take a fresh and more accurate survey, however wanting was the present one. King spoke to their practical purposes.

One of the chief dilemmas of the governors was as follows. They had perhaps £12,000 or £13,000 available each year to augment incomes. They had to decide how to use that money. In the event, they chose not to make direct payments in supplement of clerical incomes. Instead the governors used sums of £200 as individual augmentations. These sums bought pieces of land, one bit of land for each £200. Each parcel of land would yield a perpetual revenue, and that revenue was the augmentation to the maintenance of each poor clergyman.

King's comments supported the governors' notion that direct money payments would have been a poor idea. King noted how greatly the value of money had fallen since King Henry VIII's day, and King suggested that the value of money would continue to fall. He offered as illustration the example of a modus, or money payment in lieu of tithe. The real value of a clerical income must always fall when the allowance is a fixed sum of money. The value of produce from land would keep pace with inflation.

On the other hand, King suggested that the governors would be wise to buy up impropriations. These were clerical incomes that had fallen into the hands of persons or corporations that in turn hired vicars to perform the cure of souls that the money had at first been intended to support. King thought that the Bounty should buy back these impropriations so that the sums would go directly, as first intended, to the support of parish clergy. As this suggestion was perhaps radical, King both made it and also backed off a bit from it. Policy was not his province, he said.

King also rejected a still more radical scheme. He tried to prove that it would not be wise to confiscate the value of richer incomes and parcel out the money to relieve the poor clergy. Not enough money would be available, and besides, able men would not be willing to serve the church without such reward as the richer incomes offered.

There were some other important comments in this document. King remarked that the land tax suffered from the same understatement of incomes that is in evidence in the survey by the Bounty of clerical incomes.[102] King thought that the clergy lost as much as the state by this understatement. If the clergy were to get a full tithe, each clerical place would be worth over £300 per year. King thought that £100 per year would be a desirable minimum value for clerical incomes

King's comments about clerical incomes were of great importance. First, his work was an important addition to primary sources on the early years of the Bounty of Queen Anne to the poor clergy. Historians have long studied the data that was collected in connection with the Bounty of Queen Anne,[103] and King's document contains an important early analysis of some of that data. The analytical element must be welcome to students of the Bounty.

Secondly, the document had something to teach students of King's shop arithmetic. The document that King prepared for Chamberlayne was a choice example of King's use of shop arithmetic, and it illuminated some of the habits of mind that King had used in his 1696 estimates. Despite his interaction with the Learned, in 1710 King still had no interest in publication. He remained a government servant, a boffin, and his task was to provide secret data for those great and good men who formulated policy. Just as before, King had a preference for a Conversible circle over a Learned one, but Chamberlayne's role was as an intermediary for the governors. This gave King his occasion to produce the written analysis.

He retained his Conversible habits, however. He had little tendency to provide the great and good any insight into the gathering and manipulation of raw data. This was a crucial point. A hack would have taken less trouble over materials that he had no intention to display to other people. A man of less talent might have insisted on his own cleverness, might even have published his findings. King's reticence demonstrated the polish and knowledge of the world that one would expect to find in a member of Harley's circle. King magnified the wisdom and knowledge of the governors, and he minimized his own importance. He had done more or less the same not only with Harley but also with Chamberlayne, Davenant, and Arbuthnot.

We also see King's polish and skill in urging the governors to work under the aspect of eternity and to make reforms that would withstand changes of long centuries. He had insisted that statesmen be cognizant of vast periods of time in 1696, and he then made a population study that depended on Archbishop Ussher's calculations of the creation of the world and the Biblical Flood, a point to which we return in the next chapter.

King retained all his life another Conversible habit. Also among the papers in the Dr Johnson Museum were letters from King that urged officials to grant him increased income of various sorts. King was polite and reticent about policy, but he also was very forward about his own interest. He received very comfortable government salaries to the end of his life. As I said, the documents at Lichfield contributed knowledge of King's personal circumstances. As was mentioned in the well-known account of King in *The Dictionary of National Biography*, he had an official sinecure of £300 per year. If King remained in comfort to the end of his life, this Lichfield correspondence proved that he also remained in honor: High officers of state continued to consult him.

King provided the governors a brief and polished paper much like the one he had provided to Robert Harley in 1696, in sum, but King also made one important improvement in his method in the 1710 document. Robert Harley had complained that King's figures in 1696 underestimated incomes, especially those of the well to do. Subsequent historians, for instance Geoffrey Holmes, also complained that King's data understated incomes. Here in 1710 was King's reply to that complaint. He made his 1710 readers clearly understand the tendency of official documents to understate the value of individual incomes. All taxation records were liable to this fault, he said, and those for the land tax were especially defective. There was little remedy for this, however, and King held that the actual incomes were of little importance when the future revenue of taxation was correctly predicted. He thought the theoretical defect in the data about incomes would not damage policy so long as statesmen had correct estimates of future tax revenues.

# CHAPTER 8

# Gregory King's Methods of Calculation

David Glass, the leading British demographer of the middle twentieth century, discerned the outlines of the method that Gregory King used to compute the overall population of England in 1696. King began with the hearth data, a trick that he borrowed from Petty.[104] King said that the number of houses in the kingdom, charged in the books of the hearth office in 1690, were 1,319,215, and he added a few to make 1,326,000, with 1,300,000 as the round number. He calculated 105,000 hearths in greater London, 195,000 in other cities and market towns, and a round one million in villages and hamlets.[105] He then calculated population by first reducing the number of hearths to a number for households and next using the number of persons per household as a multiplier or ratio. King estimated various numbers of persons per household at various times, but, more or less, King gave 5.4 persons per hearth in London, 4 1/4 in country towns, 4.0 for villages. The mixture of decimal and vulgar or ordinary fractions was King's own.

Glass built on the earlier essay of Jones and Judges about London population. Jones and Judges had this to say about King's method of computing population. Quoting King's remark that he takes "the number of houses in the kingdom as charged in the books of the hearth office at Lady Day, 1690," and adding that the hearth tax, repealed in that year, could offer him no further assistance, Jones and Judges added that King,

> undertakes some rather ambiguous juggling to bridge the gap to 1695–6, a vital date for him, for it was then that the marriage-duty series began. He attempts a double conversion. (1) He has to allow for an increase in the number of houses during the

> five-year period in question. (2) He has also to transpose "houses" in the quotation above, where the normal unit, he explains, is the dwelling of a household, into "inhabited houses," considered as separate structures. This involves the dropping of a proportion representing the uninhabited houses included in the original estimate and the amalgamation of split dwelling places. A deduction of about 3 per cent. meets the case for adjustment on these counts. As a result of operations (1) and (2) he finds himself with a number only a little short of that with which he began. The next step is to break the national total of inhabited houses into fragments, and here the process, one is bound to say, is obscure. Most of the controversy about King's estimates has been concerned with the proportion between households and houses (of which more presently), yet there is just as much room for dispute about his method of apportionment among regions, whether it is the hearth-money local aggregates he employs, or those of the marriage duty, or whether again he fakes the sequence of his argument by coming upon an answer through a back door, to arrive later with a key to open it from the other side. The provisional result is that he succeeds in arriving at what he offers, somewhat ambiguously, as totals for inhabited houses in four agglomerations of parishes within the London Bills of Mortality; one total for the other cities and market towns; and one total for the villages and hamlets. At this point the marriage-duty assessments certainly begin to play a part. Using these, be suggests an average of 5–4 souls per inhabited house in the inner City of London, 4–6 per inhabited house in the City parishes without, and proceeds on a descending scale until the villages and hamlets are reached at 4 souls per house. It is a simple matter now to find the number of people in each division. King is satisfied that he has the houses correctly estimated; he is uncertain that all the inhabitants appear in the assessments. He adds 10 per cent. in the London area. This alters the ratios, which become "almost 6 heads per house" within the walls and "above 5 heads per house" in the City Without.[106]

There it was in a nutshell. The excellence of this analysis can best be judged by a comparison of it with that of Glass. He quoted Jones and Judges with praise, and he built his own work on King using the solid foundation that they had provided.

We know more about how King calculated the number of houses, Glass concluded, than we do about how he calculated household size, the number of persons whom he presumed to live in each dwelling. King did not tell either Harley or Davenant much about his method of the calculation. He said he worked from parish records returns and from the assessments of births, deaths, and marriages imposed by the act of 1695, but he omitted further description of his reasoning.

Considerable work has lately been done both on English household size in general and also on King's estimates of household size. Historian Richard Wall said in 1972 that "the basic structure of English households in the preindustrial era is now well known,"[107] and historian Chris Husbands explained clearly the connection of household size to the hearth tax data.[108] Elona Cuthbertson studied a partial and uncompleted list that Gregory King used to calculate household size in the village of Harefield.[109] Still, despite these additions, Glass's basic judgment stands. Richard Wall echoed it. Not all of Gregory

King's calculations were reliable, said Wall, "but in exactly what ways and to what extent it is defective may never be known."[110]

The topic of King's accuracy in his population estimates for Harley must therefore pivot on King's calculation for household size. If, as Holmes said, King intended deliberately to compute low figures for wealth, as Petty had intended to compute inflated ones, then King would have fudged his numbers for household size. Glass said, long before Holmes wrote, that King's accuracy about household size must remain an open question. King's intent will remain in dispute so long as the reasoning behind King's multipliers remains unavailable.

At the end of this chapter, I will have a few more words to say about King's calculations of household size, but I supplement Jones, Judges, and Glass in this chapter mainly by analysis of another of King's calculations, one that Glass and the others overlooked. This analysis will supply the reasoning behind another of King's computations, one similar or analogous to the calculation of household size. King used ratios to calculate population growth over time, both in the English case and also in the case of world population. He used Biblical chronologies to supply ratios or rates of doubling for world population. He then projected contemporary English population data backward and forward in time by similar calculations, extrapolating English ratios from those that he had calculated for ancient world population.

Remember that household size was also a ratio or a multiplier. To obtain population estimates, King multiplied the number of households by household size. To learn how he calculated ratios elsewhere, therefore, is to obtain valuable insight. We can do so in this case of Biblical population ratios, but we must abide King's use of Biblical and classical chronologies, a topic that would otherwise be dated and tedious.

There will be another side benefit: While Biblical chronology is, of course, now obsolete, we will see clearly by our study of it that King's use of this material was free of any intent to deceive. On the contrary, King's honesty in computation shows clearly, the very point that was obscure or disputed in the matter of English household size. Both with Biblical population data and with English population data, King calculated figures and then altered them to accord with experience and common sense, as a proper statistician might do in later time.

As we have seen already, King retained a traditional feature of shop arithmetic. Conducted on an abacus, it displayed only final results. King displayed only final results in the fair copy of his work that he presented to Robert Harley. King hid his calculations and their supporting data in manuscript notebooks, which Peter Laslett printed. While King's manuscripts are not complete, still, fortunately, large parts survived.

King needed Ussher's dates. King's work certainly implied rejection of Joseph Scaliger's different dates. Writing before Ussher, Scaliger calculated dates, and Ussher made Scaliger the foil for many points, especially the birth of Abraham. We all saw this in chapter 5. King never cited Ussher, but, in the manuscript, King used Ussher's dates. The crucial date for later population, following Ussher, was the date of Noah and the Flood. Following that catastrophe, on this argument, the world was repeopled. On both the key dates of the creation and the flood, King, then, followed Ussher. I deduce a resemblance between King and a general tradition of which Ussher was the most famous representative. King could have gotten the dates from Ussher indirectly. That is to say, King could have used another, unnamed author who cited Ussher. King did not supply footnotes, of course, and it is not possible now to know which of these calendars he used.

King's analysis of ancient population growth borrowed Ussher's dates, but neither Ussher's methods nor mathematics. King's manuscript book makes clear his entire dependence on simple shop arithmetic. In the copy that King gave to Harley, few calculations supported the bald statements of world population. The manuscript book makes clear that King left aside Ussher's whole apparatus of higher mathematical mysticism, for Ussher wanted to predict the end of the world and the Second Coming, but King ignored those predictions. Reliance on shop arithmetic shielded King's mathematics from the magic, astrology, and mysticism of Ussher's version of higher mathematics.

As Robert Record and others had done in advanced shop arithmetic, King implied algebra in his polynomial equations. King adjusted hearths to yield households on the following formula, for instance.

> To y Numbers of Chimneys add twice the numbers of houses and 1/20 part of the houses more or 5 p cent Take y difference between y numbers of chimneys, & y double Numbers of Houses so augmenting with a 20th part if the chimneys be less than y Houses so augmented add 1/2 the dif to the chimneys & houses so added together, if more subtract.[111]

Note that King used the logic of algebra but not its notation.

King used shop arithmetic to calculate from Biblical chronology in the following ways. King took his essential basic dates about early population history from the Bible. With Ussher, King dated ancient Jewish population history, and these dates enabled King to calculate world population growth rates in ancient time. King's mathematical method was clear in these calculations because the Bible presented him with many anomalies. Jewish population data were clearer from the Bible than the world data as a whole, but scripture forced King to use the Jewish data in ways he would not otherwise have done. For instance, he concluded that, for one period, the children of Israel were a greater percentage of world population than he would otherwise have made them, or than he made them in later periods. Scripture forced King to make Jews nearly one-seventh of the world's population in ancient times. He had to adjust these anomalies as he carried his population history toward his own day, and he used Jewish growth rates as a contrast for world rates. He argued that population doubled at different rates before and after the Biblical Flood. He appears to have thought that people lived longer before and so could have more children in a single lifetime, 70 or 80 instead of 12. Even after the Flood, Abraham lived a long time. By Jesus' time, human life was down to three score years and ten. King made doubling to be from 10 to 328 years before the flood and 15 to 410 years at Jesus's time, and 410 to 680 years since. He charted these ratios elaborately in the manuscript that Laslett published.

King, therefore, used experience to modify the multipliers that he extrapolated from Biblical accounts. The year 1690 had a doubling rate of 680, and the rate would continue to decline. Assuming a duration of 30 years for each human generation in his own time, and assuming that each couple then produced, one with another, 8 children in 30 years, King thought that future population growth was slowing down. As a Baconian, King observed current population. King noticed that his own scheme seemed "not to Encrease fast enough upon comparing it with the Holy Scriptures." He said, therefore, that world population doubled at a slower rate than Ussher would predict, and that the rate continued to decrease. World population took much longer to double in his day, that is to say, than Jewish population did in ancient times, and he thought that the doubling of world population would be still slower in the distant future. At no point do we see why else he should have changed the rate of doubling, but we cannot miss that he slowed it. We must conclude that he did so to accord with his observation. He was an empiricist. We also conclude of course that he did so against our notion of common sense because the larger a population, the more immune we would think it to periodic fluctuations. We would use that argument to retain King's observed current population and to dismiss estimates, based on Biblical figures, for earlier time. But King did not see things that way. He accepted Ussher but slowed doubling to fit the Biblical scheme with current population data as he observed them.

King calculated current English population from hearths and households, and he then estimated past and future world population, including past and future English population, to check his current results. To estimate population, King had to figure initial state of population, the rate of reproduction, and the carrying capacity of the land. The ratio derived from the doubling of world population was the basis for King's projection of English population in the past and future. Having a method of calculating population growth over time, he applied it to the question of English population. From the hearth data, he had calculated a current population. King used classical sources to estimate the initial date of English population history and then calculated the rate of increase to his present figure. He projected ongoing increase into the far future. In his charts, he used the number of people as the x-axis, and he plotted the rate of growth as a function of this.

King used his Biblical calculations as models for slowing the doubling of English population. He assumed that England's population growth rate was similar to that of world population, and he first calculated world population, from Ussher, and then turned to the English population. King said that England had been first populated from a handful of couples, and he estimated the rate at which English population thereafter doubled. Again, using Ussher, King applied to English population the slowing rate of doubling that he first established from his own study of population. Saying that English doubling took longer in his day than in earlier times, again probably from observation but without explanation, he indicated the change in the rate of growth, and in the change of the change. King made English population to be 1/119 or 1/120 of world population.

Now we come to a main question: Did King fudge these English figures? I suggest that he did not. I suggest, first, that the calculations were odd in appearance for reasons that have to do with shop arithmetic. King certainly used only very simple mathematics. He used addition, subtraction, multiplication, division, and a little algebra. No advanced mathematical tools appeared, although they would have eased his work. He failed to use any notion of geometric increase. All increase of population was doubling, a standard shop arithmetic calculation. He also failed, of course, to use calculus. When describing the change in a dependent variable, itself subject to change, it is useful to use a differential, which would have been called a fluent by Newton. But King did not know such things. How many English scholars in King's day could have known such calculations?

King often used the words *ad hoc* as a running head for his tables of data. It was an appropriate phrase, for he had invented *ad hoc* the mathematical methods by which he supplemented Baconian science. Borrowing from Graunt and Petty, King tailor-made or crafted a singular method of his own for his purposes. King's method was odd. As an example of oddity, we see his cumbersome and awkward calculation of "the difference of the difference." King repeatedly used this phrase to describe calculations in his analysis of ancient population. King's cumbersome calculation that he called the difference of the difference created sideways funnels or sideways pyramids of numbers on his pages of manuscript.

I judge these oddities to bear on his failure to lay out clearly his calculation of household size. While he frequently calculated difference of the difference, King seldom calculated mean averages. Undoubtedly he employed some averages as multipliers. King even supplied in decimal form some of his multipliers for household size, but I suggest those decimal multipliers were red herrings. No supporting calculations appeared, and, anyway, he much preferred to write multipliers as ordinary or vulgar fractions, such as 4 1/2, when he could, rather than decimal fractions, such as 4.5. I suggest, instead, that King was simply not at ease with decimal fractions, and that may explain his failure to detail his English multipliers. The Scottish mathematician John Napier (1550–1617) had made decimal fractions widely available, although he did not invent them.[112] King made little use of them, nor, as we saw in Chapter

6, did King use a slide rule (based on Napier's logarithms) as he could have done, nor did he calculate mean averages. King's Biblical calculations were clear with regard to method, and they lacked mean averages. He always calculated the difference of the difference, and that appears to have been his constructed rough substitute for decimal fractions. I think that he estimated averages in his head without written calculation.

Back to household size, King observed sample households and so collected the raw data for calculations of mean average household size, but I suggest he then rounded out the averages or multipliers in his head and without much formal calculation on paper. Saying this does not detract either from the value of his estimates or from his own integrity.

Observing household size carefully, and working on a basis of extensive sampling, he produced an accurate estimate of population. That is his chief claim upon our interest. However, he also used only simple shop arithmetic and so left us unfulfilled because we cannot trace how he rectified the calculations. King estimated household size by experience, and he did it well, but his calculation from observations was inadequate by later mathematical standards. Glass said as much, and so did Wall. Elona Cuthbertson recently proved it again.

I have shown in this chapter that King did leave clear records of his method of adjusting Biblical population. And, further, I have suggested King's mathematical reasoning when he calculated population history from Biblical and other classical sources. King adjusted his data to accord with his experience. I believe he adjusted his English figures for population and wealth in an analogous way, to accord with experience.

I have shown part of the case in the previous chapter. King stated clearly to John Chamberlayne and the governors of the Queen's Bounty to the clergy that they had to accept low estimates of wealth in order to obtain accurate projections of tax revenue.[113] Writing toward the end of his life to the governors of the Queen's Bounty, he said that policy was not his province. He stated that his purpose was to assess revenue so that the great and good could use his data to set policy. He told the governors that they needed conservative estimates of wealth because actual tax revenues were always only a fraction of the taxes truly due. He said for instance that returns from the land tax were only 75 percent of those that would be collected if all rents were truly declared. He told the governors to lower estimates in the one column, wealth, to achieve accurate results in the other column, revenue. Tax revenue was always merely a fraction of that which the state should have received. One must remember that King wrote for high officers of state and not, like an academic, for publication. The high officers long kept King's figures secret. However, they clearly knew what was happening in the 1696 estimates. Harley knew. He thought that if some of King's figures were consistently on the low side rather than the high side, then the revenue predictions would therefore be safe. King intended only to produce figures that would serve Harley as a basis for policy.

The purpose was to estimate the strength of the state in war, and, to that end, King estimated such things as available soldiers and sailors and the actual revenue from future tax.

This chapter has affirmed an older analysis by Jones, Judges, and Glass. I have done so by laying out something that they neglected, however, the method by which Gregory King computed population from Biblical sources. These data show that King slowed down population doubling to accord with experience.

I deduced that King estimated household size in a fashion that cannot now be recovered, but he had much systematic, empirical experience on the matter. His empiricism was superior to his mathematics, I suspect. He used only shop arithmetic supplemented by guesswork, but that did not detract from his integrity, nor did it diminish his achievement.

If King had been a Tory hack who fudged his figures, he would not have gone to such lengths in these Biblical computations. Hidden from public view, they served no party purpose. The extent and complexity of these computations, therefore, argued for the integrity of King's data and also for his skill.

We are right to think that King's estimates were sometimes low or conservative, but we would be wrong to think he intended them to be inaccurate. King intended all his calculations to yield accurate estimates, especially accurate estimates of future tax revenues. I maintain that King worked carefully and on a system: He was a man of genius and a calculator of great integrity. If he was not an inventor of mathematical probability, he was, nonetheless, an important figure from an interim period in the history of science, in this case, statistical science.

# CHAPTER 9

# What Was Political Arithmetic, Really?

As we have just seen in the last chapter, shop arithmetic was the birthright and the nemesis of the tradition in which Gregory King worked in 1696. Often called *political arithmetic*, the tradition was then vital and evolving, allowing King to do pathbreaking calculations in his estimates. His calculation of English population was an important achievement, and the observations summarized by his so-called Law of Demand or King's Law were also very important. Late eighteenth-century and early nineteenth-century practitioners of political arithmetic such as George Chalmers and Sir John Sinclair, surely able men, still used political arithmetic, but they also changed it fundamentally, as we will see more at length in the next chapter. Thereafter, notwithstanding their efforts at renewal, British political arithmetic died out, and new traditions replaced it. First it was replaced by what Sinclair called statistics and then by economics. The future of British social analysis lay with adaptation of the novel higher mathematics invented in the seventeenth century, especially in the cases of demography and economics with adaptation of mathematical probability. Using mathematical probability, demographers and economists advanced claims to be scientific, claims that their successors retain to this day. In particular, W. S. Jevons and F. Y. Edgeworth (1845–1926) in the late nineteenth century added mathematical probability to British economics. Sir Ronald Fisher's advances in mathematical probability were also especially important to twentieth-century demography.

Remember why mathematical probability would have been useful in Bacon's system and in later political arithmetic: It would allow an individual example to be seen as part of a class. If one sticks too closely to bald experience, as

Bacon rightly said, one's knowledge is merely idiosyncratic. That is to say, one will miss the forest and see only the individual trees. Petty revisited the same problem, posing it even more clearly than Bacon, and Graunt dealt with the specific difficulty of empiricism in medicine. Petty and Graunt clearly foresaw that mathematical analysis could, to some extent, allow an observer to rise above individual cases and to see larger patterns, but they hardly accomplished that. With mathematical probability, they could have done much more than they did.

Why was that next step lacking for Petty, Graunt, and King? Why did Edgeworth, Fisher, Jevons, and others add higher mathematics to social analysis, while they did not? One could argue deductively. One could say that shop arithmetic in political arithmetic was itself a part of a general pattern or class in the history of mathematics. Several schools started up, but only a few survived, and the others died out. Such things were normal in the history of thought.[114]

By contrast, recall the previous discussion in Chapters 5 and 6. They left aside the general and instead dealt only with the specific. They pointed out two details about the appropriateness of shop arithmetic in King's individual circumstance. It was far more effective for King's purposes in 1696 than would have been James Ussher's higher mathematics, for one thing. For another thing, conversation in Robert Harley's circle esteemed shop arithmetic but not higher mathematics.

So what would have happened if King and other writers in political arithmetic had nevertheless used mathematical probability? They might have encountered severe difficulty. If King had used mathematical probability, the seventeenth-century type of probability available to him, reflecting determinist theory, might also, in the case of social analysis, have entailed allied questions of free will and moral responsibility.[115] Physicists avoided such questions, but the philosopher Thomas Hobbes in particular burdened social analysis with them. The questions of free will were incapable of resolution, and many people found repugnant Hobbes's notions of moral responsibility. Sticking to shop arithmetic, King avoided these disputes.

In this chapter, we will look at these philosophical difficulties and also at Hobbes's unsuccessful efforts to apply geometry to social analysis. First, we trace Bacon's attitude toward mathematics. His praise of arithmetic and his avoidance of higher mathematics both underlay British political arithmetic, and the use of shop arithmetic by Petty, Graunt, and King was an elaboration and an advance on Bacon.

Bacon was the subject of much controversy in his own time and later, with a book lately written about the controversies themselves and not about the man or about his philosophy.[116] Several things conspired to make Bacon the subject of controversy, and among them were the following. Biographer John Aubrey said that Bacon was a pederast, and Bacon and his brother both had that reputation in their lifetimes. Furthermore, early in life Bacon abandoned his mentor and friend Lord Essex in circumstances that made Bacon seem to desire political favor and office at whatever cost. Still further, Bacon was impeached, lost very high offices, and admitted to corruption while in office: He took bribes. As students of the role of shop arithmetic in Bacon's empiricism, however, we can safely leave most of these things to those who study Bacon full time.

There are two points cannot be left aside because they were of such great importance to shop arithmetic and political arithmetic, however. Both were common knowledge. One was Bacon's respect for the work of a handful of previous thinkers, especially the astronomers Copernicus (1473–1543) and Galileo, the Neapolitan natural philosopher Bernadino Telesio (1509–1588), and the anatomist Vesalius (1514–1564), court physician to Emperor Charles V and King Philip II.[117] Bacon said that the study of nature, on models suggested by these men in particular, could vastly augment human knowledge, and he put in his most famous book an icon reminiscent of the great voyages of discovery, a picture of a ship sailing beyond the pillars of Hercules. Bacon meant that he and his handful of predecessors were like Columbus. Their discoveries would augment human knowledge as Columbus had done. Bacon's claim to be a novel writer who broke with past method must hinge on one's evaluation of his place in this distinguished company. The second point is a corollary of the first: Like the men whom he admired, Bacon did too little to champion novel higher mathematics.

Even Copernicus failed to provide Bacon a model for novel higher mathematics, for instance. Copernicus stuck to ancient higher mathematics instead, and ancient higher mathematics was not suitable for Bacon's purposes. The Polish astronomer made an essential break with past astronomy when he claimed that the fixed stars must move at an unimaginable and impossible speed where they were part of a heavenly sphere that completes a circuit around the earth each day. Copernicus reasoned that the better alternative was the ancient Greek theory that the earth circles the sun. This theory also had a difficulty: An orbit of the earth around the sun must be very large, yet the fixed stars do not appear to shift as the earth circles the sun. Copernicus came up with a novel solution, an infinite universe. He reckoned as follows: The distance of the stars, in comparison to the orbit of the earth around the sun, must be as spheres to a point, or as an infinite to a finite sum. This argument had the excitement of real astronomy, but it was a logical and philosophical argument, similar in mathematical method to those of Ptolemy and other ancient astronomers, and it involved no innovative computation. Instead, Copernicus explicitly claimed the authority of ancient higher mathematics, not novel mathematics, for his argument. He ascribed the notion about the sun as the center to the Greek mathematician Pythagoras, a murky figure about whom many myths gathered. Not only did Copernicus endorse ancient higher mathematics, but many of his empirical astronomical data were also erroneous. No wonder that Bacon found no hint in Copernicus that ancient higher mathematics could be thoroughly revised so that a new higher mathematics would become key to a new beginning in natural philosophy.

Galileo, at least, did champion novel higher mathematics some might say. Of course Galileo did. He was the exception. However, his exception proves our rule that Bacon found no model for the centrality of novel higher mathematics in the writers whose work he cited as most valuable. The most suggestive work about velocity lay in Galileo's *Two New Sciences*, a book too late to be known to Bacon. Bacon could have known only the early Galileo, probably only *The Starry Messenger.* That work had little computation. An admirably empirical work, it was a bald report of Galileo's own observations using the telescope. Galileo's work on velocity did imply that a transformed physics would depend on a transformed higher mathematics, but *The Starry Messenger* did not say that. We will come back to Galileo again when we talk about Hobbes later in this chapter and then once more in Chapter 11. Hobbes took influence from the later Galileo, but Bacon did not.

Nor was this neglect of higher mathematics Bacon's only blind spot. He lauded Telesio but failed to understand the still greater significance of William Gilbert's work on magnets. Gilbert lived from 1540 until 1603. Similarly, Bacon praised Vesalius but took too little note of William Harvey's work on the circulation of the blood, a direct outcome of theories that Vesalius advanced about veins, and Harvey was Bacon's own physician.

In sum, Bacon correctly predicted a coming transformation in natural philosophy, but he did so without grasping the central and necessary role of novel higher mathematics in the new system, and in this omission he stood with other famous men whom he took as models, and finally Bacon also failed to grasp the importance of some other innovations in his time, such as the work of Gilbert and Harvey.

Petty and Graunt made advances over Bacon. Despite his praise of arithmetic, Bacon himself mostly used verbal logic, not quantification, and his pages had few numbers or calculations. In that regard, he was like many of the men to whom he compared himself, like the Galileo of *The Starry Messenger,* for instance, and Petty and Graunt made an advance upon him. The benefit of even their shop arithmetic to social analysis was especially clear by comparison of Graunt to Bacon. Shop arithmetic allowed Graunt to do many calculations, a contrast to Bacon's mostly verbal social analysis.

With regard to the application of mathematics to social analysis in the seventeenth century, two roads diverged. One road led through shop arithmetic to political arithmetic but not on to higher mathematics. Bacon took this road, and so did Graunt in his treatise on the bills of mortality. As they traveled on this road, shop arithmetic gave their work expression but also limited its development. This road merged shop arithmetic with empiricism. Bacon and Hobbes gave form and direction to the union of shop arithmetic and empiricism. In their essay about the true greatness of states, they set forth the role of arithmetic clearly when they said, "the greatness of estate in bulk and territory doth fall under measure, and the greatness of finances and revenue doth fall under computation." They also remarked, "not anything among civil affairs [is] more subject to error than the right valuation and true judgment concerning the power and forces of an estate."[118] Bacon's *New Atlantis* was another crucial text, and it argued that practical arithmetic and empiricism informed wise statecraft.

Graunt and Petty took this road. They had direct connection with Bacon and Hobbes. Petty was Hobbes's disciple and close associate. Graunt was so closely connected to Petty that for many years most people thought Petty had actually written Graunt's treatise on the bills of mortality. Graunt said with pride that he based his argument there on Bacon's discourses, especially those on life and death, which he reckoned as natural history.[119]

By contrast, other philosophers such as Pascal took the other road, which combined empirical arguments, very similar to those of Bacon, with higher mathematics, especially mathematical probability. For instance, Pascal invented an early but brilliant and prominent version of mathematical probability. He argued that anyone who limited metaphysical claims to an epistemology of sense experience, and who therefore left transcendent claims unconfirmed, could nevertheless still subject transcendent claims to an analysis of mathematical probability. The existence of God was a metaphysical claim that transcended sense experience, for instance, and so belief in God was a calculation of probabilities. It had the qualities of a wager, but it was a wager with good odds. Pascal showed how one could also calculate the odds in many other claims that transcended sense experience. When Sir Ronald Fisher reconstructed mathematical probability, making it the basis for many experimental methods in the twentieth century, he built upon Pascal's system and transformed it.

British political arithmetic did not take that route, by contrast. Hobbes in particular tried to merge social analysis with higher mathematics, but without success. The inventors of mathematical probability studied a determined material universe in which every action had a prior material cause. Nevertheless, they avoided the entangling conclusion that human reason shared the determinism of the material universe. By contrast, Hobbes thought the mind itself was also determined.

Hobbes's notion of determinism arose directly from his interpretation of empiricism. Graunt said proudly that sense experience was his only evidence, and this emphasis on sense experience as the sole authority, which Graunt found in Bacon, implied determinism, as Hobbes construed it. Hobbes said that anyone who held human reason to have its only sure ground in sense experience must, in logic, also grant that human reason would then be itself determined by sense experience. In philosophical terms, the will would always be the last dictate of the understanding.

Like Pascal, Hobbes was led from belief in determinism to the study of probability, but Hobbes did not invent a mathematical measure of probability.

Instead, he drew lessons about moral agency from that belief. Mathematical probability was developed to solve the same problem of determinism that caused Hobbes to develop novel theories of moral agency. We have no sure knowledge of destiny or fortune beyond the facts revealed by the five senses, and it is therefore not possible to establish an accurate analytical system precisely to predict human events, Hobbes reasoned. Abstract knowledge of the material world, knowledge that transcended immediate sensation, would always be merely probable he concluded. Instead of constructing a mathematical measurement of probabilities, as I said, he posed questions of moral agency instead.

Hobbes put the cat among the pigeons.[120] If one allowed the conventional view of moral agency, then people had free will, at least some free will, and they could use it to decide freely and to act freely. One could then allow praise or blame to attach itself to those decisions. Denying free will, Hobbes came to novel conclusions on moral agency. Using empiricism, he said that it was not possible to find a sure, abstract ground of absolute moral responsibility. He found other such grounds, however. The grounds of moral agency were the good of the community and the safety of the lives and property of its citizens. Preservation of the community was something that he fully allowed to exist as an abstraction, even though he limited valid abstract claims to those that we can confirm by sense experience. He therefore judged schemes and strategies according to their tendency to advance or hinder preservation of the community, not according to other abstract moral arguments that lacked confirmation in sense experience. The underlying philosophical argument was also, to borrow a Greek word, pragmatic. In practice, preservation of the community meant the preservation of the state, and morality was, for the state, whatever the state decreed. For individuals, morality meant above all preservation of one's own life. Many people thought these views of moral agency were deeply repugnant.

As I said, Hobbes did try to combine higher mathematics with social analysis, but he failed. He made detailed study of ancient higher mathematics, especially geometry, but he rejected its epistemology. Biographer John Aubrey tells us a piquant anecdote about his discovery of Euclid's geometry.

> [Hobbes] was 40 years old before he looked on Geometry; which happened accidentally. Being in a Gentleman's Library, Euclid's Elements lay open, and 'twas the 47 *El. libri* I. He read the Proposition. By G—, sayd he (he would now and then sweare an emphaticall Oath by way of emphasis) *this is impossible!* So he reads the Demonstration of it, which referred him back to such a Proposition; which proposition he read. That referred him back to another, which he also read. Et sic deinceps [and so on] that at last he was demonstratively convinced of the truth. That made him in love with Geometry.[121]

Hobbes, as Aubrey also said, complained that algebra, although useful, was too much admired. Resisting the modern application of algebra to geometry,

Hobbes had distinguished company, of course. Galileo and his successor as the chief Florentine mathematician, Evangelista Torricelli (1608–1647), both opposed the application of algebra to geometry.[122] However, this fault stopped those who followed Hobbes from appreciating the achievements of Descartes and Pascal.

Hobbes was fascinated by Greek geometry, as Aubrey said, but he rejected the Platonic epistemology that accompanied it. The fourth and fifth chapters of part one of *Leviathan* enable us to understand the obstacle in Hobbes's attitude toward higher mathematics. His argument about sense experience forced him to discard the Platonic notion that higher mathematics dealt with truly existing entities. We certainly have no sense experience of Platonic forms. Therefore, Hobbes thought of higher mathematics as a system of signs, a merely formal system. In some respects, Hobbes made advances over past thought, but not in his thinking about mathematics. Instead, he took a step back toward the theories of medieval scholastics.

Bishop George Berkeley's (1695–1753) rejection of calculus showed what Hobbes might have done.[123] Berkeley's grounds were roughly the same as those that Hobbes sometimes used in connection with mathematics. Berkeley especially distrusted the assumptions about infinity that were necessary for calculus. He allowed that reckoning and mathematical demonstration were useful, but he denied that they set forth the true nature of things. "We have first raised a dust," Berkeley said of all philosophy, "and then complain, we cannot see."[124]

Berkeley's criticism of infinitesimal numbers was prescient, but mathematical practitioners of the time largely ignored it, and calculus became spectacularly successful at solving problems, however wise Berkeley was in attacking its philosophical foundations. Newton, Leibniz, the Bernouillis, Leonhard Euler (1707–1783), Joseph-Louis Lagrange (1736–1813), the Marquis de Laplace (1749–1827), and others all extended calculus, and, while Euler tried to put more rigor into the method of calculus, Berkeley's arguments were appreciated, although no one really responded to them. Then, in the 1820s, the French mathematician Louis-Augustin Cauchy (1789–1857) created a rigorous new definition of the integral and the limit. These are the definitions used today in most college-level textbooks. They eliminated all of Berkeley's objections. Removing some further problems, the German mathematicians Karl Weierstrass (1815–1897) and Richard Dedekind (1831–1916) created a very rigorous basis for calculus. This is the one now used in advanced texts.

Hobbes made foolish mistakes in mathematics, like his efforts to square the circle, and these mistakes diminished the force of all his other arguments, but Berkeley made lasting contributions. For instance, Berkeley raised issues about the reality and value of mathematical notions that continue to fascinate. On the one hand, mathematics may seem an ideal and beautiful system, akin to Platonic philosophy, although still better with the contributions of every generation. On the other hand, as Berkeley said, we may well seek in vain a firm basis in nature for these speculations.[125]

One answer to these questions is that some mathematical notions seem directly connected to social circumstances. They are mathematical constructs that differ in different societies. The usual example is that of base numbers in systems of mathematics. We use 10 as a base, but other cultures have used 12, 20, or other base numbers. There is mathematical consensus that the number two would provide perhaps the most useful base, and it is used in computers. No doubt, the choice of a base number both reflects and also controls social circumstances. Looking beyond Berkeley, therefore, one finds a wealth of literature asking the famous question, "What is mathematics, really?"[126]

We might well ask, "What was political arithmetic, really?" One answer was that it was the practice of statesmen. Another was that it became a collection of classic texts. We also ask again, as we did at the beginning of this chapter, however, was political arithmetic part of a general pattern? The answer must be that it had the usual mixture of abstract theory and social circumstances. Historians of mathematics nearly always find this dual character in whatever mathematical topic they investigate. I think, for instance, that social circumstances largely decided the use of shop arithmetic in the particular case of political arithmetic. Abstract discussion of shop arithmetic there was, such as that from Dee, Record, Bacon, Hobbes, and others, but little from Graunt and none at all from King. And Graunt and King were the prime users of shop arithmetic in political arithmetic. Personal convenience and social circumstances seem to me to have dictated their use of shop arithmetic. When we ask what political arithmetic was, at least for King, we have to remember what he did as well as what he wrote. He was a man of action, not theory.

# CHAPTER 10

# George Chalmers and the Stagnation of Political Arithmetic

A golden age of British political arithmetic began with John Graunt's work on the bills of mortality, 1662, and ended with the deaths of Gregory King in 1712 and Charles Davenant in 1714. That remains the conventional judgment among historians. By the same conventional judgment, political arithmetic withered away in the later eighteenth century and early nineteenth century. We take these conventional judgments from a skillful recent survey that recounted and "to an extent substantiated the common view." It also observed, "that policy makers in the eighteenth century were narrow-minded, unprincipled, and ill-informed."[127]

Accepting this conventional view of eighteenth-century political arithmetic, we will add in this chapter that political arithmetic, to use a current metaphor, missed the bus in the nineteenth century. Other disciplines replaced it, first statistics and then economics. David Hume, Adam Smith, and others developed moral philosophy into the new discipline of economics. The eighteenth-century failure to attach political arithmetic firmly to economics greatly contributed to the nineteenth-century decline of political arithmetic.[128] Although some practitioners of political arithmetic tried to adapt it to Smith's arguments about free trade, Hume and Smith deprecated political arithmetic. "You know that I have little faith in political arithmetic," Adam Smith told George Chalmers.[129] Hume's essay "The Populousness of Ancient Nations" was written in part to criticize the failure of practitioners to lay to rest the misconception that Europe's population had declined since ancient times.

Eighteenth-century political arithmetic's diffusion and its nineteenth-century decline nevertheless formed important preliminaries for twentieth-century scholarship about Gregory King's 1696 estimates. The decline of political arithmetic meant that few people thereafter gave any thought to Gregory King until the twentieth century. The nineteenth-century economic writer W. S. Jevons was the exception. Commenting on King's Law, he raised fascinating questions about a connection between the Law and mathematical probability, as we will see in the next chapter. Yet even so, King was, for the most part, neglected after the early nineteenth century, and his work was rediscovered again in the twentieth century.

Eighteenth-century political arithmetic may have been in decline, but it was also profuse. For instance, Joseph Massie (died 1784), Richard Price (1723–1791), Arthur Young (1741–1820), and others carried on the political arithmetic tradition in eighteenth-century Britain. Even the new United States had a practitioner in Thomas Cooper (1759–1839), advisor to President Thomas Jefferson.[130] Furthermore, political arithmetic remained entire and robust in Sweden. From 1740 until 1770 especially, Swedes quoted English writers and applied their notions to analyze the relation between population and the production of land.[131] Political arithmetic also was important in Germany in the eighteenth century, hanging on there until the Napoleonic period. However, these later practitioners each differed in various ways from King and from one another, and no single, clear mathematical method was common to them all.

We leave aside these and many other writers of note, and we focus only on two late eighteenth-century and early nineteenth-century Scottish practitioners, George Chalmers, whom we have just met as a correspondent of Adam Smith, and Sir John Sinclair. In Britain, they were the two later practitioners who most resembled King. They were like him in their ability to reach high policymakers with their collections of quantitative data. However, they changed political arithmetic, and their changes explained in part the decline of the discipline. Sinclair claimed to abandon political arithmetic and start a new discipline, statistics. He and Chalmers both sought to influence policy, not merely to supply data to policymakers as King had been content to do. Unlike King also, they published extensively on policy, using quantitative data to persuade the reading public. King had provided numbers to statesmen, the great and good, but he had been mostly silent on policy. We will say that Chalmers, like Sinclair, abandoned traditional political arithmetic. Like Sinclair, Chalmers also began a new discipline, although he kept the old name, political arithmetic. Unlike King, he devoted his new discipline to the open and public advocacy of policy.

Chalmers was the nineteenth-century biographer of King and champion of the 1696 estimates. Chalmers recovered the complete text of those estimates from obscurity and printed them during the wars of the French Revolution. This reprinting of King's 1696 estimates was alone sufficient to command our attention because it formed a most important preliminary topic for discussion of King's twentieth-century reputation. We will concentrate on Chalmers in this chapter; moreover our discussion of Sinclair will serve to illuminate the discussion of Chalmers.

A native Scotsman who also spent time in British North America but whose principal career was in London, Chalmers was probably educated at Aberdeen even though he did not graduate from that university, and he went on to become a lawyer in Maryland at the outbreak of the American Revolution.[132] Because he was loyal to King George III, he was a marked man in 1775. Returning to Britain, he forfeited many American fees and other assets. This loss was reimbursed with compensation, but only after much delay, so Chalmers meanwhile found employment in London as chief clerk to the Privy Council's committee on trade and plantations. This was a very respectable position, and from the start it paid him five hundred pounds per year. He was able to earn some other fees in addition, and eventually his pay and fees totaled one thousand pounds per year.

Chalmers was a client of Charles Jenkinson (1727–1808). Father of the long-serving Tory prime minister, Jenkinson specialized in debate about commerce and fisheries, and he was first a baronet, then a baron, and then earl of Liverpool. Especially influential during Lord North's supremacy, he was one of the parliamentary "friends" of King George III, becoming chief of the committee on trade. Evidently, Chalmers, who was secretary of that same committee, had considerable influence on him, and one is reminded of King's relationship with Harley. However, Jenkinson was not as influential as Harley. Further, King died before Harley's fall, but Chalmers lived sound and well during the period when ill health slowly removed Jenkinson from the scene. Naturally, Chalmers lost influence as his patron lost power, but Chalmers thereafter was paid his salary and left secure, although with little work to do, and he wrote and published many books and pamphlets on various subjects.

Even during his most active time at the committee on trade, Chalmers had many afternoons free, and he took on much work beyond his bare duties for the committee. He long acted as an agent for other Maryland Loyalists, for one thing. He also became agent for the Bahamas. (Many of his fellow Loyalists moved there, with their slaves, more than doubling the population of those islands.) Jenkinson's support of the slave trade earned him many friends, and they played a role in his rise to an earldom; Chalmers collected data and supplied them both to Jenkinson and also to other persons who supported the slave trade and opposed its abolition.

So how did Chalmers contribute to the decline of political arithmetic? His fervent support of slavery was a blot on his record, of course. It was also a measure of his limits as a writer and theorist. As he did not join the abolition movement, so he also made no bold, quick move to join with new and unconventional theory on free trade, nor did he invent or adapt any ingenious innovation in quantitative method. Instead, he used political arithmetic to support his advocacy of policy.

Above all, Chalmers used political arithmetic to support mercantilism's restrictions on trade. This association of political arithmetic with mercantilism played a role in leading Adam Smith to criticize political arithmetic. In the words of a recent economic historian, Smith feared that the state might put political arithmetic to nefarious uses.[133] The political arithmetic that he rejected was the political arithmetic of Chalmers and Sinclair, not that of Gregory King or John Graunt. Smith spoke of King himself with admiration and respect.

In exculpation of Chalmers, we could say that his Maryland experiences were a trauma that froze many of his views. He never fully transcended the loss of what he had believed were early, brilliant, American prospects. Persons he met in Maryland, Loyalists who fled like him to Britain, remained his warmest friends throughout life.

He used political arithmetic to support policy in this manner or fashion. From his American trauma, he retained a long-held and increasingly obstinate belief that navigation acts were beneficial to Britain. In particular, he favored the restriction of U.S. trade with British sugar islands in the West Indies, and he collected data to show how the exclusion of American wheat there benefited the balance of trade in Britain and Ireland. He argued that case using quantitative data. Americans used their trade with the sugar islands to cancel American debts owed to European merchants, he said.[134] He tried to prove that by admitting American wheat to the sugar islands, Britain assumed these American obligations, and Britain thus added to the vast sums it already owed to Europe.

This emphasis on a favorable balance of trade with Europe was obsolete, but it was nevertheless still consonant with the opinions of many Tory politicians, and Jenkinson shared it. For a long time, this obsolete view controlled British policy. Britain supplied the West Indies with wheat from the costly British and Irish home markets, even though American prices were much lower, and Royal Navy ships took as smugglers many Americans who tied to supply their cheaper grain to the sugar islands. Tories found in American actions arguments to support their views.[135] When Whigs allowed the trade to slip into American hands, however, Tories were not able to reclaim it.

Stubborn public adherence to mercantilism severely limited Chalmers's interest in quantification for its own sake. His views on trade were the independent variable. He used quantification as a means dependant on an end, not as a preoccupation or pastime in itself. Slowly, of course, he converted to free trade on the models of Adam Smith and others, although he long thought that free trade within British dominions would be enough. He thought it could exist there alongside traditional mercantilism. After all, he was secretary of the committee on trade, and regulation of trade was his bread and butter. He never relented on slavery, by the way, and his support of it was another example of his using quantification merely to support policies that he favored. In sum, although he slowly changed his views on trade, the change was not accompanied by any advance in quantitative analysis. Chalmers continued to use quantification merely to bolster his arguments about policy.

Chalmers also mixed quantification with antiquarian research. He started his antiquarian career when he was first in London, and he became a well-known practitioner. Perhaps because he had never graduated from Aberdeen and therefore lacked academic credentials, he was in earnest about his antiquarian work, and he valued, even flaunted, his membership in the Society of Antiquaries. As his influence on policy faded at the committee on trade, Chalmers laid ever more emphasis on his gravity and worth as an antiquary.

Dugdale or King would have recognized Chalmers's antiquarian tomes, but there were crucial differences. Chalmers was little interested in heraldry. Again, Chalmers was not as skillful with quantification as was King. Nor was Chalmers so brilliant an antiquarian researcher as Dugdale. Dugdale's books invited comparison with John Leland's *Itinerary in England and Wales* or with William Camden's *Britannia*, the greatest milestones of English antiquarianism. Dugdale also surpassed Chalmers in the connection of quantification and policy in antiquarian research. We might take Dugdale's history of draining of the fens as an example. A monumental volume, it was authoritative but also inventive and original, although a bit too heavy for easy reading.

By contrast, Chalmers was a better writer than Dugdale or King. His antiquarian books were and are easy and pleasant to read, and he was reasonably successful in obtaining money by them, even though the antiquarian researches were not exhaustive and original, as Dugdale's had been. His antiquarian books have not secured to Chalmers a lasting reputation, as they did to Dugdale.

While mentioning Chalmers's defects as an antiquarian, let me add a bit of my own guesswork. Chalmers said in his account of King's life that he, Chalmers, had in his possession King's manuscript copy of state papers concerning the reign of King Edward VI. I think Chalmers had many King papers in his possession, and they have since vanished. This would explain the relative lack of such papers in official archives. I hope a cache of King papers will turn up, and I went to Edinburgh to search for them among Chalmers's papers, but I found nothing of importance. Nevertheless, I still hope that the papers will turn up.

Antiquarianism was not a bad thing in itself, of course, but it corrupted Chalmers as a practitioner of quantification. It made him regard older quantitative data as specimens like fossils or relics. He was likely to credit numbers merely because he found them in an old book, and he too seldom calculated new ones for himself.

Chalmers did write a great work in this regard, however, *Caledonia*, an antiquarian account of Scotland. Among his many publications, this was the masterwork, and it was very impressive in its way. Yet critics condemned its inaccuracies, and it hardly survived. No current edition made it available to present-day readers. The Illinois library system for state universities, for instance, has as far as I know only one copy, a rare book, in poor condition, and difficult of access, and they were very kind to give me an extended loan of it.

As a mixture of antiquarianism and political arithmetic, Chalmers also wrote an almanac or handbook, *An Estimate of the Comparative Strength of Great Britain*, 1786. It was very successful and had many subsequent editions. King was a foundation for this handbook. Chalmers first summarized King's 1696 estimates in his 1786 edition, and then he reprinted the estimates in full in later editions. Finally, Chalmers published King's estimates in a separate pamphlet with a valuable biographical introduction. This version of the estimates and this life of King are reprinted at the back of my book. Let me add that Chalmers' life of King is valuable because he seems to have information that is no longer in the archives.

Anyway, inclusion of King's 1696 estimates separated Chalmers' *Estimate* from his other books and made Chalmers' *Estimate* of lasting interest. A reprint edition from 1979 is still generally available. In order to understand Chalmers's reprinting of the 1696 estimates, the difference between Chalmers's own work and King's work, and the nineteenth-century decline of political arithmetic, we should first compare Chalmers with Sir John Sinclair. We discuss Chalmers because of his close connection to King. We discuss Sinclair because he is essential to an understanding of Chalmers.

Sinclair descended from a noble family, and he became a politician, statistician, and agricultural reformer.[136] Although an independent member of parliament, not a party man, he was influential with the younger Pitt, and he at last obtained high office when he was appointed cashier of Excise for Scotland at six thousand pounds pay per year. "Sir John Sinclair has gotten the golden fleece at last," cried the envious Sir Walter Scott.[137]

*The Oxford English Dictionary* credited Sinclair with adapting the word *statistics* from German and making it current in English. This was the crucial turning point, I believe. Political arithmetic was tightly focused when Gregory King inherited it from Graunt and Petty. Using shop arithmetic as the language of communication, King gave quantitative advice to statesmen. Political arithmetic then lost its focus and its core of method, shop arithmetic, while at the same time becoming widely used in the eighteenth century. People changed or developed it from one thing into several others. Sinclair explained the part that he played in the alteration of political arithmetic, and we are lucky to have his clear account. The dictionary quoted Sinclair's own words.[138]

> In 1786, I found, that in Germany they were engaged in a species of political inquiry, to which they had given the name of Statistics; and though I apply a different idea to that word, for by Statistical is meant in Germany, an inquiry for the purpose of ascertaining the political strength of a country, or questions respecting matters of state; whereas, the idea I annex to the term, is an inquiry into the state of a country, for the purpose of ascertaining the quantum of happiness enjoyed by its inhabitants, and the

means of its future improvement; yet, as I thought that a new word might attract more public attention, I resolved on adopting it.

This change was the beginning of the decline of political arithmetic. The discipline that Sinclair denoted as the German referent of the word *statistical* was actually English political arithmetic by another name. Sinclair was technical and precise in calling it *statistics*. In seventeenth-century English usage, *political arithmetic* was policy itself, not discourse about policy. It was policy pursued by policymakers who had informed themselves of numerical data. When Gregory King told the governors of the Queen's Bounty that policy was not his province, he was using this distinction between political arithmetic as policy, on the one hand, and data, or what Sinclair said the Germans called *statistics*, on the other. However, many writers lost that clear distinction. Even Davenant lost it. He used the phrase *political arithmetic*, as Sinclair said, to refer to any verbal discussion of the state and its strength. When Sinclair abandoned the older words and made a new one, borrowing the word *statistics*, he avoided this confusion. Sinclair abandoned the quiet, abstract, and impartial discussion of the strength of the state. He took up a new discipline that used data publicly to advocate policy.

We find in Chalmers's books also the same change in meaning that Sinclair mentioned. Sinclair made political arithmetic into a discipline of advocacy, rejecting the older tradition of abstract and impartial analysis supplied in secret to statesmen. Chalmers also undertook to advocate policy as his primary goal, and he made his quantitative calculations as secondary supports. No wonder Hume and Smith had reservations.

To put the matter differently, we could emphasize here again the difference between the social contexts of political arithmetic in the seventeenth century and in the eighteenth century, using again the categories from David Hume quoted in Chapter 6 about the Learned and the Conversible. Gregory King's 1696 estimates had been part of a conversation of the Conversible, that is to say a spoken word and face-to-face business, and it connected to a specific and very exclusive circle of powerful policymakers. Political arithmetic was the policy made by these policymakers. Sinclair and Chalmers made political arithmetic, or statistics, or whatever one called it, into a conversation of the Learned, mostly carried on in print. It had been the secret supply of data to a high and exclusive seventeenth-century circle of policymakers, and Chalmers and Sinclair made it into the public advocacy of policy. Sinclair was right to give this different business a new name. As a conversation of the Learned, a matter of books that writers sold to booksellers, eighteenth-century political arithmetic became a public discourse, a rhetoric, and eventually a canon of books forming a tradition. The consequence was the withering of political arithmetic as Gregory King had known it, a conversation of the Conversible. Chalmers, Sinclair, and others altered or replaced it. Later, economics replaced it.

Having all along placed such emphasis on mathematical probability, we might now compare the eighteenth-century and nineteenth-century withering of political arithmetic to the present tangled state of mathematical probability as a discipline. Tightly focused, early twentieth-century mathematical probability was a set of agreed mathematical methods. Scientists in many fields used these methods with success to construct experiments. That focus was then lost, and people applied mathematical probability in so many different ways that no single core of method remained as an element common to all applications. Mathematical probability was so widely embraced and valued as a method that it became an end in itself. People came to consider the calculation of probabilities as a substitute for good data. Real statisticians abhorred this, but they became a tiny minority among users of statistical methods. Observers speculate that perhaps mathematical probability as a discipline will now disappear and be replaced by something new. Does not the similarity between the decline of political arithmetic and that of mathematical probability strike the eye?

# CHAPTER 11

# Wobbles and Perturbations

As we saw in Chapter 2, the journal *Nature* recently supplied an exchange of views concerning estimates for twenty-first-century population. The writers in *Nature* taught us to understand that their demographic estimates, although among the best available work and very valuable, were not gospel. Turning now to Roy Porter's Penguin book about English history for the eighteenth century, a standard text, we find that very same verdict in connection with King's 1696 estimates. Porter offered this evaluation of the reliability of the data in the 1696 estimates: "King's pioneer enumerations are not gospel: his sources were limited and he had biases of his own. But his general profile stands."[139]

Porter's comments on King's 1696 estimates implied a renewal of scholarly favor for the 1696 estimates. Porter repeated most of the essential elements from King's 1696 estimates, directly citing the estimates eight times. Porter often quarreled with King's data and adjusted them, of course, correlating them and correcting them where possible with other data, just as Jones, Judges, and Glass had done. Porter wrote this, for instance:

> Gregory King estimated that the nation was divided up as follows (the percentages include families and dependents):
>
> 1.2%—Landowners
>
> 14.3%—farmers and freeholders
>
> 3.4%—professionals, including clergy

3.7%—merchants and shopkeepers
4.4%—artisans and handicraftsmen
26.8%—labouring people and out-servants
29.4%—cottagers and paupers
6.8%—the armed forces

While citing these data, Porter also remarked:

These figures are clearly defective: there were far more merchants, shopkeepers, artisans and craftsmen than King noted, and domestic servants—such a large proportion of the population—do not appear as a separate category. Nevertheless, the general profile is suggestive.

Historians are right to cite King's 1696 estimates with favor, despite the weaknesses and defects of some of King's data. *Nature* and Porter gave us an accurate description of the problem posed by demographic estimates in general and by King's 1696 estimates in particular, I believe. Demographic data are to be calculated by the best methods available, and the calculations must then be evaluated or criticized by experts in order to iron out defects, but in the last analysis one has to accept uncertainty and imprecision in demographic estimates because of the inherent difficulties in the task. These difficulties made uncertainty and imprecision inseparable from King's enterprise of demographic estimation. The task was too difficult for his skills, but it remains too difficult for ours. A correct evaluation of King's 1696 estimates must read very much like the comments of Jones, Judges, and Glass, or, for that matter, much like the exchange in *Nature* cited in Chapter 1. Valuable but not gospel, that must be the evaluation.

If historians accept the 1696 estimates, as Porter did, then they also must repudiate Geoffrey Holmes's too sweeping criticism of King's 1696 methods. Further, historians also must reject another extreme, Peter Laslett's gilding of the lily, his thought that King's methods in political economy foreshadowed those of the later demographers and economists who invented or used techniques of higher mathematics.

I have associated the mistake of gilding the lily, of expecting too much of King, especially with historians and the 1696 data, but some economists made a parallel mistake with King's Law. When the economist W. S. Jevons studied variations in the price of gold and correlated them with variations in supply, working in 1871, he turned to King's Law and began a systematic study of it that has since occupied the attention of many scholars. Although few attributed mathematical probability to Gregory King, economists often interpreted the Law itself in terms of mathematical probability. They invented the economic notions of price elasticity and marginal utility, and they expected mathematical probability to clarify or resolve the puzzles posed by those notions.

Simply put, the price of wheat was elastic because it reflected the marginal value of wheat to purchasers who took into account not only the intrinsic qualities of the grain but also their subjective judgments and particular circumstances as purchasers. Purchasers paid more for wheat when they feared dearth than they did when they expected that plenty would be on hand to sate appetites. The application of mathematical probability to the Law has only revealed the weaknesses of mathematical probability, however. Mathematical probability still cannot predict precisely the interactions of supply and demand.[140]

The Law was a different kettle of fish from the 1696 estimates, therefore. King's 1696 estimates or any demographic estimates require that one accept a degree of uncertainty, of course, but the order of uncertainty in King's Law is a quantum leap greater. Further, the effort, beginning after Jevons, to apply mathematical probability to supply and demand has not clarified the uncertainties in King's Law in the same way that the subsequent application of mathematical probability refined and clarified the issues posed by Graunt and also raised by King's 1696 estimates. The distinction between uncertainty and still greater uncertainty was a familiar one in the history of sixteenth-century and seventeenth-century mathematics, and I shall try to explain it by analogy.

Take the example of Galileo and velocity. Galileo started out as an empiricist. *The Starry Messenger*, for instance, was, in a fairly basic way, empirical.[141] He constructed a telescope, looked through it, and wrote down what he saw. When he had enforced leisure at the end of his life, he returned to the questions of mathematical analysis that he had abandoned earlier. He began by using the geometry of the ancients, a method of analysis very suited to the study of static ratios.[142]

However, he wanted to study motion, not static ratios. He again constructed experiments and observed the results. Doing so, he asked the right questions, revealing the inadequacies of the ancient mathematical tradition he had inherited. I believe that Petty, Graunt, and King were like Galileo in this regard, using empirical observation to pose the right questions, revealing the inadequacies of the mathematical tradition that they inherited. In their case, it was shop arithmetic.

Galileo was on track in another regard. He avoided the mysticism in ancient higher mathematics. In this, he stood in contrast to Johannes Kepler (1571–1630), the German astronomer and mathematician who discovered the three laws of planetary motion that bear his name. Kepler also discovered the elliptical obits of the planets. He did this good work, but he could not resist the temptation to mysticism inherent in the ancient higher mathematics that he used. Ussher was like Kepler, discovering elliptical orbits in calendars as it were, and steeped all the while in ancient mysticism. On the other hand, King was like Galileo in avoiding the mysticism.

This was uncertainty of the first grade or type. In regard to it, in this case to smooth motion and to smooth changes in velocity, Galileo and his immediate successors were wonderfully successful. He defined the problems, and his successors devised novel mathematics to solve them. Galileo therefore was prescient, prefiguring. Later, novel higher mathematics evolved from his study of dynamics. That first grade or type of uncertainty was not the whole story, however.

Now for the quantum leap to greater uncertainty. It came in astronomy when people studied the wobbles or perturbations that interrupted the smooth motion of many heavenly bodies. The infinitely large and small were also problems not easily solved in the later tradition to which Galileo contributed so much. George Berkeley's formulation of these latter problems long bedeviled calculus, for instance. Some of Berkeley's puzzles were eventually solved, but others remain baffling to this day. To what extent does mathematics deal with real entities? To what extent is mathematics the product of human circumstances?

Petty's comments about the quantification of results of medical treatments, or Graunt's studies of the bills of mortality, or King's 1696 estimates were all alike in that they posed problems of the first grade or type of uncertainty. They were to mathematical probability what Galileo's studies of smooth motion were to later advances in higher mathematics. It may seem a bit much to compare King to Galileo, but I think the comparison is just. Sticking to empiricism, King (and Petty and Graunt before him) clearly stated this problem or challenge: How could quantification of information about society enable one to see large patterns instead of merely seeing discreet facts? In particular, Graunt's clear statement of the need to recognize large patterns in runs of social data directly stimulated the invention of mathematical probability by the Bernoulli brothers and others.

However, King's Law dealt with much more difficult material. The application of mathematical probability to correlate supply and demand was long delayed and remains in many ways unsatisfactory. Therefore, King's 1696 estimates, based on Graunt's work, implied the value of mathematical probability, although King himself did not use mathematical probability, but King's Law did not imply the value of mathematical probability in the same clear and simple way. King's 1696 estimates posed an uncertainty of the first grade or type, therefore, but King's Law posed one of the second grade or type.

Let me give specific examples. King's 1696 estimates depended on sampling, and sampling has since been much improved by the application of mathematical probability. King took actual enumerations within specific places, and multiplied by the numbers of such places, but he did not select his samples in a truly random manner, as later demographers would do. Improvements wrought by the later methods of sampling were clear. Economists have closely studied supply and demand, but they have yet to reach about them the level of agreement that demographers have about the application of random sampling.

When I started out to study King's Law, I remembered the doubling and the calculations of the differences that King used to compute his Biblical material for population history. I thought he might have done something similar with prices, but, upon further study, I saw no evidence of that. A few bits of scraps about prices survive among King's manuscripts, but nothing very suggestive. The contrast is very great between the scarcity of King's manuscript materials about prices, on the one hand, and his very abundant calculations about past and future population, on the other. I concluded that he relied upon guesswork; he recorded actual prices and maybe wrote them down. No mathematical analysis of ratios survived, not even analysis like that in his Biblical calculations. Maybe on the other hand he did none, and he simply came to the Law in his head, by intuition. In either case, his presentation of the Law was verbal, merely word of mouth, and Davenant was the one who wrote it down. King made, I would therefore argue also, no Law in any strict or scientific sense, merely an empirical observation on the order of *The Starry Messenger*. In this omission, King was prescient. If he had tried to formulate a full Law, he would not be taken so seriously by scholars now. He was wise to tell Davenant to write down what they saw, but wise also to keep silence thereafter. I therefore came to see the crucial importance of King's high social polish. Everywhere in his contributions to political economy, I saw the same polish. There was a circle of conversation around Harley, and King contributed both his 1696 estimates and also King's Law in the context of the social polish of that circle.

To return to the point that began this chapter, the value of King's 1696 estimates for historians, I think that the expert evaluation of the estimates by Jones, Judges, and Glass has stood the test of time; Roy Porter was right to repeat it. It still stands or ought to stand now at the beginning of our new century; future scholarship will not soon supplant it. Let me therefore repeat the judgment once again here at the end of this book. King manipulated the 1696 data in strange ways, but he did so because of the inherent difficulty of the problems for which he attempted his calculations. Mindful of these difficulties, we should accept his figures with gratitude. They are the best estimates available, and we are lucky to have them; however, we need to adjust them by our own calculations. In particular, we need to supplement the wealth estimates with other data where possible. By asking the right questions in his 1696 estimates, King did not himself develop the tools of mathematical probability, but he did pose the right problems for future investigators, and he avoided confusing the problems. He used only empiricism and shop arithmetic, but, despite the simplicity of these methods, the 1696 estimates probably were as accurate as anyone in the seventeenth century could have made them. Many of the 1696 data are low, but all are suggestive. Some of his questions, or Graunt's, led quickly to wonderful answers. By contrast, Ussher and the others who used ancient higher mathematics did not produce seventeenth-century political economy of comparable interest or importance. So much for the 1696 estimates.

King's Law posed a more difficult puzzle, as I have said in this chapter. In the case of the Law, again in summary, King made a brilliant empirical observation, and then he did not muddle it by asking the wrong questions. He did not claim to know or understand a general analysis that had eluded him. King recognized when difficulties were too great for him. Jevons noticed the same difficulties. Later work made crystal clear how great the difficulties were, and economists and mathematicians are still working on them. Despite these continuing problems, King's empiricism and shop arithmetic enabled him to produce in King's Law a contribution that will preserve his name among economists for the foreseeable future.

I said in preliminary remarks at the very beginning of this book that I would place King's contributions to political economy within the context of statistical science. I have tried my best. To paraphrase the historian of science Steven Shapin, there was no revolution to a "hard" science of statistics, and this book has been a history of Gregory King's place therein.

# APPENDIX 1

# King's Autobiography

> Vitæ Gregorij King Fecialis Armorum primo Rouge Dragon titulo deinde Lancastriensis occursus præcipui.
> *Some miscellaneous notes of the birth, education, and advancement of* Gregory King, *Rouge Dragon Pursuivant, afterward Lancaster Herald.*

The city of Litchfield has given in this 16th century two Heralds to the College of Arms, viz. Elias Ashmole, Windsor Herald, born the 23d of May, 1617, and Gregory King, Lancaster Herald, born the 15th of Dec. 1648; not to mention that the father of Mr. Camden, Clarenceux King of Arms, was also born in this city.

Mr. King was the eldest son of his father Gregory King, by Elizabeth his first wife, daughter of Mr. J. Andrews of Sandwich, whom he married in Kent 20 Jan. preceding the birth of their first born. The father was born at Leicester, where his ancestors had lived for some generations, and where some of the family yet remain. He was the son of J. King, who having only two sons, Gregory and Thomas, dyed when Gregory the eldest was only seven years of age. However, he left him a fair house, garden, and orchard, without the Northgate of that ancient borough, which he sould anno 1648, a little before the birth of this Gregory the Herald.—

Gregory the father being a good grammar scholar had applyed himself much to the mathematicks, particularly navigation, gunnery, surveying of land and dyalling, which two last parts he exercised chiefly for a livelyhood, at other times teaching to write and cast accounts, and being sometimes employed in designing of the more curious gardens. By these and other such like mathematical and ingenuous employments he maintained his family, though not in that post as his qualifications would have easily enabled him to have done, had he not been addicted to company-keeping and to that vice which to make it a vertue they call good fellowship. So that the care of the family lay wholly upon his wife, whose character would have equalled that of the best matrons, if her condition had been less obscure.

The inclinations of the father to learning led him to the care of breeding up his sons, but particularly this his eldest son the Herald, to some tolerable degree of literature, in order whereunto he was packt away to school at two years of age; at three years old he read the Psalter, and at four the Bible very distinctly; though not being very forward of his tongue, he could not then pronounce plain many words. In this year a palsey or parylitique distemper seized him, which held him half a year so violently, that by the forcible shaking of his head and hands he was not able to see to read; it drew his neck awry, and diminished his height full half an inch, and was so severe upon him that his father often prayed that God would take him out of this life, fearing a perpetual deformity. But he recovered it, and at five years and a half old was sent to the Free-School to learn his Accidence. He had not been above half a year with the usher or undermaster, before he was removed by the head-master (at that time, and indeed all the time of Mr. King's going to school) Mr. T. Bevans, who afterwards went to Kidderminster in Worcestershire. He it was, that removed him unto the head-schoole, and took a particular care to shew him more than ordinarily, and shewed him some distinguishing kindnesses—this he seemed to be induced to, not only because he found him very forward in respect to his age and very inclineable to his booke, (he never playing the truant all the time of his schooling) but being very little of the stature for his age, partly by reason of his fore mentioned sickness, and partly from the stature for his mother, (for his father was of a just stature) his schoolmaster respected him as a little wonder, and endeavoured to render him yet more agreeable by pushing him on faster than those of the same class.

The Grammar and Sententiæ Pueriles were the entertainment of his sixth year, and being arrived at his seventh year his father taught him to write, keeping him at home a month or six-weeks, least he might carry to school the infection of the small-pox, which his younger brother Thomas then five years old laboured under. His own danger of that distemper was over, he having had them at three quarters of a year old, at such time as his mother was severely visited by them, she being blind nine days with them, before which time she passed for a very prettie if not a beautiful woman—but his father never had them to his dying day.

Cordery, and Erasmus, Cato, and Ovid de Tristibus, spent the seventh and eighth years of his age, accompanied still with some portions of the Latin Grammar. Ovid's Metam. Virgil, and some other books he learnt in his ninth year, in which his schoolmaster out of a particular fancy taught him to read Hebrew, and he being still very small for his age, his master would appoint now and then some gentlemen of the town to come to school in the evening after five of the clock when the other scholars were gone home, to hear our little spark read in a great Hebrew Bible almost as big as himself. And the next year those of this form being among their exercises to bring out of the Nomenclature a certain number of English, Latin, and Greek words, his master obliged him to repeat also the Hebrew words *ex abundanti,* furnishing him with them in a paper book expressly for that purpose.

In his tenth year he entered into the Greek Grammar, and learnt books of themes and declamations, and the schoolmaster obliging his scholars to take notes of the sermons in Church on Sunday, and to repeat them on Monday evenings, and turn them into Latin against Tuesday morning, this our Herald (being put upon it by his father) took those sermon notes originally in Latin from the Minister's English, which he the schoolmaster understanding, commended him for it, and obliged all the rest of that form or class, which was then the uppermost but one, to do the like.

About this time also it was, that he obtained leave that those declamations, which the head forms had made at their breaking up school at Christmas before the magistrates of the city, might be writ in a long roll handsomely paynted and adorned, and hung up behind them during the repeating thereof, and afterward presented to the magistrates, which from that time became a custome, and was a prettie advantage to our Herald, partly by the gratuity received for his own, which used to be the finest of all the rest, and partly by what he got for writing and embellishing those of the other scholars.

In his eleventh and twelfth year he learnt Rhetoricke and Isocrates, accompanied still with his Grammar, and themes, and some other Greek books, and had the favour of his master to be dispatched sooner than ordinary, that he might have the liberty of attending some scholars of his own, which he then taught to write and cast accounts, the benefit whereof served to buy him books and other conveniencies.

Being in his thirteenth year he read Hesiod and Homer—he made Greek verses with great readiness; he undertook to survey land by himself, when his father was otherwise engaged; and he acted the fool's part by the name of Ropeny in the pastoral comedie of Amyntas, at the Free-School; which being publickly repeated two days, before the magistrates and gentry of the town and others, he gained very much applause thereby, and had money given him by divers of his friends.

He continued the fore mentioned books in his 14th year current, and learnt the Hebrew Grammar: in which year Mr. Dugdale, then Norroy King of Arms, desiring his good friend Dr. Hunter of Lichfield to enquire him out a clerk, the Doctor having taken particular notice of our Herald's acting in the play, recommended him to Mr. Dugdale as a clerk, which his parents readily enough consented to, having at that time five more children to provide for, though in truth our Herald for the last two years had been very little charge to them, and the Rev. Bishop of Litchfield, Dr. Hacket, had designed in four or five months more to have sent him to the University. But this happening in the interim, he was sent over to Mr. Dugdale the latter end of December, 1662, being then only 14 years complete and a fortnight over, and this was the first step to his future advancement in the College of Arms.

But it is to be remembered, that as our Herald was wonderfully forwarded by his father in learning, who taught him near as much at home as he learned at school till he was 10 or 11 years of age, so on the other side his being frequently abroad with his father in measuring land from twelve to 14 years old, he did not make that progress in school learning in those two years, as he might otherwise have done. However, the knowledge he had gained in the mathematics did very well recompense it, and hath been of good advantage to him in the further course of his affairs. With these qualifications, and an inclination to drawing, (for he drew the King's Arms in one of his school books at eight years old) he went out into the world under the tutelage of that great antiquary and indefatigable writer W. Dugdale, Esq. at first Blanc-Lion, afterward Rouge-Croix Pursuivant, and Chester Herald before the civil war, and deservedly made Norroy King of Arms upon the restoration of King Charles II. Mr. Dugdale had the summer before begun the visitation of his province with the counties of Notts and Derby, and in the summer 1663 made a review thereof and visited Staffordshire, taking with him this little clerk, for he was not able of two or three years after to mount a horse from the ground. As the inclinations of his clerk led him to drawing, so that he made that proficiency therein, that Mr. Dugdale contented himself with his tricking the arms into his visitation of Staffordshire that now remains in the office. 'Tis true it is but too meanly done for the publick office, being very short of the tricking which this clerk performed in the subsequent visitations.

He also applied himself to the French tongue, and to pedigree paynting, and within a year or two writ and paynted several for Mr. Dugdale, particularly a large one of Claverin of Northumberland, and after a while paynted and engrossed the several grants of arms that were passed by the said Norroy.

The transcribing the pedigrees, and tricking of the arms of the counties visited by Mr. Dugdale, was the greatest part of this his clerk's employment, saving that afterwards Mr. Norroy gave him leave to take with him into the northern counties blank scutcheons on vellome, wherein to depict the armes of such as desired an attestation of them under the King of Armes' hand—for which end he had all along before taken a paynter with him, the charge whereof this his clerk now saved him.

Mr. Dugdale visited his whole province between the years 1662 and 1666, viz. Notts, Derby, Stafford, Chester, Lancashire, Westmorland, Cumberland, Yorkshire, Durham, and Northumberland, in many of which this his clerk took the prospects of towns, castles, and other remarquables; his first attempt being a prospect of Lancaster in 1665. Besides these Mr. Dugdale visited also Shropshire for Sir Edward Byshe, Clarenceux, anno 1664, and in all these counties our Herald had the advantage to accompany him, which rendered him so much the fitter for an Officer of Arms.

But in the beginning of the year 1667 Mr. Dugdale having finished his visitation, had not occasion to keep two clerks, as he generally had done from the year 1663—and having then for his under clerk one Henry Johnstone, since a Benedictine monk, brother to Dr. Johnstone of Yorkshire, the learned physician and good historian and antiquary—at the instant request of the said Doctor, that his brother might be continued with him, whether he was allowed any thing or no, Mr. Dugdale was obliged to consent thereto, and therefore recommended our Herald to the service of Lord Hatton, who being a great lover of antiquities, and a great patron of Mr. Dugdale during the civil war, was at this time designing a collection of grants, and the arms, quarterings, and supporters of the Nobility, in which this our Herald was employed, and in some other collections, for the space of a year and a half, viz. from summer 1667 to spring 1668–9. But the materials for those collections not being so easie to be procured as was expected, the design fell, and our Herald was dismissed, with great promises of what kindness lay in his Lordship's power to do him.

Hereupon he went to Litchfield to visit his father in spring 1689, whom he expected to have found a widower, having buried his wife, the mother of our Herald, in April the year before; but he found him re-married to Margaret Place, of Yorkshire, ever since 2 Feb. 1668–9. Here he continued 'till the spring following, teaching to write and cast accounts, and employing himself in paynting coaches, signes, and other sorts of oyl paynting, as hatchments, &c. and in instructing the registrar to the Dean and Chapter, and some other inquisitous persons, to read old records, &c.

Hence he was invited by Mr. Chetwynd, of Injestry, that great ornament of his country for all sorts of curious learning, to peruse and transcribe the deeds of his family relating to his genealogy, which he did in a fair velome book, tricking also therein the most considerable seals, being now 21 years of age.

From hence, about the latter end of the year, he was desired by the Lady Dowager Gerard, of Gerard's Bromley, relict of Charles and mother of Digby Lord Gerard, to be her steward, auditor, and secretary, in the room of one Mr. Chaunce, an ingenious gentleman, deceased, who having kept his accounts, and other matters of moment, in characters, gave our Herald the trouble of decyphering them, which in a short time he did with great dexterity. Here he continued, viz. at Sandon, in the county of Stafford, the seat of George Digby, Esq. then living, father to the aforesaid Lady Gerard, till August 1672, having in the interim done many things for that Lady in paynting, drawing, &c.

From hence he removed to London, where he renewed his acquaintance with Mr. Lee, Chester Herald, Mr. Sandford, Rouge Dragon, and others of his office, after having first wayted upon his old master, Mr. Dugdale, and having amongst others visited Mr. Hollar, the eminent gentleman, in his way, for etching, who recommended him to Mr. Ogilvy to manage his undertakings. Mr. Ogilby having the King's licence to print all things of his own composing or translating, kept a presse in his house, and under the name of Leybourne, or some other master-printer, did also print any other works, and was at that time printing Sir Peter Leicester's Antiquities of Chester, wherein some old seals being to be engraved, Mr. King made his first attempt in etching upon them, and performed them to satisfaction.—After which Mr. Dugdale reprinting his folio Esop in 8vo. and reducing the sculpts to that volume, Mr. King etched several of them, as he did some of the sculpts in the History of Asia, V. 1. which was then printing at Mr. Ogilvy's, being a translation from De Meurs's impression at Amsterdam; Africa, America, the two Chinas, and Japan, being printed before.

Mr. Ogilvy having projected a new Brittannia, designed the same in three volumes, whereof one to treat of the roads of England, another of the rivers and the most remarquable things near them, and the third of towns. He had made some beginning in the measuring of the roads, and was just engraving the counties of Middlesex and Kent; he had engaged a gentleman, one Mr. Falgate, of Essex, to survey his native county. Mr. King travailed along with him, assisted him therein, and collected divers notes out of Churches and other matters of record, in order to the historical account; and in the middle of the winter 1672, in very severe cold weather, they took the inchnography of Ipswich in Suffolk, and Malden in Essex, which were afterward very curiously finished, and sent to those two places.

At Mr. King's coming to Mr. Ogilvy's he found Mr. Leybourne just newly engaged in making a map of London, and viewing the first essay of that survey he found it was projected at a scale of 50 feet to an inch, and yet particularised nothing but only the streets, lanes, &c. Whereupon Mr. King formed a new project of that survey at 100 feet per inch, and expressed the groundplot of every individual house and garden, finished two plates of 20 himself, and ordered the carrying on of the rest of the work, which was finished accordingly, and etched in copper by Mr. Hollar.

To carry on these designs of Mr. Ogilvy great sums of money were requisite, whereupon Mr. Ogilvy projected a lottery of books, principally those of his own printing and publishing, which Mr. King contrived, and assisted at the management thereof. He also framed for Mr. Ogilvy a lesser lottery of books for Bristol fair at St. James's tide, 1673, which turned to a good advantage, Mr. King managing it there.

All this while many surveyors were employed by Mr. Ogilvy, by Mr. King's direction, to measure the principal roads of the kingdome, and they being directed to collect principal notes as they passed along, Mr. King alone digested the notes, and directed the engraving of the plates, and engraved three or four of them with his own hand, being his first attempt at handling the graver. Mr. Ogilvy was very sensible of Mr. King's great assistance to him, and was very kind to him on all occasions, allowing him a musicke master to teach him to play on the violin, and offering to renew the patent of his place of cosmographer to the King, and to put Mr. King in jointly or in reversion; but Mr. King declined that proposition.

Whereupon Mr. Ogilvy proposed to Mr. King to undertake wholly, on his account, the survey of Westminster, &c. on the same scale as London, viz. 100 feet to an inch, which Mr. King accepted, and taking to his assistance the aforementioned Mr. Falgate, compleated the same in about a twelvemonth's time; this being undertaken in spring 1674, occasioned Mr. King to take a lodging in or near the middle of the said work, and having seen several he at last fixed on one in James-street, Covent-Garden, at one Mrs. Anne Powel's, a maiden gentlewoman, whom after three months he married, scilicet 20 July 1674, in the 26th year of his age, a person of a gentleman's family in Gloucestershire, being the daughter of Mr. J. Powel of Tirley, in the parish of Forthampton, on the further side the Severn, descended from the Powels of Denbighshire.

The survey of Westminster being finished, Mr. King betook himself to engraving principally the letter-work in maps, and performed many things of that kind, as Mr. Holams's great 20 sheet map of England, his little and sheet map of England, and a single sheet map of Barbadoes, with divers other single sheet maps, besides Mr. Morgan's map of London, and many other things of other natures, as the geographical cards published by Mr. Broome the bookseller, but composed by Sir Peter Wyche, which was the parent of all the cards of that kind.

He also now and then was employed in surveying, particularly Soho Fields, whose streets and square were all projected by him, and most of the first articles for building thereof, drawn up by him also.—But though he principally employed his time in engraving from 1675 to 1680, yet it must be remembered, that Mr. Sandford, Rouge-Dragon Pursuivant, and afterward Lancaster Herald, being at the time of his being made Lancaster (scilicet 1685) engaged in the printing of his genealogical history, and shortly after being visited with sickness, desired Mr. King to proceed in the compiling of the said historical part, and to prepare copy for the press, it being then about the fourth book, which Mr. King did accordingly 'till such time as Mr. Sandford's health permitted him to go on with it himself.

Mr. Sandford was then at his lodgings in the Herald's Office, which being upon the same floor with those of Mr. Lee, Chester Herald, was the occasion of Mr. King's renewing his acquaintance with Mr. Lee, who also employed him in many little things, and recommended him to Mr. Andrew Hay, secretary to Henry Earl of Norwich, then Earl Marshal (Thomas Duke of Norfolk, the lunatic, being then living) Mr. King was often made use of by Mr. Hay in many things relating to the affairs of the Earl Marshal's office, all which Mr. Lee designed expressly as a step to introduce Mr. King into the Herald's Office.

Mr. Lee also put Mr. King upon paynting of funeral scutcheons, and to that end put into his hands the funeral work for Sir Edward Sawyer, father to Mr. Robert Sawyer, which was in the year 1676, which Mr. King, being then removed from his house in the middle of James-street, Covent-Garden, to the corner house of the long piazza, next the said street, performed accordingly at home, with his own hands, being his first undertaking of that kind.

Mr. Lee had at this time a great animosity to Sir Edward Walker, Garter, by reason he opposed or disputed in many things the authority of the Earl Marshal, which Mr. Lee studied earnestly to improve and maintain. This occasioned Mr. Lee to make use of Mr. King more intimately in relation to those disputes, and many times brought him into the Earl Marshal's presence; but these disputes ended shortly after with Sir Edward Walker's death, who deceased at Whitehall 16 February 1676–7.

This begat a great dispute with the King and Earl Marshal, touching the disposition of the office of Garter, the Marshal clayming the nomination thereof as of all officers of arms, while Sir William Hayward, one of the Gentlemen of the King's Privy Chamber, and Mr. Ashmole, late Windsor Herald, (before his resignation thereof to Mr. J. Dugdale, son to Mr. Dugdale, Norroy) sett up the King's title, each of them for themselves—Mr. Lee defended the Earl Marshal's title by arguments in writing, in which he all along made use of Mr. King, who attended the cabinet council thereupon more than once. The King at last giving up the point to the Earl Marshal, his Lordship made offer of the place to Mr. Lee, but he refused it, being very ill in health. Whereupon the Earl Marshal asked him, how he should otherwise recompense him for the services he had done him—he answered, if your Lordship will take care of my son, Mr. May, (who was then Rouge Dragon Pursuivant) and of this gentleman, meaning Mr. King, (who was then in Mr. Lee's chamber with the Earl Marshal) I shall think myself sufficiently recompensed.

This piece of justice must be done Mr. Lee, because there were several afterwards who pretended to be particularly instrumental to Mr. King's coming into the Office of Armes, whose concurrent favour Mr. King does nevertheless very gratefully resent, but must always own his promotion purely to Mr. Lee's friendship and favour.

The vacancy of Garter was supplied by Mr. Dugdale, Norroy, Henry Dethick, Rouge Croix, was made Richmond, and Henry Ball, Rouge Rose extraordinary, was made Rouge Croix. But before these gentlemen had passed their patents Mr. Lee departed this life also, viz. on 23 April 1677, whereupon the Earl Marshal gave his warrant the very next day to Mr. May to succeed his father in law in the place of Chester, and the like to Mr. King to succeed Mr. May in the office of Rouge Dragon. However, if this last vacancy had not happened, Mr. Lee had taken care that Mr. King should have been Blanch Lion Extraordinary, and a warrant was prepared for that purpose. Mr. May's patent was passed the 6th of May, and Mr. King's the 7th of May, and these officers, together with Francis Burghill, Mowbray Herald extraordinary, were all created together at the College of Arms by the Earl of Peterborough, Deputy Earl Marshal, the 24th of June 1677.

The fees and profits of the Officers of Arms were at this time so low, that in the first two years after Mr. King's admittance his dividends in the office came but to 11l. and the salaries not payd at all, (though a pursuivant's is but 20l.) This obliged Mr. King still to continue his employment of engraving and herald paynting, designing at that time a map of Staffordshire. Not but that the business of the office did share a good part of his time, which was generally brought to him by Sir Henry St. George, Norroy, neither was Sir William Dugdale wanting to assist his old clerk in what lay in his power. To these two Mr. King was most particularly obliged, they having often occasion to make use of him about the affairs of the office, pressed him very much to remove thither, which he did at Lady-Day 1680, Sir William Dugdale accommodating him with a chamber and some other conveniences, and Sir Henry St. George with a kitchin.

Sir Henry St. George was now Clarenceux, having succeeded Sir Edw. Bysshe in that office, who died anno 1678, and being under a kind of obligation to make a promise of his predecessors of giving the profits of the visitations of certain counties of his province towards rebuilding that part of the College which was then unbuilt, Sir Henry St. George accordingly assigned six counties of his province for that purpose, viz. Northamptonshire, Rutlandshire, Leicestershire, Warwickshire, Gloucestershire, and Worcestershire. Mr. King being in a manner the only officer that understood the method of visitations, was resolved on to be one (whoever was the other) to visit those counties. Accordingly he and Mr. Burghill, Somerset, were deputed anno 1681, into Northamptonshire and Rutlandshire, but Mr. Somerset left him at the beginning of the journey, and Mr. King prosecuted it by himself. The times indeed were not well settled, and Northamptonshire was much divided into factions, so that the clear profit was not above 30l. and the charges about 80l.

In the spring 1682 Mr. King, with Mr. May, Chester, were deputed to visit Leicestershire and Warwickshire, and to review Northamptonshire and Rutlandshire. This brought in clear about 130l. and the latter end of the same year they were further deputed to visit Gloucestershire and Worcestershire, and to review Leicestershire and Warwickshire; which journey brought in clear 300l. But Mr. May falling ill of an ague upon his return, which held him a long season, Mr. Dethick, Richmond, and Mr. King, were deputed the next summer to review those last four counties for the Office, and to visit Herefordshire and Monmouthshire for Mr. Clarenceux upon his own account, which they did, and brought clear into the office about 70l. beside what Sir Henry St. George cleared. This, making 530l. built up the west side and southwest corner of the Herald's College, from Garter's staircase. 'Tis true Mr. King out of his zeal for the publick pressed on these visitations somewhat earnestly, which Mr. Clarenceux seemed to resent, for Mr. King easily perceived, that Mr. Clarenceux grew cold to him from that time forward.

About this time, scilicet upon the death of the Duke of Norfolk, Earl Marshal, who succeeded his brother Thomas, that honor and office came to Henry Lord Mowbray, his eldest son, commonly called Earl of Arundel in his father's time, who having taken notice of Mr. King's qualifications constituted him registrar of the College of Arms, in the room of Mr. Devenish, York Herald, who being nephew to Sir Thomas and Sir Henry St. George, at that time Kings of Arms, obliged him to oppose it, alledging, that no Pursuivant was ever made registrar. But the Earl Marshal demanding, whether he might not make a Pursuivant registrar if he pleased, and they answering yes, Mr. King had quickly his Grace's warrant thereupon: indeed he was in fact registrar before, being employed by his predecessor to enter most things that belong to the registrars to enter. Now though Mr. Clarenceux's affection towards him seemed yet colder and colder, yet it hindered not but that Mr. Clarenceux desired his company along with him anno 1684 into Cambridgeshire, upon his visitation of that county, and Huntingdonshire, which Mr. King readily afforded him.

Not long after which, scilicet the 6th of February, we were all surprized with the sudden demise of that gracious Prince Charles II. Mr. King was found amongst those Officers of Arms, who proclaimed his successor King James II. but it was observed, that Mr. King's countenance was very sad, even during the solemnity, for the loss of so good a King and master. Mr. King was likewise at the funeral of that good Prince, and bore no small share in the management thereof, and particularly by Sir William Dugdale's direction prepared the funeral escocheons for the same.

That solemnity being over, King James presently entered upon the consideration of his own and the Queen's coronation, and the Heralds being often ordered to attend the commyttee of the councill for that affair, were directed to make ceremonials and schemes for the proceeding thereto, which Mr. King certainly prepared, and upon King James's declaring he would have the account of that coronation printed, Mr. Sandford and Mr. King had the Earl Marshal's consent for the doing thereof, which they did accordingly, the greatest part passing through the hands of Mr. King, and indeed the whole management and œconomy of it was purely owing to him; though he avoided being mentioned in the title page, contenting himself with one third part of the propriety therein, and leaving the honour and two thirds of the propriety to Mr. Sandford—well foreseeing, that they would be maligned for it by others of their office, as it fell out afterwards, for Mr. Sandford having opposed the Earl Marshal's appointing Mr. Burghill to be the receiver of fees of honour for the heralds, and endeavoring to vest it in the King, so as that the affair was brought to the councill table; the Earl Marshal suspended him, at the insinuation of some of the heralds, for not having finished the history of the coronation; but Mr. Sandford submitting himself to the Earl Marshal, the suspension was soon taken off.

This book answered not the advantage that Mr. Sandford and Mr. King proposed, for the sculps being many and tedious, the book was not finished 'till Christmas, 1687, viz. the Christmas before the Revolution, so that there was not time enough after the publishing for disposing thereof before it was too late, whereby the authors did but just save themselves, for the charge amounted in all to near 600l.

In the year 1687 Mr. Clarenceux began his visitation of London, in which he again desired the assistance of Mr. King, Rouge Dragon, as the entries in Mr. King's handwriting do plainly show, as well as in Cambridge and Huntingdon. In 1685, upon Sir William Dugdale's decease, Sir Thomas St. George came to be Garter; Mr. Dugdale, Windsor, was made Norroy, who was thereupon knighted. Mr. Dugdale had all along a particular respect for Mr. King, which did in some measure recompence the loss of so good a friend as Sir William had been always to him, and on the other side, Mr. King's gratitude to Sir William Dugdale prompted him to do all good offices to his son Sir John, who declared he would not have accepted of a King of Arms' place, but in confidence to Mr. King's friendship in the management thereof—he himself not having addicted himself much to matters of heraldry.

Mr. King had long struggled in the world to make himself master of some little fortune, but his kindness to his relations had carried away all that he could spare from time to time before his marriage; and though by his marrying he layd a good foundation for the time to come, yet the continual care of his relations, and Mr. Ogilby's dying above 100l. in his debt, (whereof he never got one farthing) joyn'd to a generous way of living, to which both his own and his wife's inclinations led them, and the charge of near 60l. in passing his patent for Rouge Dragon, by reason he presented the Earl Marshal's secretary with 20 guineas—these things, I say, kept him from laying up any thing considerable, so that the first attempt to improve what money he could spare was the lending 100l. upon houses in Southwark, in the beginning of the year—the next was his purchasing 21l. 10s. per ann. in land, in the parish of Holy-Cross, Waltham, in Essex—and the last was the purchasing a lease for 33 years of near 60 houses in St. Catherine's, held of the hospital there, the value of which purchase was about 1260l.—but to this he was over persuaded by some of his friends, it being much above his then condition to compasse, so that he was obliged to borrow more than half the purchase money at interest of five per cent.—for all the time of the purchase he did not reckon himself worth in all above 800l. The purchase of the houses in St. Catherine's promised a good income, the rental being 220l. per ann. and for 10 years before they had yielded clear 160l. per ann. it being just before the Revolution, and the taxes in William and Mary's time running very high, and rents falling, it did not prove so well as otherwise it would. It was in this year, 1688, that King James sent several Bishops to the Tower for refusing to give order for reading his declaration for liberty of conscience, upon which Mr. King, being at that instant in company, cryed out, "Then farewell to popery in England," easily foreseeing that such bold steps as those would inflame the people of England against the Roman Catholics, to whose counsels all those violent proceedings were attributed. The consideration whereof did shortly after ground Mr. King in his opinion, which he declared publiquely upon his first reading of the Prince of Orange's declaration, that the Prince came not without expectation of the Crown.

Now though Mr. King had a great respect to the succession of the Crown by legal descent, and therefore could not but have a due resentment for the misfortunes of King James, yet it hindered not but that in obedience to the Earl Marshal's order, grounded upon a particular order from the House of Lords, he assisted at the proclaiming of King William and Queen Mary; and afterward in his own person proclaymed the order for the court of clayms as previous to the coronation, and assisted at several fittings of the committee of Bishops for drawing up the coronation service, and prepared four books for that ceremonie, viz. one for the King, another for the Queen, a third for the Princess Anne, and a fourth for the Bishop of London, as he had done before the coronation of King James. He also gave more than ordinary assistance at the office in forming the ceremonial of that solemnity, and upon the Coronation Day undertook the fatigue of calling into order the Peers and Peeresses in the House of Lords and Paynted Chamber, their Majesties sitting by; and took upon him the principal care of managing that solemnity, having the Earl Marshal's order to attend thereat as Lancaster Herald, which place Mr. Sandford, Lancaster, had a little before resigned to him, though his patent was not passed till July after, so that for three or four months he was in effect both Lancaster and Rouge Dragon. This resignation cost Mr. King 220l. besides his patent, which was about 40l. more, only he had an allowance from his successor, Mr. Mauditt, of 100l.

The 1st of January following, the Elector of Brandenburgh was chosen into the order of the Garter. Sir Thomas St. George, by reason of his age, being then 75, and by reason of the sitting of the Parliament, desired to be excused from carrying the Garter in his own person to that Elector, especially being so long a journey, and thereupon proposed it to Mr. King, whose qualifications for that employment were without dispute, having Latin and French sufficient, and having for some years before addicted himself very much to the study of this order; however, Mr. King desired Sir Thomas St. George to think of some other of the Heralds that were his seniors, and particularly to offer it to Sir Henry St. George, Clarenceux, but he replied to Mr. King, that if he would undertake it, he would trouble himself no further.

Hereupon Mr. King accepted the employment, and Mr. Johnston, nephew to the Bishop of Salisbury, (and afterwards Secretary of State of Scotland) was joyned with Mr. King in the commission for that affair. The commission itself, credential, letter, and instructions, were all drawn up by Mr. King, and being approved of by the Chancellor, were also engrossed by Mr. King for the King's signing.

Having received into his hands the whole habit and ensigns of the order, and prepared his equipage, he kissed the King's hand upon his departure, on the 4th of February, 1689, and having received 250l. advance upon his allowance of 30s. per diem, he set forward with his colleague on the 12th of March following, and passing through Holland, Westphalia, and the Lunenburgh territories, (Mr. King having all along the favour of Mr. Johnston's own coach) they arrived at Berlin on the 20th of May, and after a private audience of the Elector and Electress and the severall Princes and Princesses of the Electoral family, to which they were conducted with all the ceremonies used to embassadors, (their character being oratores, legati, et deputati) they invested his Electoral Highness with the order with all possible splendor and magnificence on Friday the 6th of January, and dined with the Elector; and within a few days Mr. King was presented by the Elector with 500 gold ducats, and 150 more as a composition for his upper garment, &c. and with his Electoral Highness's sword, value about 10l. His secretary, Mr. Samuel Stebbing, who had been his servant near seven years, was also presented with 75 ducats, and each of his footmen with 15 ducats.

Mr. King having his audience of leave returned by Hamburgh, (Mr. Johnston staying behind as Envoy) and having been very nobly entertained by Sir Paul Rycaut, their Majesties' resident there, and by all the principall English marchants there, whilst he wayted for a passage by sea to England, which at length he met with; so that leaving Hamburgh on the 22nd of July, he arrived at Hull in August, from whence he rode post to London, leaving his secretary, and servants and baggage to come round by sea, who arriving at London in August, Mr. King kissed her Majesty's hand at Whitehall, (the King being then in Ireland) and having made the Elector's and Electrice's compliments to the Queen, and those others he was charged with, he presented her Majesty with the amber cabinet which the Electress sent by him; and so concluded his negotiation.

Shortly after which, he accounted with Sir Thomas St. George for the moiety of the presents which the Elector made him on that occasion; and upon the King's return from Ireland, was introduced by the Chancellor into his Majesty's presence, to whom he delivered the Elector's letter, and made his Majesty the like compliments in behalf of the Elector, Electress, and Electoral family, as he had done before to the Queen.

Shortly after which he delivered in his bill of extraordinaries for that journey, which amounting in all to 500l. whereof 250l. only had been advanced, he received the remainder.

The Duke of Zell was elected Knight of the Garter, and the King declaring he would invest him at the Hague with his own hands, Sir Thomas St. George thought he was obliged in honor to carry over the habit and ensigns of the order himself in person, and being only commissionated himself for that service, desired Mr. King's company as his assistant; Sir Thomas St. George kissed the Queen's hand upon his departure, (the King being gone before into Holland) and in March 1690–1 set forwards for Holland by the way of Harwich, accompanyed by Mr. King, and attended by his secretary, one Mr. Chamberlain, and two servants in livery. They arrived at the Hague just the day after the King left it in order to attempt the raysing of the siege of Mons, just newly invested by the French. This occasioned his staying at the Hague till the King returned; shortly after which, viz. on the 8th of May, 1691, the King invested the Duke of Zell in his bedchamber there with the Garter and George, the Dukes of Norfolk and Ormond and the Earl of Devonshire assisting thereat, with Sir Thomas St. George, and Mr. King carried him the habit of the order, which he essayed to put on, but without any ceremony, and the Duke presented Sir Thomas with 16 gold medals to the value of 380l. and 73 guineas as a composition for his habit. Mr. King was presented with eight of the same gold medals, value about 148l. the secretary had 50 guineas, and each of the footmen five guineas. They missed their opportunity of returning with the King, and so were forced to stay till the King came back to Holland again, and then went over in one of the yachts, not caring to venture over in the pacquet boat, having been frighted with a French privateer in their going thither. They arrived at London in 1691, and within two days Sir Thomas kissed the Queen's hand, and concluded that embassy.

In July and August this year, Mr. King having long before promised that he would make a survey for Jesus College, in Cambridge, of certain lands in Oxfordshire, Glocestershire, and Glamorganshire, (as he had done for them in Northamptonshire) took with him one Mr. Fuller, a very good artist in that way, and dispatch't those in Oxfordshire and Glocestershire, and being at Glocester engaged one Stephen Jeffreys, an ingenious Quaker, to undertake that in Glamorganshire, computed at 800 acres, but measuring 1200 acres; Mr. King, at Mr. Fuller's request, agreed to Mr. Fuller's re-return to London from Glocester, himself proceeding forwards to Glamorganshire, and taking an exact account of the severall particulars saw the work begun by Jeffreys, and so returned to London; but the wet he met with in this journey brought upon him, as he guessed, the next spring a most violent sciatica.

This year the Parliament sitting, Mr. Felton, who married the younger of the two daughters and co-heiresses of James Earl of Suffolk, petitioned the King for the barony of Lord Audley of Waldon, being a barony by writ descendible to the females; the Lady Essex Griffin thereupon, as being the elder daughter and co-heir, counterclaimed the said barony, and the Earl of Suffolk claimed it in the third place as heir male. The Earl of Thanet (whose claim to the barony of Clifford I had managed and got allowed the year before) recommended my Lady Essex Griffin to me. I drew up their case, proposed arguments, got it printed, and seconded with another paper of arguments, instructed their counsel with precedents, and attended the several hearings; but the Parliament breaking up before it came to any conclusion, Mr. Felton thought it not fit to renew it the next sessions.

In 1691 the Elector of Saxony, and the Earl of Dorset, Lord Chamberlain, were elected Knights of the Garter. The Earl of Dorset hastened his installation, and Mr. King having prepared the atchievments and other things of that kind for his Lordship, the installation was performed at Windsor. But the King gave no directions for carrying the order to his Electoral Highness of Saxony till the latter end of the summer.

Now whether any neglect of himself in the hurry of my Lord Dorset's installation, or the wet that he took in his journey to Wales the year before, might be the cause of that violent illness which Mr. King fell into this spring, is hard to say, but he was seized about Easter with a sciatica, which for seven or eight weeks together encreased to that degree, that he was obliged to make use of crutches, and was proof against all the prescriptions of physicians, apothecaries, and surgeons; finding no ease or relief by any thing but liquid laudanum, though he underwent all degrees of pharmacy. However, it pleased God to restore him to the use of his limbs again about the latter end of July. Soon after which the King sent orders over for carrying the Garter to the Elector of Saxony; but it being some months after before that affair was ready, Mr. King in the mean time dispatched the pedigree of Sir Richard Newdigate, which had been long in hand, but was now finished with great exactness, accompanied with extracts of many deeds pertinent thereto, and the draughts of severall monuments of the family.

But to come to the affair of the Elector of Saxony's Garter. Sir Thomas St. George, who had now been a year a widower, was engaged in a new amour, so that he could have no thoughts of going to Saxony himself in person; besides he foresaw it would be a winter journey, and he knew the length of the way, having had the honor, when he was Somerset Herald, anno 1669, to carry the order in the room of Sir Edward Walker, the then Garter, to this Elector of Saxony's grandfather. There could be no difficulty in the choice of the person to supply the place of Sir Thomas St. George on this occasion, Mr. King having approved himself an absolute master of that affair by his late conduct therein, so that Mr. King was presently addressed unto for the undertaking thereof; but Mr. King's late violent illness, whereof some unhappy effects had scarce yet left him, for it had interrupted his very speech and memory, made him not easily resolve to accept of it, least his distemper might return in the journey; but Sir Thomas telling him, that he would not think of any body else, and therefore if Mr. King declined it, he should be obliged to undertake it himself, which at his age, being then 77 or 78, would not be very agreeable to him; Mr. King adventured upon it.

Hereupon Mr. King prepared, by the Chancellor of the Order's directions, the commission, credential, letter, and instructions, which were signed by the Queen the 20th of August, 1692. By which commission Sir William Colt, Knt. their Majesties' Envoy residing with the Princes of the house of Lunenburgh, and who principally had promoted this affair, was joyned with Mr. King for the performing that ceremony. This being a piece of justice claimed by Sir William Colt, by reason he was not inserted in the commission for carrying the Garter to the Duke of Zell, being the Prince at whose court he most ordinarily resides.

The passing a privy seal for Mr. King's allowance and advance on this occasion spent a great deal of time, Mr. King expecting the same allowance as Sir Thomas St. George had the year before, viz. 40s. per diem; but in that pressing circumstance of affairs, occasioned by the excessive charge of the war, it could not be obtained, so that at Mr. Garter's instance Mr. King accepted the old allowance of 30s. per diem, and his privy seal was passed about Michaelmas accordingly.

But the difficulty of getting the money still remained, and Mr. King was obliged to stay till his Majesty's return from Flanders, so that he did not kiss his Majesty's hand upon his departure till the 27th of November, and though he received not his advance money till the 2d of December, yet he departed on his journey the 3d of December, 1692, and passing through Holland arrived at Osnaburg the 15th, at Hanover the 18th, and at Cell the 19th of December, where Sir William Colt received him with extraordinary kindness. But the King's affairs in relation to the ninth electorate, then newly conferred on the Duke of Hanover, detained Sir William Colt till the 31st of December, when setting forwards for Saxony, they came to Leipsick January 6, and to Dresden Jan. 9, Mr. King having the favour of Sir William Colt's own coach.

The court of Saxony had long expected them, so that now no time was to be lost in compleating the ceremonie; whereupon they had their first audience the 13th of January, their second, at which the Elector received the Blue Ribband, Garter, and Lesser George, on the 20th of January, and the grand ceremony was performed the 26th of January with all splendor and magnificence, the Elector resolving to outdo the Exemplar of Brandenburg. The carousell, the fireworks, the glorious opera, the masquerade, and the other diversions which followed in honor of this solemnity were very extraordinary, and the Elector did somewhat outdo the Elector of Brandenburgh even in the presents; for Mr. King was presented, in right of Garter King of Arms, with 50 pieces of gold purposely coynd, each of the value of 10 ducats, in an imbroidered crimson velvet purse, and in another curious purse of nuns work 200 ducats as a composition for his habit. His secretary was presented with six large silver beakers partie gilt, and his footmen with 15 dollars apiece.

The two commissioners only, as the custome is, dined with the Elector on the day of the ceremony, and on Sunday the 5th of February they had their audience of leave, and dined again with his Electoral Highness; Sir William Colt at the same time taking his audience as Envoy, that he might immediately enter upon the treatie for the Elector's forces to serve upon the Rhine against the French the ensuing campaigne, which treaty was concluded accordingly.

Mr. King being handsomely conducted out of Dresden, left that place the 13th of February, arrived at Hamburgh the 26th of February, at Amsterdam the 15th of March, and at the Hague, where staying till his Majesty's arrival there from England, he wayted on his Majesty, and having given his Majesty an account of his legation, and made their Electoral Highnesses' complements, he delivered the Elector's letter to his Majesty, and so took his leave, returning to England the 19th of April, and kissing her Majesty's hand the 23rd of April, whereby he concluded his embassy, but had not his bill of extraordinaries of 344l. 9s. 5d. for that journey ordered him till the 26th of July, 1694.

Mr. King, while he was at the Hague, put into Mr. Blathwayt's hands a memorial touching the installation of these three foreign Princes at Windsor by proxie; and visiting the Ministers of those foreign Princes there, advised them to second the said memorial; whereupon, in May following, his Majesty's pleasure was signified over to England for their instalment; whereupon Mr. King, by the Chancellor's directions, computed the charge at 552l. 10s. besides the dinner, which was imprest into the Chancellor's hands for the use of the severall officers and persons concerned in the fees, and for the atchievements, which atchievements Mr. King also prepared. But the fixing of proper proxies, and the adjusting the dinner, gave some delay to the said instalment. In the mean time Mr. King employed himself in finishing the draughts of the surveys he made two years before for Jesus College; and in a large pedigree for the Earl of Thanet, and other business for the Office.

The said installation being received, and a day nominated by the Chancellor for the ceremony, Mr. King payd the fees to the Dean and College of Windsor, amounting to 200l.; but the Chancellor interesting himself in the plate money for the altar, which then lay in the Dean's hands undisposed, would have stopt these fees upon the Dean, so that the day being put off, Mr. King was obliged to take security of the Dean for the said 200l. the Chancellor requiring Mr. King to make it good. The want of money for a dinner delayed these installations for some time, but 100l. being ordered by the treasury in September, 1693, the season of the year was then the pretence for delaying them. And so it stood all winter; but in March the day was appointed for the 5th of July, 1694, and all the necessary instruments signed by the King. But in the mean time the Elector of Saxony dyed. Upon which Mr. King represented to the Chancellor, how reasonable it was that all the honor should be payed to the Elector that might be, since his not being installed was not the Elector's fault; and this happening at the time when a committee of the Garter was to meet upon the score of the Earl of Shrewsbury's election into the order, (upon the death of the Duke of Hamilton) the said committee agreed, that it was fitt the Elector of

Saxony's atchievements should be hung up for form sake, and directed Mr. King to draw up an act of dispensation thereupon: which the Chancellor opposing, as willing to save their Majesties those installation fees, amounting to 126l. 13s. 4d. the matter was re-committed to the Knights committee of the Garter, who on May 29 reported it to the Queen according to the order which Mr. King had drawn up, whereupon the installation of the Elector of Brandenburgh and the Duke of Zell, and Earl (but then Duke of) Shrewsbury, was performed at Windsor June 5, 1694, and the atchievments of the Elector of Saxony having first been hung up for form sake, were taken down, and offered, together with the Duke of Hamilton's, immediately before the installation. At which ceremonie Mr. King officiated asassistant to Sir Thomas St. George, Garter, who was not yet perfectly recovered of his indisposition, the Queen having passed a warrant for Mr. King to have officiated absolutely for Garter, and to have worne the mantle if the case had required it.

About Christmas, 1693, Sir John Dugdale, Norroy, proposed to resign his place to Mr. King on several considerations, and all things being adjusted between Sir John and Mr. King, Sir John addressed himself by letter to the Earl Marshal for leave; but could not obtain leave, notwithstanding divers applications were made to his Grace in Sir John's behalf.

The latter end of summer, 1694, Mr. King sollicited the King's coronation fees to to the heralds; but while it was depending the Queen dyed, scilicet 28 of December, 1694, after an indisposition of eight days (of the small pox). Shortly after which Mr. King was sent for by the officers of the wardrobe to undertake the scocheons and other heraldry work for the funerall, and having given them a scheme of what was necessary for Whitehall, received the several quantities of silk necessary for the same; but the Earl Marshal having, by order of council of Jan. 9, the direction as to the number and manner of the escocheons and other trophies for that occasion committed to him, and being willing to gratify Mr. Pink, who was his Grace's coach-paynter (and one of the arms-paynters who principally promoted the decree of 1683) his Grace claymed the nomination of the paynter, which the Earl of Montagu claymed also as master of the wardrobe. At last they each resolved to nominate one, Jan. 19, 1694–5; but the next day the E. M. prevayld upon the Master of the Wardrobe to let him have the sole nomination, whereupon Mr. Pink was nominated entirely with a reservation that what had been delivered to Mr. King should be made use of. Whereupon (on considerations valuable) it was agreed that Mr. King should perfect what he had begun, which he ordered his paynter, Mr. Campion, to do accordingly, but it amounted onely to the value of 200l. which was not above an 8th part of the whole heraldry work done upon this occasion.

Mr. King's employing Mr. Campion, who was no friend to the agreement between the heralds and the painters as being a considerable looser thereby, gave occasion to incense the Earl Marshal against Mr. King for undertaking this funeral work, insomuch that he transferred the Register's place of the office from Mr. King to Dr. Plott, who was then newly nominated Moubray Herald Extraordinary, but Mr. King's qualifications were so well known to the Earl Marshal, that his Grace through all this affair, trated Mr. King with a handsom respect, as Mr. King on the other side expressed all suitable deference to his Grace.

# APPENDIX 2

# King on the Naval Trade of England

## OF THE NAVAL TRADE OF ENGLAND A.° 1688 AND THE NATIONAL PROFIT THEN ARISING THEREBY.

Gr King
Lanc Herald
1697

From a general Consideration of the following particulars. viz.[t]

The Increase of Our Shipping both for War and Trade.
The Increase of the Old Customes
The Increase of Coynage
The Increase of Plate
The Increase of Sumptuous Buildings, Forteresses etc.[a]
The Increase of Luxury both Forreign and Domestick
The Improvement of Waste Land
The Advance of the Purchase of Land, and price of Wages and Comodities
The Advance of Marriage Portions
The Lowering of Interest, and many other Circumstances of like nature.

We must allow this great Fundamental Truth

That the Trade and Wealth of England did mightily advance between the years 1600 and 1688

1st Fundamental Position

And from a more particular Reflexion upon the Premisses

We may reasonably conclude

| | General Rental | Years Purchase | Capital Stock | Increase of the Capital Stock | Yearly Increase of the Capital Stock | |
|---|---|---|---|---|---|---|
| 1. That a.° 1600 the gen.ll Rental of England in Lands, Tenem.ts Hereditaments and Personal Estates was but ............. | 6,000,000£ | at 12 | 72 Millions | | | |
| That a.° 1630 the a.d gen.ll Rental was ......................... | 8,000,000 | at 14 | 112 Millions | in 30 y | 40 Millions | 1,300,000 |
| That a.° 1660 the a.d Rental was .............................. | 10,500,000 | at 16 | 168 Millions | in 30 y | 56 Millions | 1,870,000 |
| And y.t a.° 1688 the a.d Rental was ........................ | 14,000,000 | at 13 | 252 Millions | in 23 y | 84 Millions | 3,000,000 |
| | | | | | 180 Millions | |

| | Actual Stock | Increase of the Actual Stock | Yearly Increase of the Actual Stock |
|---|---|---|---|
| 2. That the Actual Stock of the National Wealth of England in Gold and Silver Coyn, in Bullion, Plate, Jewels Furniture, Apparell, Shipping and other Carriages, Engines and Instrum.ts in Trade, Arts and Imployments In Naval and Military Stores, Foreign and Domestick Wares Comodities or Provisions, Live Cattel etc. Was a.° 1600 not above........................ | 25 Millions | | |
| That a.° 1630 the same was .................. | 37 Millions | 30 y. 12 Millions | 400,000£ |
| That a.° 1660 the same was .................. | 58 Millions | 30 y. 21 Millions | 700,000£ |
| And a.° 1683 .............................. | 86 Millions | 28 y. 28 Millions | 1,000,000£ |
| | | 61 Millions | |

Which if so, Then it follows,

1. That both the Actual Stock of National Wealth, and the Capital Stock of the whole Nation have Increased in one and the same Proportion between the Years 1600 and 1688 viz.t from 1 to 3½.
2. That the Actual Stock is Increasd from 4 to 6 times the general Rental.
3. That the Capital Stock being much about treble to the Actual Stock Every Million Increase of the Actual Stock does Increase the Capital Stock about 3 Millions.

3. That the Coyn of the Nation (being a.° 1688 in Tale about a 5.th part of the Actual Stock, and a 15.th part of the Capital Stock) seems to have Increased much in the Same proportion with the Actual Stock and Capital Stock viz.t

| | Stock of Money | Increase of the Stock of Money | Yearly Increase of the Stock of Money |
|---|---|---|---|
| That it was a.° 1600 ....... | 5 Millions | | |
| a.° 1690 ....... | 7½ Millions | 30 y. 2½ Millions | 083,000£ |
| a.° 1660 ....... | 11½ Millions | 30 y. 4 Millions | 133,000£ |
| a.° 1688 ....... | 17 Millions | 28 y. 5½ Millions | 196,000£ |
| | | 12 Millions | |

4. That the Trade of England, viz.t its Exports and Imports in money or other adequate Treasure, and in Wares and Commodities in Gross was during the said Term of years between 1600 and 1688 at a Medium One Eighth part of the Actual Stock of the Nation and near 3 Fifths of the Stock of Money, and was Carryed on by about one fourth part of the Stock of Money; But has risen of later years somewhat faster in proportion than the Stock of Actual Wealth; So as that a.° 1600 such Bulk of Trade in gross was between an 8.th and 9.th part of the whole Actual Stock of the Nation, or near 3 Millions ꝑ annum Carryed on by somewhat above one Million of Money ꝑ annum and in a.° 1688 was between a 7.th and 8.th part of the Whole

Actual Stock or near 11½ Millions ꝑ annum Requiring about 4 Millions ꝑ annum in Money to Carry it on, according to the following Scheme

| | Actual Stock | Stock of Money | Bulk of Trade | Gross Exports | Gross Imports | Originall Exports in Wares | Re Exports in Wares | Exports in Money or adequate Treasure |
|---|---|---|---|---|---|---|---|---|
| A°1600 | ........25 Mill. | 5 Mill. | 3 Mill. | 1,400,000£ | 1,600,000£ | 1,000,000£ | 0,300,000£ | 100,000£ |
| 1690 | ........37 Mill. | 7½ Mill. | 4½ Mill. | 2,000,000 | 2,500,000 | 1,300,000 | 0,500,000 | 200,000 |
| 1688 | ........86 Mill. | 17 Mill. | 11½ Mill. | 4,310,000 | 7,120,000 | 1,800,000 | 0,750,000 | 350,000 |
| 1660 | ........58 Mill. | 11½ Mill. | 6½ Mill. | 2,900,000 | 3,850,000 | 2,600,000 | 1,160,000 | 550,000 |

5. That as to the Increase of the Actual Stock of Wealth about the year 1688 particularly We are to Observe, That The Plague the Fire of London and the Foreign Wars which happend between 1664 and 1670, did diminish or hinder the Increase of the Capital Stock of the Nation about 30 or 40 Millions and the actual Stock about 18 Millions Whereof the actual Decrease was above 12 Millions viz.t from above 62 Millions anno 1664 to 50 Millions anno 1667; So that whereas by the year 1670 the Actual Stock ought to have been 71 Millions the same was not above 53 Millions, viz.t but about equal to the Actual Stock a.° 1655. And this seems to be the Reason why some persons in their Discourses on Trade, reckoning the Kingdome to be Richer anno 1656 or thereabouts then it was a.°1670 or 1680 made Conclusions to the Prejudice of our Foreign Trade; Whereas allowing the Nation to be no Richer (as to its Actual Stock) a.° 1670 then it was a.° 1655 by reason of the foresaid Accidents; And that till the year 1676 it had not Recoverd to the Condition it was in a.° 1664 yet the great Increase of the Actual from 1677 to 1688 must be attributed chiefly to Our Increase of Foreign Trade; and Consequently being Increased to 86 Millions by the year 1688, It made an Increase of 33 Millions in the 18 years between 1670 and 1688, or at a Medium near 2 Millions ꝑ annum viz.t about 1,300,000£ ꝑ annum anno 1670 and 2,400,000 anno 1688.

6. That if the Increase of the Actual Stock of Wealth was anno 1688 . . . . . . . . . . 2,400,000£ ꝑ an.
We may reasonably allow the Increase by Foreign Trade was . . . . . . . . . . 1,700,000£ ꝑ an.
And by Inland Trade and Labour . . . . . . . . . . 0,700,000 ꝑ an.

Lastly
That if the Increase of the Actual Stock of Wealth by Forreign Trade was Anno 1688 . . . . . . . . . . 1,700,000 ꝑ an.
The increase of Gold and Silver Coyn might well be . . . . . . 550,000 ꝑ an.
The Increase of Treasure adequate to Gold and Silver Coyn, as Bullion, Plate, Jewells etc.[a] . . . . . . . . . . 150,000 ꝑ an.
The Increase of Foreign Comodities layd by as Treasure or Applyed to the Increase of the National Stock . . . . . . . . . . 1,000,000 ꝑ an.

Thus having Calculated the Quantum of the Increase of the Actual Wealth of the Nation by Foreign Trade in General a.°1688 to be 1,700,000£ ꝑ an. We Shall lay down this Second Fundamental Position, viz.t

2d Fundamental Position

That by how much the Nation does not Consume of its Imports, but either lays up, or Increases the Stock of Gold or Silver or other adequate Treasure, or of Durable Commodities in Specie by so much at least does the Nation gain by Forreign Trade besides all other Advantages of Navigation

And upon a due Consideration of the Trade of the Nation anno 1688 We have Stated the General Ballance thus

1.st The National Increase of Money or Adequate Treasure Imported by Trade anno 1688

| | |
|---|---|
| Gross Imports of Money or Adequate Treasure | 1,250,000£ |
| Gross Exports of Money or Adequate Treasure | 550,000 |
| Increase of Money or Adequate Treasure | 700,000 |

2 The National Increase of Wares and Commodities Imported by Trade over and above Our Re Exports and Home Consumption anno 1688

| | |
|---|---|
| Gross Imports of Wares and Comodities | 5,870,000£ |
| Deduct Imports Re Exported | 1,280,000 |
| Remains neat Imports of Wares and Comodities | 4,590,000 |
| Gross Exports of Wares and Comodities | 3,760,000£ |
| Deduct Imports Re Exported | 1,280,000 |
| Remains Neat Exports of Wares and Commodities | 2,480,000 |
| Neat Imports of Wares and Comodities | 4,590,000£ |
| Neat Exports of Wares and Commodities | 2,480,000 |
| Increase of Wares and Commodities by Imports | 2,110,000 |
| And the Neat Imports of Wares and Commodities being | 4,590,000£ |
| Whereof Consuming at Home within the year | 3,590,000 |
| The Increase of the National Stock by Wares and Comodities Imported, and not Consumed within the year was | 1,000,000 |
| But the Increase of Money or Adequate Treasure Imported being | 0,700,000£ |
| And the Increase of Wares and Comodities Imported over and above the Exports being | 2,110,000£ |
| The general Increase of Profit by Forreign Trade in a larger Sence was anno 1688 | 2,810,000£ |
| But the National Gain or Increase of the National wealth, by Money or Adequate Treasure Imported being | 0,700,000£ |
| And by Wares and Commodities Imported and not Consumed within the year | 1,000,000£ |
| The Actual Increase of the National Wealth by Forreign Trade was in all but | 1,700,000£ |

| | |
|---|---|
| So that though the Value of our Neat Exports in Wares and Comodities was then but | 2,480,000£ |
| And in Money or Bullion but | 550,000£ |
| In all | 3,030,000 |

Yet the said 3,030,000£ So Exported in Money or Commodities Enabled Us

| | |
|---|---|
| 1.st to Consume in Forreign Commodities not only the full Value of our Neat Exports in Wares and Commodities, viz.t | 2,480,000£ |
| But also to Consume in like Forreign Commodities, over and above the full Value of Our Exports, the further Value of | 1,110,000£ |
| Consumed in all | 3,590,000 |
| 2 To Treasure up in forreign Commodities applyed to the Increase of the Actual Stock of the Nations Wealth | 1,000,000£ |
| And in Money or Adequate Treasure | 0,700,000 |
| Increase in all | 1,700,000 |
| Consumed and Increased together | 5,290,000 |

But note that out of this Increase of Money or Adequate Treasure which is here Calculated to be 700,000£ for the year 1688 There must be at least 100,000£ deduted for the Natural yearly decay and Diminution of the Species of Gold and Silver by its Fabrication into Coyn, Plate Wyre &c by the wear of all things made of Gold and Silver by Gilding and by other means and Accidents within the Realm For as to the Several occasions of Drawing Money or Adequate Treasure out of the Realm in times of Peace, otherwise then by trade, we reckon it is Sufficiently ballanced by the like Occasions for bringing it in, as by Travailers Intelligence money, Rewards to Ambassadors etc.[a]

Lastly having considerd the Nature of Trade, and the Subserviency of the Trade of one Country to that of another, or to Trade in general, We are of opinion that it may be laid down as another Fundamental Truth, viz.t

That all the Branches of Our Foreign Trade, which have admitted a Series of Increase of Trafique, are Nationally profitable

Whereupon dividing Forreign Trade into these 3 Principal Branches viz.t

1. The Trade to Europe, Africa and the Levant
2. The Trade to the Plantations
3. The Trade to the East Indies.

We have formd the following Scheme of the Trade of England to and from each of those parts for the year 1688 according to the Value of the Commodities here at home Distinguishing the Exports and Imports into Money or Adequate Treasure, and into Wares and Commodities; Meaning by Adequate Treasure whatsover is Gen.lly Esteemed equal to Money as Bullion, Plate Gold Dust, Jewels Bills of Exchange &c.

## A Scheme of the Trade of England anno 1688

| | Exports in Gross £ | Exports in Money or Adequate Treasure £ | Exports in Wares and Comodities £ | Imports in Gross £ | Imports in Money or Adequate Treasure £ | Imports in Wares or Commodities £ | Imports Consum'd at Home £ | Imports Re export'd to other parts £ | Imports applied to the Increase of the National Stock £ |
|---|---|---|---|---|---|---|---|---|---|
| Original Exports to Europe Africa and the Levant.................... | 2,340,000 | 0,140,000 | 2,200,000 | 2,870,000 | 0,720,000 | 2,150,000 | 1,610,000 | 0,000,000 | 0,450,000 |
| Original Exports to the Plantations......................... | 0,310,000 | 0,010,000 | 0,300,000 | 0,950,000 | 0,030,000 | 0,020,000 | 0,280,000 | 0,600,000 | 0,040,000 |
| Original Exports to the East Indies .............................. | 0,500,000 | 0,400,000 | 0,100,000 | 1,700,000 | 0,100,000 | 1,600,000 | 0,900,000 | 0,500,000 | 0,200,000 |
| | 3,150,000 | 0,550,000 | 2,600,000 | 5,520,000 | 0,850,000 | 4,670,000 | 2,790,000 | 1,190,000 | 0,600,000 |
| Re Exports of Plantation Goods to Europe Africa and the Levant ............................. | 0,600,000 | 0,000,000 | 0,600,000 | 0,750,000 | 0,210,000 | 0,540,000 | 0,370,000 | 0,020,000 | 0,150,000 |
| Re Exports of East India Goods to Europe, Africa & the Levant ............................. | 0,500,000 | 0,000,000 | 0,500,000 | 0,650,000 | 0,180,000 | 0,470,000 | 0,320,000 | 0,020,000 | 0,150,000 |
| Re Exports of European, African or Levant Goods to the Plantations or East Indies ...... | 0,060,000 | 0,000,000 | 0,060,000 | 0,200,000 | 0,010,000 | 0,190,000 | 0,110,000 | 0,060,000 | 0,080,000 |
| | 4,310,000 | 0,550,000 | 3,760,000 | 7,120,000 | 1,250,000 | 5,870,000 | 3,590,000 | 1,280,000 | 1,000,000 |

D.r Chamb. reckons the Wollen Manufactures Exported at 2 Millions ℘ ann. Sterling Lead, Tin and Coals at 500,000£ ℘ annum

Besides, Hops, Flax, Hemp, Hatts, Shoos, Ale, Beer, Herrings Pilchards, Salmon, Oysters, Saffron Liquorice, Watches Ribbands, Toys &c.

Cloths and Houshold Stuff sent to America are reckond at 200,000£

England Produces yearly 50,000,000 Chaldrons of Sea Coal, 1,200,000 Pounds of Tin, 800 Fodders of Lend, 800 Furnaces of Iron, 800 Tuns of Allom, much whereof is Exported.

We Transport of Irish Comodities in Wool, Butter Hydes Tallow Beef Herrings Pilchards & Salmon 500,000£ ℘ ann we Transport from America besides our own Consumption, in Sugar Indico Tobacco Cacao Nutts &c 600,000£ ℘ annum Besides in Fish Pipe Staves, Masts, Bever etc.[a] from New England and North America 200,000£ ℘ annum

In the Infancy of the East India Trade in one year 1613 we Reexported in Pepper 200,000£

Of late our Reexports from India in Pepper, Salt Petre, Callicoes, Silks, Druggs, Diamonds, Pearls, comp. at 800,000£ ℘ annum

[The table on p. 118 comes here in the MS.]

| | |
|---|---|
| So that if the General Increase by Money or Adequate Treasure Imported was anno 1688 | 0,700,000£ |
| And the Increase of Wares and Commodities over and above the Value of our Exports in Wares or Commodities was | 2,110,000£ |
| In all | 2,810,000 |

We must conclude as follows viz.[t]

1 That as to the European, African and Levant Trade

| | |
|---|---|
| The Original Exports in Money or Wares being | 2,340,000£ |
| Re exports in Plantation Goods | 0,600,000 |
| Re Exports in East India Goods | 0,500,000 |
| Exports in all | 3,440,000 |
| Imports in gross from Original Exports | 2,870,000£ |
| Imports from Plantation Goods Re Exported | 0,750,000 |
| Imports from East India Goods Re Exported | 0,650,000 |
| Imports in all | 4,270,000 |
| Exports deducted | 3,440,000 |
| The general Increase was | 0,830,000 |

2 That as to the Plantation Trade

| | |
|---|---|
| The Original Exports in Money or Wares being | 0,310,000£ |
| Re Exports of European, African, Levant or East India Goods | 0,040,000 |
| Exports in all | 0,350,000 |
| Imports in gross from Original Exports | 0,950,000 |

Imports from European, African Levant or East India Goods Re Exported . . . . . . . . . . 0,120,000

Imports in all . . . . . . . . 1,070,000
Exports Deducted . . . . . . . . 0,350,000

The General Increase was . . . . . . . . 0,720,000

3 That as to the East India Trade
The Original Exports in Money or Wares being . . . . . . . . . . 0,500,000£
Re Exports of European, African Levant or Plantation Goods . . . . . . 0,020,000

Exports in all . . . . . . . . 0,520,000

Imports in gross from Original Exports . . . . . . . . . . 1,700,000
Imports from European, African, Levant or Plantation Goods Re Exported . . . . . . . . . . 0,080,000

Imports in all . . . . . . . . 1,780,000
Exports Deducted . . . . . . . . 0,520,000

The General Increase was . . . . . . . . 1,260,000

But if the National Profit by Trade be allowd to be no more than what remains unconsumed or un exported of Our Imports notwithstanding we are thereby enabled to Spend, and do actually consume 1,110,000£of such Imports over and above the Value of Our Wares and Commodities Exported; Then the said National Profit must be thus proportion'd or Ballanced.

| 1st Ballance | General Increase | Deduct for Freight etc. | | National Profit |
|---|---|---|---|---|
| The European, African and Levant Trade | 0,830,000£ | at 13 ℘ Cent or | 110,000£ | 720,000£ |
| The Plantation Trade | 0,720,000 | at 30 ℘ Cent or | 220,000 | 500,000 |
| The East India Trade | 1,260,000 | at 62 ℘ Cent or | 780,000 | 480,000 |
| | 2,810,000 | at 38 ℘ Cent or | 1,110,000 | 1,700,000 |

But whereas in the 2,810,000£ Calculated to be the General Profit or Increase by Trade in Money or Adequate Treasure or Wares, over and above Our Exports, the European African and Levant Trade, Including the Plantation and East India Re Exports brought in anno 1688 an Increase of 830,000£ We are to observe
That the Returns of the Plantation Re Exports brought in an Increase . . . . . . . . . . 0,150,000£
And the Returns of the East Indian Re Exports bringing in likewise an Increase of . . . . . . . . . . 0,150,000

In all . . . . . . . . . . 0,300,000

| | |
|---|---|
| The said General Profit or Increase arising by the European African and Levant Trade from our Original Exports was but . . . . . . . . . . . . . . . . . . . . . . . . . . . . . . . . . | 0,530,000$^{£}$ |
| And that if the said 300,000$^{£}$ arising by the Ruturns of the Re Exports of the Plantation and East India Goods be transferred equally to the proper account of the Plantation and East India Trades | |
| Then the general Profit or Increase by the Plantation Trade will be . . . . . . . . . . . . . . . . . . . . . . . . . . . . . . . . . | 0,870,000$^{£}$ |
| And the General Profit or Increase by the East India Trade will be . . . . . . . . . . . . . . . . . . . . . . . . . . . . . . . . . | 1,410,000$^{£}$ |
| In all . . . . . . . . . . . . . . | 2,810,000 as before |

Consequently in the 1,700,000$^{£}$Calculated to be the National Profit by Trade, the 3 Branches of Our Trade as aforesaid (Applying the Returns of the Plantation and East India Re Exports to the proper Accompt of those 2 Trades) will hold this Proportion or Ballance

| 2.$^{d}$ Ballance | Generall Increase | Deduct for Freight etc.[a] | | Nationall Profit |
|---|---|---|---|---|
| The European African and Levant Trade. . . . . . . . . . | 0,530,000$^{£}$ | at 12 per Cent | 65,000$^{£}$ | 0,465,000$^{£}$ |
| The Plantation Trade with the Returns of Plantation Goods Re. Exported . . . . . | 0,870,000 | at 26 per Cent | 225,000 | 0,645,000 |
| The East India Trade with the Returns of East India Goods Re-Exported . . . . . | 1,410,000 | at 58 per Cent | 820,000 | 0,590,000 |
| | 2,810,000 | at 39 per Cent | 1,110,000 | 1,700,000 |

From these two several Ballances of Trade, arising from the different application of the Returns of the Plantation and East India Re Exports either to the Profit of the European, African and Levant Trade, or to the Profit of the Plantation and East India Trades respectively

We may observe, as follows,

| | By the First Ballance | By the 2.$^{d}$ Ballance |
|---|---|---|
| 1. That the general Profit or Increase of Money and Wares by the European African and Levant Trade is. . . . . . . . . . . . . . . . . . . . . . . . . . . . . . . . . | Near a. 4.$^{th}$ of the gen.$^{11}$ Exports and Re-Exports in those Trades | Between a 6.$^{th}$ & 7.$^{th}$ of the Exports |
| By the Plantation Trade . . . . . . . . . . . . . . . . . . . . . . . . . . . . . | Above double the Exports | Between double & treble the Exports |
| By the East India Trade | Between double and treble the Exports. . . . . . . . . . . . . . . . . . . . . . . . . . . . . | Near treble the Exports |

| | | |
|---|---|---|
| 2. That the National Profit by the European, African and Levant Trade was................ | Between a 4.th and 5.th of the gen.[11] Exports in those Trades | Almost a 6.th of the Exports |
| By the Plantation Trade ............................. | Oone and a half of the Exports | Almost double the Exports |
| By the East India Trade ............................. | Near equal to the Exports | Near 1¾ of the Exports |

3. That the Exports to the Plantations and East Indies together, being little more than one Fourth of the European, African and Levant Exports yet the Plantation and East India Imports are 2 Thirds of the European African and Levant Imports.

We come now to Consider the general Scheme before going by the ordinary method of Stating the Ballance of Trade, whereby to find how it affects the Increase or Decrease of Money or Adequate Treasure, viz.t (Agreeing the Exports and Imports, and what Proportion therof is Navigated or Carryed by Our own Shipping, and what by Forreigners) To Compute the Exports and Imports in Our Own Shipping according to the Value of the Markets abroad And the Exports and Imports in forreign Shipping according to the Value here at home.

1. As to the Bulk of Trade arising from Our Gross Exports and Imports in Money or Adequate Treasure, or in Wares or Commodities following the former Scheme, It Stands thus,

| | Gross Exports | Gross Imports | Both together |
|---|---|---|---|
| The European African and Levant Trade amounts to . . . . . . . . . . . . . . . . . . . . . | 3,440,000£ | 4,270,000£ | 7,510,000£ |
| The Plantation Trade . . . . . . . . . . . . . . . . | 0,350,000 | 1,070,000 | 1,420,000 |
| The East India Trade . . . . . . . . . . . . . . . . | 0,520,000 | 1,780,000 | 2,300,000 |
| In all. . . . . . . . . . . | 4,310,000 | 7,120,000 | 11,430,000 |
| Whereof Money or Adequate Treasure . . . . | 0,550,000 | 1,250,000 | 1,800,000 |
| Wares and Commodities . . . . . . . . . . . . . | 3,760,000 | 5,870,000 | 9,630,000 |

But in this Calculation We Shall esteem Money or Adequate Treasure as a Comoditie only, and shall take the Gross Exports and Imports in their Greatest Latitude.

2. As to what Proportion was Navigated by Our Selves a.o 1688 and what by Forreigners, We are of Opinion, That with Relation to the Value of Our whole Trade here at Home, Our Own Navigation was Somewhat more than 3 Fourths, and the Forreign Navigation near one Fourth; But reckoning the Value of the Forreign Navigation at the Market here and of Our own, at the Markets abroad, Then the Forreign Navigation seems to have been at that time in Proportion to Our Own as 1 to 2¾, And with respect to the Tunnage of Ships Our Own Navigation seems to have been at that time Two thirds, and the Forreign Navigation one third.

[The table on p. 123 comes here in the MS.]

And the Advantage to Forreigners Trading to England in their own Ships was, at that time, in general, thus

According to the following Scheme.

| | Value here | Value abroad | Value upon the balance | | Gain by Freight &c | |
|---|---|---|---|---|---|---|
| Exported By Our Selves | 3,310,000£ | 4,120,000£ | Value abroad | 4,120,000£ | To our Selves | 0,810,000£ |
| By Forreigners | 1,000,000 | 1,250,000 | Value here | 1,000,000 | To Forreigners | 0,250,000 |
| | 4,310,000 | 5,370,000 | | 5,120,000 | | 1,060,000 |

| Imported | Value here | Value abroad | Value upon the ballance | | Gain by Freight &c | |
|---|---|---|---|---|---|---|
| By Our Selves | 5,570,000£ | 2,870,000£ | Value abroad | 2,870,000£ | To our Selves | 2,700,000£ |
| By Forreigners | 1,550,000 | 1,150,000 | Value here | 1,550,000 | To Forreigners | 0,400,000 |
| Gross Imports | 7,120,000 | 4,020,000 | Gross Imports | 4,420,000 | Gross Imports | 3,100,000 |
| Gross Exports | 4,310,000 | 5,370,000 | Gross Exports | 5,120,000 | Gross Exports | 1,000,000 |
| In all | 11,430,000 | 9,390,000 | | 9,540,000 | | 4,100,000 |

| | | | |
|---|---|---|---|
| | Value abroad | | Value abroad |
| So the Exports by our Own Shipping being | 4,120,000 | In all | 6,990,000£ |
| Imports by Our Own Shipping | 2,870,000 | | |
| The National gain by Our Own Shipping in the ballance of Trade | 1,250,000 | | |
| | Value here | | Value here |
| And the Exports by Forreign Shipping being | 1,000,000 | In all | 2,550,000£ |
| Imports by Forreign Shipping | 1,550,000 | | |
| The National loss by Forreign Shipping in the Ballance of Trade is | 0,550,000 | In all | 9,540,000 |

Whence it follows,

| | |
|---|---|
| That our gain upon the Ballance by our own shipping being | 1,250,000£ |
| And our Loss upon the Ballance by Forreign Shipping being | 0,550,000£ |
| The Increase of Money or Adequate Treasure by the Balance of our Trade in general was a.° 1688 | 0,700,000 |

| | |
|---|---|
| By Freight or Advance of the Price of our Commodities Exported by them above the Value here | 250,000£ |
| By Freight or Advance of the Prize of their own Commodities Imported here above their Value abroad | 400,000£ |
| In all | 650,000 |
| Besides the Increase of Goods Imported to their own Countreys over and above their own Exports according to the Value of them in their Countreys | 100,000£ |
| In all | 750,000 |

Upon the whole we Conclude

| | |
|---|---|
| 1. That the General Increase of Our Money or Adequate Treasure, and of Wares and Commodities over and above the Value of Our gross Exports was a.º 1688 | 2,810,000£ |
| And the gain made by Forreign Nations Trading with England in their own Shipping was | 0,750,000£ |
| So that the Naval Trade of England is generally Profitable to our Selves and Forreigners, in all | 3,560,000£ |
| 2. That the National Profit to England by Forreign Trade was then at least | 1,700,000£ |
| Whereof in money or Adequate Treasure | 0,700,000 |
| And in Wares or Commodities Treasured up, or applied to the Increase of the National Stock | 1,000,000 |

# APPENDIX 3

# King's Natural and Political Observations 1696

### NATURAL AND POLITICALL OBSERVATIONS AND CONCLUSIONS UPON THE STATE & CONDITION OF ENGLAND

*By Gregory King Esq.ʳ Lancaster Herald of Armes, A.ºD. 1696.*

## PREFACE.

If to be well apprized of the true State and Condition of a Nation, Especially in the Two maine Articles of it's People, and Wealth, be a Piece of Politicall Knowledge, of all others, and at all times, the most usefull, and Necessary; Than surely at a Time when a long and very Expensive Warr against a Potent Monarch (who alone has stood the shock of an allyance, & Confederacy of the Greatest part of Christendome) Seems to be at it's Crisis, Such a Knowledge of our own Nation must be of the Highest concern: But since the attaining thereof (how necessary & disireable soever) is next to impossible, We must Content our selves with such near approaches to it as the Grounds We have to go upon will enable us to make.

However if having better Foundations than heretofore for Calculations of this kind, We have been Enabled to come very near the Truth; Then doubtlesse the following observations & conclusions will be acceptable to those who have not entirely given up themselves to an Implicit Beleif of Popular Falcehoods. But the Vanity of People in overvaluing their own Strength is so natural to all nations as well as ours; That as it has influenc'd all former Calculations of this Kind both at Home and Abroad, So if these, even these Papers may be allowed not to have erred on that hand, I am of opinion they will not be found to have Erred on the other.

## THE CONTENTS.

1. The Number of People in England & Wales, calculated from the Assessments, on Marriages, Births, & Burials.
2. The Proportion of England in Acres & people, to France & Holland, To Europe, & to the world in generall, with a Calculation of the number of People, now in the World.
3. The Several Distinctions of the People, as to Males, & Females, married, & unmarried, children, Serv.[ts] & Sojourners.
4. The Several ages of the People.
5. The origination, & Increase of the People of England with some Observations about Procreation.
6. The annual Income, & Expence of the Nation A.[o] 1688. with a Scheme of the Income, & Expence of the Several Families respectively; And a calculation of the Quantity of Silver & Gold in England, France & Holl.[d] In Europe and in the world in General, and of the Increase and Consumption thereof.
7. The Several Sorts of Land in Eng.[d] & the value & Product thereof, with a Scheme of the Live Stock of the Nation in Cattle &c. and of the Flesh yearly consum'd as Food.
8. The Beer, Ale, & malt, annually consum'd in England, & the Revenue of Excise, ariseing thereby.
9. A Calculation of the Produce of the Poll Bills, & some other Taxes viz.[t] The Tax on Marriages, Births, & Burials and on Houses, & Windows; And what may be Rais'd on some commodities not yet Taxed.
10. The State of the Nation A.[o] 1695. And what may be the Effect of continuing the Warr to 1698. Inclusive.
11. The State of France & Holland in 1688 & 1695.
12. The State and condition of the three Nations of England, France, & Holland compar'd one with another with respect to the years 1688 & 1695.

## NATURAL AND POLITICAL OBSERVATIONS, UPON THE STATE, AND CONDITION OF ENGLAND.

Whereas the ensuing Treatise depends chiefly upon the Knowledge of the true Number of People in England, and such other circumstances relating thereunto, as have been collected from the assessments on Marriages, Births, and Burials, Parish Registers, & other publick accounts; We shall first exhibit the calculation of the Number of People, as they appear by the said Assessments

1. As to the Number of the People of England.

In this Calculation, We shall consider.

1. The Number of Inhabited Houses.
2. The Number of People to each House.
3. The Number of Transitory People, & vagrants.

The Number of Houses in the Kingdome, as charg'd in the Books of the Hearth Office at Lady Day 1690. Were .................................. 1,319,215.

The Kingdome increasing at this time about 9000 People ℘ ann. as will appear in the ensuing Discourse.

The Increase of Houses should be about 2000 ℘ ann. But by reason of the Present Warr with France not much above 1000 ℘ ann So that by the year 1695 The Increase cannot have been above 6 or 7000. Which makes the present Number of Houses, that is to say such as were so charged in the Books of the Hearth office to be about.................................. 1,326,000.

But whereas the chimney Mony being charg'd on the Tennant or Inhabitant, The Divided Houses stand as so many distinct Dwellings in the Accounts of the said Hearth office; And whereas the Empty Houses, Smiths shops &c. are Included in the said account, All which may very well amount to 1 in 36 or 37 (or near 3 ℘ Cent) which in the whole may be about 36,000 Houses, It Follows

That the true Number of Inhabited Houses in England, is not Above ........................................................................ 1,290,000

Which however in a Round Number, We shall call ..................... 1,300,000

And shall thus apportion,

| | Houses |
|---|---|
| London & the Bills of Mortality | 105,000 |
| The other Cities, & Markett Towns | 195,000 |
| The Villages & Hamletts | 1,000,000 |
| In all, | 1,300,000 |

Haveing thus adjusted the Number of Inhabited Houses, We come to proportion the number of Souls to each House according to what we have observed from the said assessments on Marriages, Births, & Burials, in Several parts of the Kingdome viz.[t]

That London within the Walls produc'd at a medium almost..... 5½ Souls ℘ House.
The 16 Parishes Without the Walls ........................... Full 4½ Souls ℘ House.
And the Rest of the said Bills ............................... almost 4½ Souls ℘ House.
That the other Cities and Markett Towns produc'd at a medium .......................................................... 4⅓ Souls ℘ House.
And the villages & Hamletts at a Medium ................ about 4 Souls ℘ House.
Accordingly the Number of People computed from the said assessments amounts to............................................... 5,318,100 Souls.

As by the following Scheme.

| | Inhabited Houses. | Souls ℘ House. | Number of Souls. |
|---|---|---|---|
| The 97 Parishes within the Walls.................. | 13,500 | at 5′4 | 72,900 Souls. |
| The 16 Parishes without the Walls. ................ | 32,500 | at 4′6 | 149,500 |
| The 15 Out Parishes in Midd.$^{x}$ & Surrey......... | 35,000 | at 4′4 | 154,000 |
| The 7 Parishes in the City & Liberties of Westm.$^{r}$ ............................................. | 24,000 | at 4′3 | 103,200 |
| So London & the Bills of Mortality contain...... | 105,000 | at 4′57 | 479,600 |
| The other Cities & Market Towns ................ | 195,000 | at 4′3 | 838,500 |
| The Villages & Hamletts ............................ | 1,000,000 | at 4 | 4,000,000 |
| In all | 1,300,000 | at 4′9 | 5,318,100 |

But considering that the omissions in the s.$^{d}$ assessm.$^{ts}$ may well be,

| | | |
|---|---|---|
| In London & the Bills of Mortality ........................ | 10 ℘ Cent or | 47,960 Souls. |
| In the Cities & Towns.......................................... | 2 ℘ Cent or | 16,500 Souls. |
| In the Villages & Hamletts.................................. | 1 ℘ Cent or | 40,000 Souls. |
| | In all | 104,460 Souls. |

It follows that the True number of People dwelling in the 1,300,000 Inhabited Houses should be 5,422,560 Souls.

According to the following Scheme

| | People by the Assessm.$^{ts}$ | Omissions in the Assessm.$^{ts}$ | Number of People in all. | | |
|---|---|---|---|---|---|
| The 97 Parishes .......... | 72,000 | 7,200 | 80,100 | at almost 6 | Heads ℘ House. |
| The 16 Parishes .......... | 149,500 | 14,950 | 164,450 | at above 5 | Heads ℘ House. |
| The 15 Parishes .......... | 154,000 | 15,400 | 169,400 | at above 4′8 | Heads ℘ House. |
| The 7 Parishes............ | 103,200 | 10,820 | 113,520 | at almost 4¾ | Heads ℘ House. |
| The Bills of Mortal........ | 479,600 | 47,960 | 527,560 | at above 5 | Heads ℘ House. |
| The Cities & Towns ...... | 838,500 | 16,500 | 855,000 | at almost 4′4 | Heads ℘ House. |
| The Villages .............. | 4,000,000 | 40,000 | 4,040,000 | at 4′4 | Heads ℘ House. |
| Total ................. | 5,318,100 | 104,460 | 5,422,560 | at above 4′17 | Heads ℘ House. |

Lastly Whereas the Number of Transitory People as Seamen, & Souldiers, may be accounted 140,000 Whereof near onehalf or 60,000 have no place in the said assessm.$^{ts}$ And that the number of vagrants viz.$^{t}$ Hawkers, Pedlars, Crate Carriers, Gipsies, Theves & Beggars may be Reckond 30,000. Whereof above one half or 20,000 may not be taken notice of in the s.$^{d}$ assessm.$^{ts}$ making in all 80,000 Persons.

It follows that the whole number of the People of England is much about.......................................................................5,500,000 Souls.

| | |
|---|---|
| viz.$^{t}$ London & the Bills of Mortality ...................................... | 530,000 Souls. |
| The other Cities & Markett Towns.................................... | 870,000 Souls. |
| The Villages, & Hamletts................................................ | 4,100,000 Souls. |
| In all | 5,500,000 Souls. |

2. The Proportion of England in Acres & People, To France and Holland, To Europe, & to the World in General, with a Calculation of the Number of People Now in the World

That England is in Proportion

| | In Acres. | In Souls. |
|---|---|---|
| To the Globe of the Earth & Seas as.......................... | 1 To 3,300 | 1 To 130 |
| To the known habitable World as.............................. | 1 To 600 | 1 To 110 |
| To Europe (Includ.$^{g}$ Muscovy) as .............................. | 1 To 43 | 1 To 18 |
| To France as........................................................ | 1 To 3¼ | 11 To 30 |
| To Holland as...................................................... | 9 To 2 | 5 To 2 |
| To France & Holl.$^{d}$ Together as ............................... | 1 To 3½ | 10 To 32 |

That England haveing but 7 Acres of Land to Each head.

It is between 5 & 6 Times better peopled than the Known world in General.
Above twice, but not 3 times better Peopled than Europe in General.
About 1½ Times better peopled than Germany.
Above 3 Times better Peopled than Ireland Now is.
Almost 3 Times better Peopled than Scotland, or Spain.
Somewhat better Peopled than France, That Kingdome haveing at Least 9 Acres ꝑ head, as Italy likewise hath.
About as well Peopled as the Spanish Netherlands now are, or as the Countries about the Rhine, viz.$^{t}$ Alsatia, The Palatinate, Lorrain &c.
And Exceeded only in populousnesse by Holland & China, of all the Nations in the World.
That England hath 5 Times the number of People now in Scotland, and 6 times the number of People now in Ireland.
That Scotland & Ireland Together are near equall to England in number of Acres, but not 2/5.$^{ths}$ of Engl.$^{d}$ in Number of People.
That England Scotland & Ireland Together contain
About 75 Millions of Acres.
Somewhat more than 7 Millions of People.
Somewhat above 10 acres to Each Head.

About the 23.$^{d}$ part of Europe in Acres. And the 13.$^{th}$ or 14.$^{th}$ part of Europe in People.
Somewhat more than Half France in Acres & People.
Nine Times the bigness of the 7 Provinces of Holland in Acres.
And more than 3 Times, but not near 4 times the People of those Provinces
And in Proportion To France and Holland Together, as 10 To Nineteen in Acres, and as 10 To 22 in People.

As to the Number of People now in the World.
We are to consider.

1. The Number of Acres in the Habitable World.
2. The Proportion of People to the Number of Acres.

As to the Number of Acres.

1. The superficiall content of the Globe of Earth & Water at 69½ miles to a Degree of Latitude, is 200 Millions of Square Miles, or 128,000 Mill.$^{s}$ of Acres, at 640 Acres to a square Mile.
2. The Land Discover'd & Undiscover'd is now Generally presum'd to be one Moity of the Globe, or 64,000 Mill.$^{s}$ of Acres.
3. The known part of the world contains about.................. 23,000 Mill.$^{s}$ of acres.
   And the Unknown Part ............................................. 41,000 Mill.$^{s}$ of acres.
4. That of the known part of the world............. 20,000 Mill.$^{s}$ of acres is habitable.
   And..........................................................3,000 Millions Uninhabitable.
5. That of the unknown part..................25,000 Mill.$^{s}$ of acres may be Habitable.
   And.................................................. 16,000 Mill.$^{s}$ of acres Uninhabitable.

As to the Proportion of People to the Number of Acres.

1. That where there is more than 100 Acres to each Head, Such Country is Little better than Desert.
2. That there is no country besides Holland & China so Populous, as to have but 4 Acres ℘ head.
3. That England haveing about 7 acres ℘ head, France about 9 And Scottland & Ireland Together about 18 or 20 Acres ℘ head we cannot suppose Europe in General has above 15 or 20 acres ℘ Head.
4. That Asia being generally very rich & Populous, Especially India, Persia, & China, (w.$^{ch}$ last is said to have 10 Millions of Large Families Containing 59 Millions of Men, besides Women & children, whereby the Number of Souls in China should be at Least 230 Millions for 1000 Millions of Acres) We cannot suppose but Asia must be near as well, if not better Peopled pro Rato than Europe.
5. That allowing Europe & Asia to be about 3 Times better Peopled pro rato than Affrica, and 6 Times better peopled pro Rato than America, It follows that the number of People in the Known part of the World should be about 600 Millions

of Souls; And in the Unknown Part, above 100 Millions, In all ........................ 700 Millions of Souls.

| | Acres. | | Souls. |
|---|---|---|---|
| Europe ........................... | 1,700 Millions at | 17 Acres ℘ Head. | 100 Millions. |
| Asia ............................... | 6,800 Millions at | 20 Acres ℘ Head. | 340 Millions. |
| Affrica ............................ | 6,100 Millions at | 64 Acres ℘ Head. | 95 Millions. |
| America .......................... | 8,400 Millions at | 129 Acres ℘ Head. | 65 Millions. |
| In all | 23,000 Millions at | 38 Acres ℘ Head. | 600 Millions. |

3. The several Distinctions of the People, as to Males, & Females, Married, and unmarried, Children, Servants, & Sojourners

That the 5 Millions and a half of Souls in England Including the Transitory People, & vagrants, appear by the assessm.[ts] on Marriages Births and Burials, to bear the following proportions in Relation to Males & Females viz.[t]

| | Males. | | Females. | Males. | Females. | Both. |
|---|---|---|---|---|---|---|
| In London & the Bills of Mortal .................... | 10 | To | 13 | 230,000 | 300,000 | 530,000 |
| In the other Cities & Market Towns.......... | 8 | To | 9 | 410,000 | 460,000 | 870,000 |
| In the Villages & Hamletts ................ | 100 | To | 99 | 2,060,000 | 2,040,000 | 4,100,000 |
| | 27 | To | 28 | 2,700,000 | 2,800,000 | 5,500,000 |

That as to other Distinctions, they appear by the said Assessm.[ts] to bear these Proportions.

| | | People. | Males. | Females. |
|---|---|---|---|---|
| Husbands & Wives at above .......................... | 34½ ℘ Cent. | 1,900,000 | 950,000 | 950,000 |
| Widdowers at above........... | 1½ ℘ Cent. | 90,000 | 90,000 | ........... |
| Widdows at almost ............ | 4½ ℘ Cent. | 240,000 | ........... | 240,000 |
| Children at above .............. | 45 ℘ Cent. | 2,500,000 | 1,300,000 | 1,200,000 |
| Servants at almost.............. | 10½ ℘ Cent. | 560,000 | 260,000 | 300,000 |
| Sojourners & Single Persons......................... | 4 ℘ Cent. | 210,000 | 100,000 | 110,000 |
| | 100 | 5,500,000 | 2,700,000 | 2,800,000 |

And that the Different Proportions in each of the said Articles Between London, The great Towns, & the villages may the better appear, We have exhibited the Following Scheme.

| | London & Bills of Mortallity. | | The other Cities & great Towns. | | The Villages & Hamletts. | |
|---|---|---|---|---|---|---|
| | | Souls. | | Souls. | | Souls. |
| Husband & Wives | 37 ℘ Cent | 196,000 | 36 ℘ Cent | 313,200 | 34 ℘ Cent | 1,394,000 |
| Widdowers........ | 2 ℘ Cent | 10,600 | 2 ℘ Cent | 17,400 | 1½ ℘ Cent | 61,500 |
| Widdows .......... | 7 ℘ Cent | 37,100 | 6 ℘ Cent | 52,200 | 4½ ℘ Cent | 184,500 |
| Children........... | 33 ℘ Cent | 174,900 | 40 ℘ Cent | 348,000 | 47 ℘ Cent | 1,927,000 |
| Servants ........... | 13 ℘ Cent | 68,900 | 11 ℘ Cent | 95,700 | 10 ℘ Cent | 410,000 |
| Sojourners &c....[a] | 8 ℘ Cent | 42,400 | 5 ℘ Cent | 43,500 | 3 ℘ Cent | 123,000 |
| | 100 | 980,000 | 100 | 870,000 | 100 | 4,100,000 |

4. The Several Ages of the People.
That the Yearly Births of the Kingdome Being 190,000 Souls

| | In all. | Males. | Females. |
|---|---|---|---|
| Those under 1 year old are .......................... | 170,000 | 90,000 | 80,000 |
| Those under 5 years old are ......................... | 820,000 | 415,000 | 405,000 |
| Those under 10 years old are........................ | 1,520,000 | 764,000 | 756,000 |
| Those under 16 years old are........................ | 2,240,000 | 1,122,000 | 1,118,000 |
| Those above 16 years old are........................ | 3,260,000 | 1,578,000 | 1,682,000 |
| Those above 21 years old are........................ | 2,700,000 | 1,300,000 | 1,400,000 |
| Those above 25 years old are........................ | 2,400,000 | 1,150,000 | 1,250,000 |
| Those above 60 years old are........................ | 600,000 | 270,000 | 330,000 |

So that the Number of Communicants is in all...........................3,260,000 Souls
And the Number of Fighting men between 16 & 60 is ........................ 1,310,000.
That the Bachelors are about 28 ℘ Cent of the Whole.
Whereof those under 25 years are 25½ ℘ Cent.
And those above 25 years are..............................2½ ℘ Cent.
That the Maidens are about 28½ ℘ Cent of the whole.
Whereof those under 25 years are.............................. 26½ ℘ Cent.
And those above 25 years are................................ 2 ℘ Cent.
That the Males & Females in the Kingdome in General are Aged one with another 27½ years.
That in the Kingdome in General there is near as many People liveing under 20 years of age, as there is above 20. Whereof, one Half of the Males is under 19 Years, and one half of the Females, is under 21 Years.

| At a Medium | | | | | Years. |
|---|---|---|---|---|---|
| That the Husbands are aged | 43 | Years apiece w.ch at | 17¼ | p Cent Makes | 742 |
| The Wives .................. | 40 | Years apeice .............. | 17¼ | ............... | 690 |
| The Widdowers ............ | 56 | Years apeice .............. | 1½ | ............... | 84 |
| The Widdows............... | 60 | Years apeice .............. | 4½ | ............... | 270 |
| The Children ............... | 12 | Years apeice .............. | 45 | ............... | 540 |
| The Servants................ | 27 | Years apeice .............. | 10½ | ............... | 284 |
| The Sojourners ............. | 35 | Years apeice .............. | 4 | ............... | 140 |
| At a Medium | 27½ | | 100 | Persons. | 2750 Years. |

5. The Origination & Increase of the People of England.

That if the World was Repeopled from 8 Persons after the Floud and that England was peopled originally by Two Persons, or by a number not exceeding 20 Persons; such first peopling was about the year of the World 2200 or 2300 viz.[t] 600 years after the Floud; & 16 or 1700 Years before the birth of our Saviour at which time the World had between one and two millions of People only.

But if the first Peopling of England was by a colony or colonies consisting of a number between 100 & 1000 People (w.[ch] is most Probable) Such colony or colonies were brought over between the year of the World 2400 & 2600 viz.[t] about 8 or 900 years after the Floud, and 14 or 1500 years before the Birth of our Saviour at which time the World had about a Million of Families, and 4 or 5 Mill.[s] of People.

From Which Hypothesis it will follow by an orderly series of Increase.

That when the Romans Invaded England 53 years before our Saviors Time, The Kingdome had about 360,000 People & at our Saviors Birth about 400,000 People.

That at the Norman conquest a.[o] Christi 1066 The Kingdome had somewhat above Two Mill.[s] of People.

That a.[o] 1260 or about 200 Years after the Norman conquest the Kingdome had 2,750,000 People, or half the present Number so that the People of England have doubled in about 435 Years last past.

That in Probability the next doubling of the People of England will be in about 600 years to come, or by the year of our Lord 2300. At which time it will have 11 Mill.[s] of People; But that the next doubling after that, will not be (in all probability) in lesse than 12 or 1300 Years more, or by the Year of our Lord 3500 or 3600. At which time the Kingdome will have 22 Mill.[s] of Souls, or 4 times it's present number in case the World should last so long.

Now the Kingdome containing but 39 Mill.[s] of acres, it will then have Lesse than 2 Acres to each head, & consequently will not then be capable of any further Increase.

That the Increase of the Kingdome for every 100 Years of the Last preceeding Term of Doubling, and the Subsequent Term of Doubling, has been, and in probability will be according to the following scheme.

| An.[o] Christi. | Number of People. | Increase every 100 Years. |
|---|---|---|
| 1300 | 2,860,000 | 440,000 |
| 1400 | 3,300,000 | 540,000 |
| 1500 | 3,840,000 | 780,000 |
| 1600 | 4,620,000 | 880,000 |
| 1700 | 5,500,000 | 920,000 |
| 1800 | 6,420,000 | 930,000 |
| 1900 | 7,350,000 | 930,000 |
| 2000 | 8,280,000 | 925,000 |
| 2100 | 9,205,000 | 910,000 |
| 2200 | 10,115,000 | 885,000 |
| 2300 | 11,000,000 | .......... |

Whereby it appears, That the Increase of the Kingdome being 880,000 People in the last 100 Years, & 920,000 In the next succeeding 100 Years. The annual Increase at this time is about 9000 Souls ꝑ ann.

But whereas the Yearly Burials of the Kingdome are about, 1 in 32 or 170,000 Souls; And the yearly Births 1 in 28 or 190,000 Souls Whereby the yearly Increase Should be...................... 20,000 Souls.

It is to be noted.

1. That the Allowance for Plagues, & great Mortalities comes to at a Medium .................................................................. 4,000 ꝑ ann.
2. Forreign or Civil Warrs at a Medium.................................... 3,500 ꝑ ann.
3. The Sea constantly imploying about 40,000 Precipitates the Death of about.................................................................. 2,500 ꝑ ann.
4. The Plantations (over & above the accession of Forreigners) carry away.................................................................. 1,000 ꝑ ann.

In all.......11,000 ꝑ ann.

Whereby the Neat annual Increase is but..................................... 9,000

In all...........20,000

That of these 20,000 Souls which would be the annual Increase of the Kingdome by Procreation, were it not for the Forementon'd abatements.

The Country increases annually by Procreation............................. 20,000 Souls
The Cities & Towns (Exclusive of London).................................. 2,000 Souls
But Lond.° & the Bills of Mortality decrease annually..................... 2,000 Souls

So that London requires a Supply of 2000 ꝑ ann. to keep it from Decreasing, besides a further Supply of about 3000 ꝑ ann. for its increase at this time. In all 5000 or a Moity of the Kingdoms Neat Increase.

That allowing London and the Bills of Mortality to have contain'd in Iulius Cæsars time between 4 & 5000 Souls; and at the Norman Conquest about 24,000 Souls, and at this time about 530,000 Souls. The Increase thereof hath been, and in probability will be according to the following Scheme of the Duplication of its Inhabitants.

| Number of Souls. | Anno Christi. | Number of years in w.h the People of Lond.° have doubled. |
|---|---|---|
| 8,280 | 330 | |
| 16,560 | 830 | 500 |
| 33,120 | 1230 | 400 |
| 66,240 | 1500 | 270 |
| 132,480 | 1585 | 85 |
| 264,960 | 1621 | 36 |
| 529,920 | 1695 | 74 |
| 1,059,840 | 1900 | 205 |
| 2,119,680 | 3000 | 1100 |

Whereby it appears that London has doubled 3 Times since the year 1500. So that it is now 8 times as bigg as it was then. And the Present yearly Increase of London, and the Bills of Mortality would have been (had it not been for the Present Warr) 3000 Souls ℘ ann.

But in Relation to the Present Warr we are to consider,

| | |
|---|---|
| That if the Nation do at this time Contain | 5,500,000 Souls |
| It did contain An.º 1688 about 50,000 more or | 5,550,000 Souls |
| For that Instead of a decrease of 11,000 ℘ ann out of the yearly Increase by Procreation of 20,000. The said Decrease has been at a Medium 19,000 ℘ ann. In all for 7 years | 133,000 |
| And that Instead of an Increase of 20,000 ℘ ann by Procreation, the s.d Increase has been at a Medium but 12,000 ℘ ann In all for 7 years | 84,000 |
| So that the Kingdome has decreased in 7 years | 49,000 |

Observations about Procreation
Accounting the People to be 5,500,000 souls

By the foremention'd Assessments on Marriages Births and Burials, & the Collectors Returns thereupon, and by the Parish Registers, It appears that the Proportions of Marriages Births and Burials, is according to the following Scheme.

| People. | | Annual Marriages. | | | | |
|---|---|---|---|---|---|---|
| 530,000 | London & Bills of Mortal | 1 in 106 | In all 5,000 | Producing | 4 | children each. |
| 870,000 | The Cities & Market Towns | 1 in 128 | In all 6,800 | Producing | 4′5 | children each. |
| 4,100,000 | The Villages & Hamletts | 1 in 141 | In all 29,200 | Producing | 4′8 | children each. |
| 5,500,000 | | 1 in 134 | 41,000 | | 4′64 | |

| | Annuall Births. | | | Annual Burials. | | |
|---|---|---|---|---|---|---|
| London & Bills of Mortal | 1 in 26½ | In all | 20,000 | 1 in 14′1 | In all | 22,000 |
| The Cities & Market Towns | 1 in 28½ | In all | 30,000 | 1 in 30′4 | In all | 28,600 |
| The Villages & Hamlets | 1 in 29′4 | In all | 139,400 | 1 in 34′4 | In all | 119,400 |
| | 1 in 28′85 | | 190,000 | 1 in 32′35 | | 170,000 |

Whence We may observe That in 1000 coexisting Persons.

| | | | |
|---|---|---|---|
| There are 71 or 72 | marriages in the Country | Producing | 34′3 children. |
| 78 | marriages in Towns | Producing | 35′2 children. |
| 94 | marriages in London | Producing | 37′6 children. |

Whereby It followes.

1. That tho' each marriage in London produceth fewer people than in the Country, Yet London in General haveing a greater proportion of Breeders is more Prolifick than the other great Towns, and the great Towns are more Prolifick than the country.

2. That if the People of London of all Ages were as long liv'd as those in the Country, London would Increase in People much faster Pro rato than the Country.
3. That the Reason why each marriage in London produces fewer children, than the Country Marriages, seems to Be,
1. From the more frequent Fornications and Adulteries.
2. From a Greater Luxury & Intemperance.
3. From a Greater Intensnesse or Businesse.
4. From the Unhealthfullnesse of the Coal Smoke.
5. From a greater Inequality of age Between the Husbands & Wives.

And that it may appear what the effect is of the Inequality of ages in Married Couples, I have collected the following observations from a certain great Town, in the Middle of the Kingdome, consisting of Near 3000 Souls.

Litchfield

1. That there is no child of any Parents now Liveing in the said Town where the Wife is 17 years older than the Husband, or the Husband 19 years older than the Wife.
2. That the whole Number of children being 1060 the number of those where the Mother was older than the Father is 228 and where the Husband was older than the Wife 832.
3. That one Moity of the whole number of children in the said Town are the Product of such Parents, where the Husband is 4 or more years older than the Wife.
4. That the greatest Number of children with respect to any one number of years of Difference in age between the Husband and Wife, is where the Husband is Two years older than the Wife, the Product whereof is 147 or a 7.th Part of the whole.
5. That an Equality in age in the Husband, & Wife, is not so Prolifick, as an Inequality, Provided that Inequality exceed not a Superiority of 4 Years in the Wife, or 10 Years in the Husband; For the equality of years produced but 23 children, whereas one years Inequality in the age of the Parents either way produc'd above 60.
6. That of the said 1060 Children in the whole Town near 3 Quarters of them are the Product of Coalitions from 2 years superiority of age in the Wife inclusive to 6 years superiority of age in the Husband Inclusive.
7. That the highest Powers in men & Women for Procreation is in that Town at 31 years of age in the Husband and 28 in the Wife, the Produce of the former being 86 children, & of the Latter 83.
8. That one moity of the said 1060 children are the Product of Fathers from 28 to 35 years of age Inclus. and of mothers from 25 to 32.
   Whence it followes that a just equality or too great an inequality of age in marriages, are prejudicial to the Increase of Mankind.
   And that the early or Late marriages in Men and Women, do tend little to the Propagation of Humane Race.

Lastly, From a consideration of the Male & Female children in the said Town, and the ages of their Parents, at the time when such children were respectively conceiv'd; A Scheme may be establish'd of the Powers of Generation, and the Inclination of the

Several coalitions towards the Producing the one or the other Sex, according to the Superiority of Power in either Sex, at the time of Such respective coalitions.

6. The Annual Income, & Expence of the Nation as it stood An.° 1688.

| | | |
|---|---|---|
| That the Yearly Income of the Nation a.° 1688 Was | 43,500,000 | Sterlg. |
| That the Yearly Expence of the Nation Was | 41,700,000 | |
| That then the Yearly Increase of wealth was | 1,800,000 | |
| That the Yearly Rent of the Lands were about | 10,000,000 | |
| of the Burgage or Houseing about | 2,000,000 | |
| of all other Heriditaments about | 1,000,000 | |
| In all | 13,000,000 | |
| That the yearly Produce of Trade arts & Labour was ab.$^{t}$ | 30,500,000 | |
| In all | 43,500,000 | |
| That the Number of Inhabited Houses being about | 1,300,000 | |
| The Number of Families about | 1,360,000 | |
| And the Number of People about | 5,500,000 | |

The People answer to 4¼ ꝑ House, & 4 ꝑ Family.

That the Yearly Estates or Income of the several Families answer

| | £ | s. | d. | |
|---|---|---|---|---|
| In common To about | 32 | .. | .. | ꝑ Family |
| And about | 7 | 18 | .. | ꝑ head |
| That the yearly expense of the Nation is about | 7 | 11 | 4 | ꝑ head |
| And the yearly Increase about | | 6 | 8 | ꝑ head |

| | £ | |
|---|---|---|
| That the whole Value of the Kingdom in Gen.$^{ll}$ is about | 650,000,000 | Stlg. |

Viz.$^{t}$

| | | |
|---|---|---|
| The 13 Millions of yearly Rents, at about 18 years Purchase | 234,000,000 | Sterlg. |
| The 30 Millions and a Half ꝑ annum by Trade, arts, Labour &c. at near 11 years Purchase (which being the Value of the 5 Mill.$^{s}$ & a half of people at 60$^{£}$ ꝑ head) comes To | 330,000,000 | |
| The Stock of the Kingdome in mony Plate Jewells and Household Goods about | 28,000,000 | |
| The Stock of the Kingdome in Shipping, Forts, Ammunition, Stores, Forreign or home Goods, Wares, and Provisions for Trade abroad, or consumption at home, and all Instruments, & Materialls relating thereunto | 33,000,000 | |
| The Live Stock of the Kingdome in Cattle, Beasts, Fowle, &c. | 25,000,000 | |
| In all | 650,000,000 | Sterlg. |

## A Scheme of the Income & Expence of the several Families of England Calculated for the Year 1688.

| Number of Families. | Ranks Degrees Titles and Qualifications. | Heads ℘ Family. | Number of Persons. | Yearly Income ℘ Family. | | Totall of the Estates or Income. | Yearly Income ℘ Head. | | Expence ℘ Head. | | | Increase ℘ Head. | | | Totall Increase ℘ annum. |
|---|---|---|---|---|---|---|---|---|---|---|---|---|---|---|---|
| | | | | £ | | £ | £ | | £ | | | £ | s | d | |
| 160 | Temporall Lords | 40 | 6,400 | 2800 | | 448,000 | 70 | | 60 | | | 10 | .. | .. | 64,000£ |
| 26 | Spirituall Lords | 20 | 520 | 1300 | | 83,800 | 65 | | 55 | | | 10 | .. | .. | 5,200 |
| 800 | Baronets | 16 | 12,800 | 880 | | 704,000 | 55 | | 51 | | | 4 | .. | .. | 51,200 |
| 600 | Knights | 13 | 7,800 | 650 | | 390,000 | 50 | | 46 | | | 4 | .. | .. | 31,200 |
| 3,000 | Esquires | 10 | 30,000 | 450 | | 1,200,000 | 45 | | 42 | | | 3 | .. | .. | 90,000 |
| 12,000 | Gentlemen | 8 | 96,000 | 280 | | 2,880,000 | 35 | | 32 | 10 | | 2 | 10 | .. | 240,000 |
| 5,000 | Persons in offices | 8 | 40,000 | 240 | | 1,200,000 | 30 | | 27 | | | 3 | .. | .. | 120,000 |
| 5,000 | Persons in offices | 6 | 30,000 | 120 | | 600,000 | 20 | | 18 | | | 2 | .. | .. | 60,000 |
| 2,000 | M.rch.ts & Traders by Sea | 8 | 16,000 | 400 | | 800,000 | 50 | | 40 | | | 10 | .. | .. | 160,000 |
| 8,000 | M.rch.ts & Traders by Sea | 6 | 48,000 | 200 | | 1,600,000 | 33 | | 28 | | | 5 | .. | .. | 240,000 |
| 10,000 | Persons in the Law | 7 | 70,000 | 140 | | 1,400,000 | 20 | | 17 | | | 3 | .. | .. | 210,000 |
| 2,000 | Clergy Men | 6 | 12,000 | 60 | | 120,000 | 10 | | 9 | | | 1 | .. | .. | 12,000 |
| 8,000 | Clergy Men | 5 | 40,000 | 45 | | 360,000 | 9 | | 8 | | | 1 | .. | .. | 40,000 |
| 40,000 | Freeholders | 7 | 280,000 | 84 | | 3,360,000 | 12 | | 11 | | | 1 | .. | .. | 280,000 |
| 140,000 | Freeholders | 5 | 700,000 | 50 | | 7,000,000 | 10 | | 9 | 10 | | .. | 10 | .. | 350,000 |
| 150,000 | Farmers | 5 | 750,000 | 44 | | 6,600,000 | 8 | 15 | 8 | 10 | | .. | 5 | .. | 187,000 |
| 16,000 | Persons in Sciences & Lib. arts | 5 | 80,000 | 60 | | 960,000 | 12 | | 11 | 10 | | 1 | 10 | .. | 40,000 |
| 40,000 | Shopkeep.rs & Tradesmen | 4½ | 180,000 | 45 | | 1,800,000 | 10 | | 9 | 10 | | .. | 10 | .. | 90,000 |
| 60,000 | Artizans & handycrafts | 4 | 240,000 | 40 | | 2,400,000 | 10 | | 9 | 10 | | .. | 10 | .. | 120,000 |
| 5,000 | Naval officers | 4 | 20,000 | 80 | | 400,000 | 20 | | 18 | .. | | 2 | .. | .. | 40,000 |
| 4,000 | Military officers | 4 | 16,000 | 60 | | 240,000 | 15 | | 14 | .. | | 1 | .. | .. | 16,000 |
| 511,586 Fam. | | | | £ | | | £ | s | £ | | | | | | |
| | | 5¼ | 2,675,520 | 67 | | 34,495,800 | 12 | 18 | 12 | .. | | .. | 18 | .. | 2,447,000£ |
| | | | | £ | | £ | £ | | £ | s | | £ | s | d | Decrease |
| 50,000 | Common Seamen | 3 | 150,000 | 20 | | 1,000,000 | 7 | .. | 7 | 10 | | .. | 10 | .. | 75,000£ |
| 364,000 | Labour.s People & outserv.ts | 3½ | 1,275,000 | 15 | | 5,460,000 | 4 | 10 | 4 | 12 | | .. | 2 | .. | 127,500 |
| 400,000 | Cottagers & Paupers | 3¼ | 1,300,000 | 6 | 10 | 2,000,000 | 2 | .. | 2 | 5 | | .. | 5 | .. | 325,000 |
| 35,000 | Common Souldiers | 2 | 70,000 | 14 | | 490,000 | 7 | | 7 | 10 | | .. | 10 | .. | 35,000 |
| 849,000 Fam.s | | 3¼ | 2,795,000 | 10 | 10 | 8,950,000 | 3 | 5 | 3 | 9 | | .. | 4 | .. | 562,000£ |
| .............. | Vagrants | ... | 30,000 | ... | ... | 60,000 | 2 | .. | 3 | .. | | 1 | .. | .. | 60,000 |
| | | | | £ | s | | | | | | | | | | |
| 849,000 | | 3¼ | 2,825,000 | 10 | 10 | 9,010,000 | 3 | 3 | 3 | 7 | 6 | .. | 4 | 6 | 622,000£ |

### So the General Account is

| Number of Families. | | Heads ℘ Family. | Number of Persons. | Yearly Income ℘ Family. | | Totall of the Estates or Income. | Yearly Income ℘ Head. | | Expence ℘ Head. | | | Increase ℘ Head. | | | Totall Increase ℘ annum. |
|---|---|---|---|---|---|---|---|---|---|---|---|---|---|---|---|
| | | | | £ | | | £ | s | £ | s | d | £ | s | d | |
| 511,586 Fam. | Increasing the wealth of the Kingd | 5¼ | 2,675,520 | 67 | | 34,495,800 | 12 | 18 | 12 | .. | .. | .. | 18 | .. | 2,447,100£ |
| 849,000 Fam. | Decreas.g the wealth of the Kingdom | 3¼ | 2,825,000 | 10 | 10 | 9,010,000 | 3 | 3 | 3 | 7 | 6 | .. | 4 | 6 | 622,000 |
| 1,360,586 Fam. | Neat Totalls .... | 1½ | 5,500,520 | 32 | | 43,505,800 | 7 | 18 | 7 | 11 | 3 | .. | 6 | 9 | 1,825,100£ |

A Calculation of the Quantity of Silver & Gold in England, France, & Holl.$^{d}$ in Europe; & in the world in General, & of the Increase, and consumption thereof An.$^{o}$ 1688.

This calculation is built upon this Hypothesis.

1. That the Silver and gold in Europe at the discovery of the West Indies near 200 Years ago was but 45 Mill.$^{s}$ sterlg, But is now about 5 Times as much, or 225 Millions.
2. That there has been 520 Mill.$^{s}$ of Silver & gold, Imported into Europe from america, within these Last 180 years Besides what has been produc'd in Europe or Imported into it from asia, & africa.
   Whereby the Account of Europe Stands Thus.

| | | |
|---|---|---|
| The Existing Stock of Silver and Gold in Europe 180 years ago ... | 45 | Mill.$^{s}$ Sterlg. |
| Produc'd in Europe within these Last .......... 180 years .......... | 8 | Mill.$^{s}$ |
| Imported into Europe from Asia in Manufactures .................... | 2 | Mill.$^{s}$ |
| From Affrica in Gold Dust &c. .................................. | 15 | Mill.$^{s}$ |
| From America in Specie .......................................... | 520 | Mill.$^{s}$ |
| In all | 590 | Mill.$^{s}$ |

Whereof 545 Mill.$^{s}$ having been produc'd in Europe or Imported into it within these Last 180 years, viz.$^{t}$

| | | £ |
|---|---|---|
| In the First Eighty years | 205 Mill.$^{s}$ | or 2,560,000 ℘ ann. |
| And in the Last hundred years | 340 Mill.$^{s}$ | or 3,400,000 ℘ ann. |

We may conclude, That the Existing Stock of Silver & Gold in Europe,

| | | It has Increas'd |
|---|---|---|
| Being 200 Years ago | 45 Mill.$^{s}$ | |
| Was 100 Years ago 100 Mill.$^{s}$— | | £ |
| In the 1.$^{st}$ 80 years, | 55 Mill.$^{s}$ | or 700,000 ℘ ann. |
| And is at Present 225 Mill.$^{s}$— | | |
| In the Last 100 years, | 125 Mill.$^{s}$ | or 1,250,000 ℘ ann. |
| | 180 Mill.$^{s}$ | |

So this Last 100 Years Europe has

| | | £ |
|---|---|---|
| Produc'd & Imported........ | 340 Mill.$^{s}$ | or 3,400,000 ℘ ann. |
| Increas'd....................... | 125 Mill.$^{s}$ | or 1,250,000 ℘ ann. |
| Consum'd & Exported ...... | 215 Mill.$^{s}$ | or 2,150,000 ℘ ann. |

Now before We come to the Particulars how this 215 Millions in Gold & Silver has been consum'd in Europe within this last 100 Years, We shall consider in what the 225 Millions Which We Estimate to be the Present Stock of Europe, in Gold & Silver and things made thereof, doth consist Viz.$^{t}$

| | In Europe In General | In England £ | In France £ | In Holland £ |
|---|---|---|---|---|
| Coyn'd Silver | 110 Mill.$^{s}$ | 8500000 | 18000000 | 7000000 |
| Coyn'd Gold | 28 Mill.$^{s}$ | 3000000 | 5000000 | 2000000 |
| Bullion | 8 Mill.$^{s}$ | 1000000 | 1500000 | 1500000 |
| Lay Plate | 46 Mill.$^{s}$ | 4000000 | 9000000 | 1500000 |
| Church Plate | 20 Mill.$^{s}$ | 200000 | 3000000 | 100000 |
| Medalls and Rarities | 5 Mill.$^{s}$ | 200000 | 900000 | 300000 |
| Gold & Silver thread & Wire and things made thereof in Wear | 6 Mill.$^{s}$ | 400000 | 1400000 | 100000 |
| D.$^{o}$ in stock for Trade | 2 Mill.$^{s}$ | 200000 | 600000 | 300000 |
| | 225 Mill.$^{s}$ | 17500000 | 39400000 | 12800000 |

Whereupon We have Estimated the consumption of the 315 Mill.$^{s}$ of Gold & Silver in Europe within this Last 100 Years, w.$^{ch}$ is 3,150,000$^{£}$ ℘ ann. as followeth.

| | | In Europe In Generall £ | In England £ | In France £ | In Holland £ |
|---|---|---|---|---|---|
| By The wear of Silver coyn | a 1000.t$^{h}$ part of the 110 Mill.$^{s}$ | 110,000 | 8,500 | 18,000 | 7,000 |
| The wear of Gold coyn | a 1000 part of 28 Mill.$^{s}$ | 28,000 | 3,000 | 6,000 | 2,000 |
| Wast in Coynage | a 200 part of 2 Mill.$^{s}$ | 10,000 | 1,250 | 2,500 | 800 |
| Wast in working of Plate | a 150 part of 3 Mill.$^{s}$ | 20,000 | 1,600 | 4,000 | 700 |
| The Wear of wrought plate | a 800 part of 66 Mill.$^{s}$ | 82,000 | 4,000 | 12,000 | 1,600 |
| The Wear of things made of Gold & Silver thread or Wire | a. 10.$^{th}$ part of 6 Mill.$^{s}$ | 600,000 | 60,000 | 180,000 | 20,000 |
| Leaf & Shell gold & silver | The whole of 50000£ | 50,000 | 6,000 | 20,000 | 3,000 |
| Lost in casualties at Sea | a 70.$^{th}$ part of 2 Mill.$^{s}$ | 30,000 | 7,000 | 10,000 | 10,000 |
| Lost by Fires Inundations &c.$^{a}$ | a 40000.$^{th}$ pr.t of 200 Mill.$^{s}$ | 5,000 | 1,000 | 2,000 | 500 |
| Liquid Gold & Silver | The ½ of 10000£ | 5,000 | 500 | 1,500 | 200 |
| Buried & Lost not known How | a 7000.$^{th}$ part of 140 Mill.$^{s}$ | 20,000 | 2,000 | 5,000 | 500 |
| Export.$^{d}$ out of Europe by Trade &c.$^{a}$ | | 1,190,000 | 240,000 | 160,000 | 300,000 |
| | In all | 2,150,000 | 334,850 | 420,000 | 346,300 |

Whereby it appears That the Two Principall Articles by w.$^{ch}$ the Gold and Silver of Europe is consum'd, is in things made of Gold & Silver thread & Wire, and in Coyn or Bullion exported in Trade; These Two articles alone being 7 parts in 8 of the whole consumption of the Gold and Silver of Europe.

As to the World in General, I compute the existing Stock 180 years ago at 500 Mill.$^{s}$

The Produce this Last 180 Years 1200 Millions The Consumption 850 Mill.$^{s}$

The Increase 350 Mill.$^{s}$ w.$^{ch}$ added to the 500 Millions makes the present Stock 850 Mill.$^{s}$

7. The Several Sorts of Land in England, with the Value & Product thereof.
England and Wales contains. 39 Mill.$^{s}$ of acres viz.[t]

| | Acres. | Value. | Rent. |
|---|---|---|---|
| Arrable Land | 11,000,000 | at 5.$^{s}$ 10.$^{d}$ ⅌ Acre | 3,200,000£ |
| Pasture & Meadow | 10,000,000 | at 9.$^{s}$ ⅌ Acre | 4,500,000 |
| Woods & Coppices | 3,000,000 | at 5.$^{s}$ ⅌ Acre | 750,000 |
| Forrests Parks & Commons | 3,000,000 | at 3.$^{s}$ 6.$^{d}$ ⅌ Acre | 550,000 |
| Heaths Moors Mountains & barren Land | 10,000,000 | at 1.$^{s}$ ⅌ acre | 500,000 |
| Houses & Homesteads Gardens & Orchards, Churches & churchyards | 1,000,000 | { The Land | 450,000 |
| | | The Buildings | 2,000,000 |
| Rivers Lakes Meres & Ponds | 500,000 | at 2.$^{s}$ ⅌ acre | 50,000 |
| Roads Ways & Waste Land | 500,000 | at ... ⅌ acre | ........ |
| In all | 39,000,000 | at 6.$^{s}$ 2.$^{d}$ ⅌ acre | 12,000,000£ |

| | True yearly value. | Value as rated to the 4.$^{s}$ Tax. | Produce of the 4.$^{s}$ Tax. |
|---|---|---|---|
| So the Yearly rents or Value of the Land is | 10 Mill.$^{s}$ | 6,500,000 | 1,300,000 |
| The Houses & Buildings | 2 Mill.$^{s}$ | 1,500,000 | 300,000 |
| All other Hereditaments | 1 Mill.$^{s}$ | 500,000 | 100,000 |
| Personal Estates &c.[a] | 1 Mill.$^{s}$ | 550,000 | 100,000 |
| In all | 14 Mill.$^{s}$ | 9,050,000 | 1,800,000 |

So that whereas the Tax of 4.$^{s}$ ⅌ Pound produces but ........................ 1,800,000£
It should Produce (if duly assess'd)................................................ 2,800,000

The Produce of the Arrable Land I thus Estimate.

| | of Bushells | ⅌ Bush.$^{ll}$ | Value |
|---|---|---|---|
| Wheat | 12 Millions | at 3.$^{s}$ 6.$^{d}$ | 2,100,000£ |
| Rye | 8 Millions | at 2.$^{s}$ 6.$^{d}$ | 1,000,000 |
| Barley | 25 Mill.$^{s}$ | at 2.$^{s}$ | 2,500,000 |
| Oats | 16 Mill.$^{s}$ | at 1.$^{s}$ 6.$^{d}$ | 1,200,000 |
| Peas | 7 Mill.$^{s}$ | at 2.$^{s}$ 6.$^{d}$ | 875,000 |
| Beans | 4 Mill.$^{s}$ | at 2.$^{s}$ 6.$^{d}$ | 500,000 |
| Vetches & c.[a] | 1 Mill.$^{s}$ | at 2.$^{s}$ | 100,000 |
| | 73 Millions | at 2.$^{s}$ 3.$^{d}$ | 8,275,000 |

This is only the neat Produce Exclusive of the Seed Corn w.$^{ch}$ in some sorts of grain being near a 4.$^{th}$ of the Produce in others a 5.$^{th}$ may in general be reckoned about 17 mill.$^{s}$ of Bushells more, which makes the whole produce to be 90 Mill.$^{s}$ of Bushells w.$^{ch}$ at 2.$^{s}$ 3.$^{d}$ ⅌ Bush in common is Full 10 millions Sterlg.

These 73 Mill.[s] of Bushels of Grain are the Product of 10 of the 11 Mill.[s] of Acres of Arrable Land, The other Million of Acres producing Hemp, Flax, Woad, Saffron, Dying Weeds &c.[a] The value of the Product whereof is about 1 Million Sterling.

So that the Rent of the Corn Land being under 3,000,000£ ℘ ann and the Neat Produce thereof above 8 Millions, The Produce is near Treble to the Rent

Now the Rents or Yearly Value of the Pasture & meadow, woods, Coppices, Forrests, Parks, Commons, Heaths & Moors Mountains, and Barren Land Being ............................................. 6,250,000£ Sterlg.

The Produce can Scarce make above Two Rents or 12 Millions. There being little charge either in cultivating the Land or Gathering the Product thereof, comparatively to what there is in the Arrable Land.

This Produce is Principally in and by Cattle, Hay, Timber & Firewood.

| | |
|---|---|
| The Produce by Cattle in Butter, cheese & Milk is about | 2,500,000£ |
| The value of the Wool yearly shorn is about | 2,000,000 |
| The value of the Horses yearly bred is about | 250,000 |
| The value of the Flesh yearly spent as Food is about | 3,350,000 |
| The value of the Tallow & Hides of the cattle | 600,000 |
| The value of Hay Yearly consumed by horses about | 1,300,000 |
| The Hay yearly consum'd by other cattle | 1,000,000 |
| The Timber yearly Fell'd for building & such uses | 500,000 |
| The Wood yearly spent in Firing & Petty uses | 500,000 |
| So the Produce (Including 1 Mill. Sterlg. in hay spent by cattle) is in all | 12,000,000£ |

An Estimate of the Live stock of the Nation.

| | Yearly breed or Increase | The whole Stock | Value of each besides the skin £ | s | d | Value of the Stock. |
|---|---|---|---|---|---|---|
| Beeves Sterks & Calves | 800,000 | 4,500,000 | 2 | .. | .. | 9,000,000£ |
| Sheep & Lambs | 3,200,000 | 11,000,000 | .. | 8 | .. | 4,400,000 |
| Swine & Piggs | 1,300,000 | 2,000,000 | .. | 16 | .. | 1,600,000 |
| Deer & Fawns | 20,000 | 100,000 | 2 | ... | ... | 200,000 |
| Goats & Kidds | 10,000 | 50,000 | ... | 10 | ... | 25,000 |
| Hares & Leveretts | 12,000 | 24,000 | ... | 1 | 6 | 1,800 |
| Rabbits & Conies | 2,000,000 | 1,000,000 | ... | ... | 5 | 21,100 |
| | 7,342,000 | 18,074,000 | | | | 15,247,900£ |

| | |
|---|---|
| So the value of the Live Stock for Food is | 15,247,900£ |
| The value of the Horses (and asses) Being 1,200,000 at 2£ 10[s] each Breeding annually 100,000 is | 3,000,000.. |
| The value of the Pelts & Skins (over & above the wool) | 2,400,000 |
| | 20,647,900 |

| | |
|---|---|
| The value of the Wool yearly shorn (or Pelted) 10,000,000 fleeces, 2,000,000.$^{lb}$ at 4.$^{s}$ ℘ Fleece or 28.$^{s}$ ℘ Todd at 12.$^{d}$ ℘ lb .............. | 2,000,000 |
| The value of the whole Stock of Tame Fowl as Geese, Turkeys, Hens, Ducks, Pigeons, Swans, & Peacocks...................................... | 460,000 |
| The whole Stock of Wild Fowle about........................................ | 12,000 |
| In all.... | 23,119,900$^{£}$ |

An Estimate of the yearly consumption of Flesh in the Nation

| | Number of the yearly consumption | W.t of each carcass | Price of a pound weight | Price of each beast | Value of the yearly consumption | Weight of the yearly consumption |
|---|---|---|---|---|---|---|
| Beeves & Calves .......... | 800,000 | 200 $^{lb}$. w.t | 1⅓ d. | 1 18 .. | 1,520,000 | 208,000,000 w.$^{t}$ |
| Sheep & Lambs........... | 3,200,000 | 32 | 2¼ d. | .. 6 .. | 960,000 | 102,400,000 |
| Swine & Piggs............ | 1,300,000 | 46 | 3 .. | .. 11 6 | 750,000 | 59,800,000 |
| Deer & Fawns............ | 20,000 | 70 | 6 .. | 1 15 .. | 35,000 | 1,400,000 |
| Goats & Kidds............ | 10,000 | 36 | 2½ | .. 7 6 | 4,000 | 360,000 |
| Hares & Leveretts ........ | 12,000 | 2½ | 7 .. | .. 1 6 | 900 | 30,000 |
| Rabbits & Conies......... | 2,000,000 | ¾–½ | 6 .. | .. .. 5 | 42,100 | 1,700,000 |
| | 7,342,000 | | | | 3,302,000 | 373,690,000 |
| Tame Fowle......................................... | | | at 6.$^{d}$ ℘ pound | | 600,000 | 24,000,000 |
| Wild Fowle ......................................... | | | at 12.$^{d}$ ℘ pound | | 20,000 | 400,000 |
| | | | | In all.... | 3,922,000£ | 398,090,000 w.$^{t}$ |

Which for 5½ Mill.$^{s}$ of People is,

| | £ | s. | d. | | | lb | oz. | |
|---|---|---|---|---|---|---|---|---|
| In value | .. | 14 | 3 | ℘ ann. | In weight | 72 | 6 | ℘ ann. |
| | .. | .. | ½ | ℘ diem fere | | .. | 3⅙ | ℘ diem. |

But for 2,700,000 Persons being the value of those who eat flesh constantly, the foresaid Proportion of 398,090,000 Pound weight of Flesh yearly spent as Food comes to 6⅖ ounces ℘ head ℘ diem & 147½ pound weight ℘ head ℘ annum; Besides Dutch Beef, Westphalia Bacon &c.[a]

The remaining 2,800,000 Persons not eating of Flesh being these.

| | |
|---|---|
| 200,000 | Infants under 13 months old. |
| 40,000 | Sick Persons. |
| 260,000 | Part of 700,000 Persons, who feed on fish at Least 2 days in 7. |
| 1,280,000 | Part of 1,760,000 Persons contain'd in 440,000 Families who by reason of their Poverty do not contribute to church or Poor, & consequently eat not flesh above 2 days in 7. |
| 1,020,000 | Part of 1,200,000 Persons contain'd in 400,000 Families who receive Alms & consequently eat not flesh above once a Week. |
| 2,800,000 | |

8. The Beer Ale & Malt annually consumed in England, & the Revenue of Excise ariseing thereby.

| | | |
|---|---|---|
| That the Arrable Land of Eng.$^{d}$ is near……… | 11 Mill.$^{s}$ of Acres. | |
| Of which the Barley Land is almost a Third or……… | 3,200,000 Acres. | |
| Whereof somewhat above Two thirds being yearly Sowed, and the other Third Fallow, The Land Yearly Sowed with Barley is about……… | 2,200,000 Acres. | |
| Which at 15 Bushells ⅌ Acre is……… | 33 Mill.$^{s}$ of Bush.$^{lls}$ | of Barley. |
| viz.$^{t}$ Malted & Brew'd into ale & Beer……… | 21½ Mill.$^{s}$ of Bush.$^{lls}$ | mill.$^{s}$ 22½ malted |
| Malted & made into Spirits & for other uses……… | 1 Mill. Of Bush.$^{lls}$ | |
| Seed corn at near 4 Bushells ⅌ Acre……… | 8½ Mill.$^{s}$ of Bush.$^{lls}$ | 10½ unmalt.$^{d}$ |
| Barley for Bread, feeding of Poultry &c.$^{a}$……… | 2 Mill.$^{s}$ of Bush.$^{lls}$ | |
| In all | 33 Mill.$^{s}$ of Bushells. | |

| | |
|---|---|
| Which 22½ Millions of Bushells of malted Barley may well Produce……… | 24 Mill.$^{s}$ of Bush.$^{lls}$ of malt |
| That the Malt brew'd into Ale & Beer is……… | 23 Mill.$^{s}$ of Bush.$^{lls}$ |
| Whereof the Malt Brew'd for sale is much about……… | 13,500,000 Bush.$^{lls}$ |
| And for Private use……… | 9,500,000 Bush.$^{lls}$ |

And That the difference between the years 1688 & 1695 is according to the following Scheme

| | Bush.$^{lls}$ of malt. | | Barr.$^{lls}$ | | Barr.$^{lls}$ | | |
|---|---|---|---|---|---|---|---|
| A.° 1688… | 15,900,000 | Producing… | 5,300,000 Strong | Excised……. | 4,800,000 | at 2.$^{s}$ 6.$^{d}$ ⅌ Bar.$^{ll}$ | 600,000£ |
| | | | | Not Exc.$^{d}$….. | 500,000 | | |
| | 7,100,000 | Producing… | 7,100,000 Bar.$^{lls}$ Small | Excis'd…….. | 2,400,000 | at .. 6.$^{d}$ ⅌ Bar.$^{ll}$ | 60,000 |
| | | | | Not Exc.$^{d}$….. | 4,700,000 | | |
| | 23,000,000 | | 12,400,000 | | | | 660,000£ |
| A.° 1695… | 14,500,000 | Producing… | 3,850,000 Barr.$^{lls}$ Strong | Excised……. | 3,200,000 | at 4.$^{s}$ 9.$^{d}$ ⅌ Bar.$^{ll}$ | 766,100£ |
| | | | | Not Exc.$^{d}$….. | 620,000 | | |
| | 7,500,000 | Producing… | 7,500,000 Bar.$^{lls}$ Small | Excis'd…….. | 2,200,000 | at 1.$^{s}$ 3.$^{d}$ ⅌ Bar.$^{ll}$ | 137,500 |
| | | | | Not Exc.$^{d}$….. | 5,300,000 | | |
| | 22,000,000 | | 11,350,000 | | | | 903,600£ |

Whence it Followes.

That if the drink Brew'd for Private use a.$^{o}$ 1688 had pay'd the then duty of Excise, It had come to 180,000$^{£}$ and in the whole...................... 840,000$^{£}$
That if the Drink brew'd, for Private use a.$^{o}$ 1695 should pay the Present duty it would come to 408,250$^{£}$ And in the whole......................... 1,311,850

That raising the Excise has reduc'd the consumption of malt from 23 millions of Bushells to 22 Mill.$^{s}$
That it has reduc'd the quantity of Drink brew'd From 12,400,000 Barrells to 11,350,000 Barrells.
That it has decreas'd publick Brewing from 4,800,000 Bar.$^{lls}$ of Strong Drink To 3,233,000 Bar.$^{lls}$ And from 2,400,000 Bar.$^{lls}$ of Small To 2,200,000 Barrells.
And that it hath increas'd Private Brewing from 500,000 Barr.$^{lls}$ of Strong, to 620,000 Barr.$^{lls}$ And from 4,700,000 Barr.$^{lls}$ of small to 5,300,000 Barrells
Lastly that 9.$^{d}$ ℘ Bushell on Malt at the Kiln, is much about equivalent to the present Excise, And that 18.$^{d}$ ℘ Bush.$^{l}$ on malt at the Mashfatt would come to one mill.$^{n}$ Sterlg.

9. A Calculation of the Poll Bills and some other Taxes and what may be rais'd by some Commodities not yet Taxed.

That the Produce of the 12.$^{d}$ Poll 1.$^{st}$ W.$^{m}$ & Mary Being...................... 288,300$^{£}$
And of the Quart.$^{ly}$ Poll 3.$^{d}$ W.$^{m}$ & M ............................................. 597,500
The People of Eng.$^{d}$ do not appear by the 1.$^{st}$ Poll Bills to be above................................................................ 5,400,000 Souls.
Tho' in the consumption & Expence of the Nation they answer to near................................................................ 5,500,000 Souls.

As by the following Scheme.

| | 12.$^{d}$ Poll First W.$^{m}$ & Ma. | Quart.$^{ly}$ Poll 3.$^{d}$ W. & Ma. |
|---|---|---|
| The number of People as they answer'd in the Poll-Tax.................................................... | 5,400,000 | 5,390,000 |
| viz.$^{t}$ Persons Receiving Alms................................ | 600,000 | 620,000 |
| Their children under 16 years ........................ | 300,000 | 310,000 |
| Persons not paying to church & poor (660,000) ... | ........ | 670,000 |
| Their children under 16 years ........................ | 600,000 | 610,000 |
| Children under 16 of Day Labourers ................ | 240,000 | 260,000 |
| Children under 16 of Serv.$^{ts}$ in husbandry.......... | 140,000 | 160,000 |
| Children under 16 of such as have 4 children or more, & are not worth 50$^{£}$ (150,000 Parents .... | 180,000 | 200,000 |
| Omitted by neglect or otherwise deficient ......... | 100,000 | 120,000 |
| So the number of those that were excus'd or Insolvent is ........................................................ | 2,150,000 | 2,950,000 |
| The Number of the Solvent People........................ | 3,250,000 | 2,440,000 |
| In all .......... | 5,400,000 | 5,390,000 |

| | At 12.$^{d}$ ℘ head | At 4.$^{s}$ ℘ Head |
|---|---|---|
| So the Common duty of the Solvent People amounted to........................................................ | 162,500£ | 488,000£ |
| And all other parts of the said Polls ........................ | 125,800 | 109,500 |
| In all.......... | 288,300£ | 5 97,500£ |

Note, That the Quart.$^{ly}$ Poll excus'd all such as by reason of their Poverty did not contribute to church & Poor, Whereas the 12 penny Poll excus'd only their children under 16 years,
But not the Parents themselves, Whereby the Quarterly Poll excus'd 600,000 Persons, more than the 12 Penny Poll by that Single Article.
That if all Persons had paid the common duty only upon the 12 peny Poll, without any thing for Degrees, Titles or qualifications it would have rais'd near as much as it did or..........................................................................................275,000£
And that if all Persons had paid only the common duty of 4.$^{s}$ upon the Quarterly Poll, It would have rais'd near twice as much as it did, or........................... 1,100,000£

Of the Present Duty on Marriages, Births, & Burials, Accounting the People To Be 5,400,000 Souls.

| As a Medium in times of Peace. | | In all. | Common duty. | | But An.$^{o}$ 1695. | Thus. | |
|---|---|---|---|---|---|---|---|
| Yearly Burials | 1 in 32 | 170,000 at 4.$^{s}$ | Each | 34,000£ | 1 in 29 ½ | 183,000 | 36,600£ |
| Births | 1 in 28 | 190,000 at 2 | Each | 19,000 | 1 in 30 ½ | 177,000 | 17,700 |
| Marriages | 1 in 132 | 41,000 at 2 | 6.$^{d}$ | 5,125 | 1 in 140 | 39,000 | 4,875 |
| Bachelors | 1 in 40 | 140,000 at 1 | | 7,000 | 1 in 40 | 140,000 | 7,000 |
| Widdowers | 1 in 200 | 27,000 at 1 | | 1,350 | 1 in 200 | 27,000 | 1,350 |
| | | | | In all 66,475 | | | 67,625 |

Omissions Frauds & Insolvent.

| | | | | | |
|---|---|---|---|---|---|
| In Burials | 6 | ℘ Cent | 10000 | at 4.$^{s}$ each | 2000£ |
| Births | 3 | ℘ Cent | 6000 | at 2 | 600 |
| Marriages | 2½ | ℘ Cent | 1000 | at 2.$^{s}$ 6.$^{d}$ | 125 |
| Bachelors | 10 | ℘ Cent | 14000 | at 1 | 700 |
| Widdowers | 5 | ℘ Cent | 1500 | at 1 | 75 |
| | | | | | In all 3500 |

Excus'd by Receiveing Alms.

| | | | | | |
|---|---|---|---|---|---|
| In Burials | | | 00000 | | 00000£ |
| Births | 30 | ℘ Cent | 60000 | at 2.$^{s}$ each | 6000 |
| Marriages | 10 | ℘ Cent | 4000 | at 2.$^{s}$6.$^{d}$ | 500 |
| Bachelors | 5 | ℘ Cent | 7000 | at 1 | 350 |
| Widdowers | 20 | ℘ Cent | 5000 | at 1 | 250 |
| | | | | | In all 7,100£ |

So the Common duty comes To .....................................................66,475
And the deductions ..........................................................................10,600

Whereby The Neat Produce of the common duty is ..............................55,875£

The Persons charg'd For Quality are about 1 in 10 of the whole.

| | | | | |
|---|---|---|---|---|
| viz.$^{t}$ Burials | 17000 | at 14.$^{s}$ | each | 11900£ |
| Births | 19000 | at 8.$^{s}$ | each | 7600 |
| Marriages | 4000 | at 10.$^{s}$ | each | 2000 |
| Bachelors | 14000 | at 5.$^{s}$ | each | 3500 |
| Widdowers | 3000 | at 5.$^{s}$ | each | 1500 |
| | | | In all for Quality | 26500£ |
| Omissions Frauds & Insolvents in Quality a 20.$^{th}$ part, or | | | | 1325£ |
| Whereby the Neat Produce for Quality Is | | | | 25175 |
| And the Neat Produce of the Common duty | | | | 55875 |
| So the Neat Produce in all Should be | | | | 81050 |
| Whereas it is given for | | | | 130000£ |

Of the Present duty on Houses & Windows for Supplying the Deficiency of the Clip't Mony.

The Number of Inhabited Houses is near ........ 1,300,000
The Number of Windows under ........ 9,000,000

| | Houses | | | |
|---|---|---|---|---|
| Whereof | 980,000 | under 10 Windows at | 2.$^{s}$ ꝑ house | 98,000£ |
| | 270,000 | under 20 Windows at | 6.$^{s}$ ꝑ house | 81,000 |
| | 50,000 | above 20 Windows at | 10.$^{s}$ ꝑ house | 25,000 |
| | 1,300,000 | | | 204,000£ |

Out of Which Deducting.

| | Houses | | |
|---|---|---|---|
| For those who receive Alms | 330,000 | at 2.$^{s}$ ꝑ house | 33,000£ |
| Those who do not pay to Church & Poor | 880,000 | at 2 4.$^{d}$ | 44,000 |
| Omissions Frauds & Defaulters | 40,000 | at 4 | 8,000 |
| Insolvent In all | 750,000 | | 85,000£ |
| Solvent In all | 550,000 | | 119,000 |
| So that the Neat Produce Is But | | | 119,000£ ꝑ annum. |
| Whereas It being Granted for 7 years & valued at 1,200,000£ It is given for above | | | 170,000£ ꝑ annum. |

But Whereas the Premium & Interest mony upon advanceing Such part of the Summ (which the act hath given credit for) as the Fund will bear; may be Estimated at 12 or 13 ꝑ Cent, & the collecting and other Charges 5 or 6 ꝑ Cent in all 18 or 19 ꝑ Cent It follows that the Neat Produce to the Excheq.$^{r}$ will be but 100,000£ ꝑ ann. applicable to the Discharge of Principall & Interest; But if one Half of the 1,200,000£ be advanced the First year upon the Credit of the Act, and that a 4.$^{th}$ part of the said 119,000£ should be paid in the First year in Light hammerd Mony worth only ¾.$^{th}$ of the Tale, The Produce of the First year applicable to discharge of Principall mony will not be above ........ 50,000£

So that if the whole Deficiency of the clipt mony Should instead of 1,200,000$^{£}$ amount to 2,400,000$^{£}$ It will be about 24 years before the said duty will discharge the Principall & Interest, tho' there should be no further Anticipations thereon than 5, or 600,000$^{£}$ at the first; and though the said Duty Should produce by the end of the said 24 years 11400$^{£}$ ℘ Ann clear, applicable to the discharge of the Principall.

As to some Commodities not Yet Taxed.

| | | |
|---|---|---|
| That a Half Penny ℘ lb w.$^{t}$ on common soap & a penny ℘ lb w.$^{t}$ on Castile Soap will raise near ........ | £ 50,000 | ℘ ann. |
| That a Half Penny Per lb on Candles will raise about ........ | 70,000 | ℘ ann. |
| That 3 half pence in the shill.$^{g}$ on Leather Parchm.$^{t}$ & Velome will be ........ | 100,000 | ℘ ann. |
| That 1.$^{d}$ ℘ Bush.$^{ll}$ on Malt will raise 100,000$^{£}$ ℘ ann. Consequently 3.$^{d}$ ℘ Bush.$^{ll}$ will raise 300,000 ℘ ann ........ | 300,000 | ℘ ann. |
| That 3.$^{d}$ ℘ Bush.$^{ll}$ on Wheat will raise ........ | 150,000 | ℘ ann. |
| That 2.$^{d}$ ℘ Bush on Rye will raise ........ | 67,000 | ℘ ann. |
| That 1.$^{d}$ ℘ Bush.$^{ll}$ on all Barley & oats bro.$^{t}$ to the mill, will raise .. | 13,000 | ℘ ann. |
| In all ........ | 750,000 | ℘ ann. |
| That 1.$^{d}$ in the crown of the value of all Live cattle will raise ........ | 400,000 | ℘ ann. |
| That 1.$^{d}$ in the Shill.$^{g}$ on all Flesh spent as Food will raise ........ | 3000,000 | ℘ ann. |
| That 3.$^{d}$ ℘ Flecce for each Fleece of Wool Shorn will raise ........ | 100,000 | ℘ ann. |
| In all | 800,000 | ℘ ann. |
| That 2.$^{s}$ ℘ lb on all Materiall for Building or Repairs will raise ..... | 300,000$^{£}$ | ℘ ann. |
| That 10 ℘ Cent upon all wool consum'd or Manufactur'd will raise ........ | 500,000 | ℘ ann. |

10. The state of the Nation An.$^{o}$ 1695.

| | | |
|---|---|---|
| That the Present Income of the Nation is a Million lesse than it was A.$^{o}$ 1688 and is now but about ........ | 42½ | Mill.$^{s}$ Sterlg. |
| That the Yearly Expence is about 40½ Mills. & the Taxes 5 Millions In all ........ | 45½ | Mill.$^{s}$ Sterlg. |
| That the Kingdome does now yearly decrease ........ | 3 | Mill.$^{s}$ Sterlg. |
| That if the Warr continue to An.$^{o}$ 1698 Inclusive The Yearly Income will in Probability Be But ........ | 38½ | Mill.$^{s}$ Sterlg. |
| The Expence ........ 38½ Mill.$^{s}$ / Taxes ........ 4 Mill.$^{s}$ } In all ........ | 42½ | Mill.$^{s}$ Sterlg. |
| The Yearly Decrease ........ | 4 | Mill.$^{s}$ Sterlg. |

According to the Following Scheme.

| An.$^{s}$ | Annuall Income of the Nation. | Annuall Expence of the Nation. | Ordinary Revenue of the Crown. | Extraord.$^{ry}$ Taxes actually raised | Annuall Expence In all. | Increase or Decrease of the Nation. |
|---|---|---|---|---|---|---|
| 1688 ........... | 43,500 | 41,700.$^{m}$ | 2,000,000 | ......... | 41,700,000 | Incr. 1,800,000 |
| 1689 ........... | 43,600 | 41,500.$^{m}$ | 1,800,000 | 3,000,000 | 44,500,000 | Decr. 900,000 |
| 1690 ........... | 43,700 | 41,500.$^{m}$ | 1,800,000 | 4,000,000 | 45,500,000 | Decr. 1,800,000 |
| 1691 ........... | 43,800 | 41,400.$^{m}$ | 1,700,000 | 4,000,000 | 45,400,000 | Decr. 1,600,000 |
| 1692 ........... | 43,800 | 41,200.$^{m}$ | 1,700,000 | 4,000,000 | 45,200,000 | Decr. 1,400,000 |
| 1693 ........... | 43,600 | 41,000.$^{m}$ | 1,600,000 | 4,000,000 | 45,000,000 | Decr. 1,400,000 |
| 1694 ........... | 43,100 | 40,800.$^{m}$ | 1,600,000 | 5,000,000 | 45,800,000 | Decr. 2,700,000 |
| 1695 ........... | 42,500 | 40,500.$^{m}$ | 1,500,000 | 5,000,000 | 45,500,000 | Decr. 3,000,000 |
| 1696 ........... | 41,000 | 40,100.$^{m}$ | 1,500,000 | 4,500,000 | 44,600,000 | Decr. 3,000,000 |
| 1697 ........... | 40,200 | 39,300.$^{m}$ | 1,400,000 | 4,500,000 | 43,800,000 | Decr. 3,600,000 |
| 1698 ........... | 38,500 | 38,500.$^{m}$ | 1,400,000 | 4,000,000 | 42,500,000 | Decr. 4,000,000 |

Hence We may Inferr.

That in 7 years From 1688 To 1695 Inclusive the Taxes have amounted to effectually ................................................ 29 Mill.$^{s}$ Sterlg.
But that the Kingdome is scarce actually decreased...................... 13 Mill.$^{s}$
So that by Industry & Frugality there has been saved full............. 16 Mill.$^{s}$
That by the year 1698 Inclusive The Taxes will in 10 Years have amounted to in all probability effectually ........................... 42 Mill.$^{s}$

And the Kingdome will be actually Decreas'd 23½ Millions That after the Year 1695 The Taxes actually rais'd will fall short every year more & more to that Degree, That the Warr cannot well be sustain'd beyond the year 1698 upon the Foot it now stands, unlesse

1. The Yearly Income of the Nation can be Increas'd.
2. Or the Yearly Expence Diminish'd.
3. Or a Forreign or Home Credit be obtain'd or Establish'd.
4. Or the Confederacy be Inlarg'd.
5. Or the State of the Warr alter'd.
6. Or a General Excise, in effect Introduc'd.

Now whereas by the Foregoing Scheme, The Wealth of the Kingdome seems to be actually Decreas'd almost 13 Mill.$^{s}$ Sterlg. between 1688 & 1695 Inclusive, And will Probably decrease by 1698 Inclusive above 10 Mill.$^{s}$ & a half More, In all about 23 Mill.$^{s}$ and a half in 10 Years; The said Decrease seems to be thus chargeable.

| | The Stock of the Kingdom 1688. | Decrease by the year 1695. | Remain.g Stock an.o 1695. | Decrease by the year 1698. | Remaining Stock anno 1698. |
|---|---|---|---|---|---|
| Coyn'd Silver | 8,500,000 | 4,000,000 | 4,500,000 | 1,500,000 | 3,000,000 |
| Coyn'd Gold | 3,000,000 | ......... | 3,000,000 | 1,500,000 | 1,500,000 |
| Uncoynd Silver & gold | 500,000 | 400,000 | 100,000 | 100,000 | ......... |
| Wrought Plate Rings &c.a | 4,000,000 | 1,600,000 | 2,400,000 | 1,200,000 | 1,200,000 |
| Jewells | 1,500,000 | 500,000 | 1,000,000 | 200,000 | 800,000 |
| Furniture Apparell &c.a | 10,500,000 | 2,500,000 | 8,000,000 | 1,500,000 | 6,500,000 |
| | 28,000,000 | 9,000,000 | 19,000,000 | 6,000,000 | 13,000,000 |
| Stock for Trade Consumption &c.a | 33,000,000 | 3,000,000 | 30,000,000 | 3,500,000 | 26,500,000 |
| The Live Stock in Cattle &c.a | 25,000,000 | 1,000,000 | 24,000,000 | 1,000,000 | 23,000,000 |
| | 86,000,000 | 13,000,000 | 73,000,000 | 10,500,000 | 62,500,000 |

Hence it follows That if the stock of the Nation which was 86 Millions Sterlg. A.o 1688 viz.t about double to the yearly Income & expence, shall be decreas'd to 62 Mill.s & a Half by A.o 1698. The Warr cannot well be sustain'd longer than that year for these Reasons.

1. For that the Mony of the Kingdome will then be but 4½ Millions viz.t but one Tenth of the annual Expence, Lesse then which cannot circulate the Whole.
2. That the Wrought Plate will be little above a Million Consequently nothing to be spar'd further than that article.
3. That 7 Mill.s in Jewells, Household stuff, Furniture, Apparell &c.a is the least quantity We can imagine that Article reduceable unto, The bedding of the Kingdome amounting to one Half of that Summ.
4. That if the stock of the Kingdome, in Shipping, Forts & castles and in naval and military stores and appointments, & for Forreign Trade, and home consumption, and all the Branches of that Article be reduc'd from 33 to 26 Millions; If it should be further Lessen'd, the Nation cannot be secure, Trade cannot be carried on, Nor a Sufficient Stock of Provisions left to supply us in times of Difficulty.
5. That if the Live Stock of the Nation which will then be Diminish'd a 12.th part, should be further Diminish'd, It may occasion an excessive Rice of the Price of Wool, Leather, Flesh, Butter, and cheese, not much short of a Famine; Unless the Number of People Decrease Proportionably; The effect whereof will be equally pernitious.

11. The State of France & Holland An.o 1688 And An.o 1695.

As to the State of France An.o 1688.

| | |
|---|---|
| That France contains about | 126 Mill.s of Acres. |
| Which at about 40 Acres ℘ Family is | 3,200,000 Faml.s |
| And allowing Full 9 Acres ℘ Head, & 4⅓ Heads ℘ Family is | 14,000,000 of Souls.. |
| That the Yearly Rents of the Lands & other Heriditaments of France at 5.s ℘ acre is | 32,000,000 Sterlg. |
| The Trade & Businesse of France | 52,000,000 Sterlg. |
| In all | 84,000,000 Sterlg. |

Which is for every head in France about ........................................6£ ℘ annum.
Of this 86 Mill.s Income ℘ ann. in Times of Peace.

| | | | £ | s | d | |
|---|---|---|---|---|---|---|
| The Taxes & Revenue of the Crown is about 10½ Mill.s Sterlg ................................ | 10½ Mill.s Sterlg | or | .. | 15 | .. | ℘ h.d |
| The Consumption over & above Taxes &c.a .. | 70 Millions, | or | 5 | .. | .. | ℘ h.d |
| The Yearly Increase................................ | 3½ Millions, | or | .. | 5 | .. | ℘ h.d |
| In all | 84 Millions, | or | 6 | .. | .. | ℘ h.d |

As to the 10½ Mill.s Sterlg for the ordinary Taxes & Publick Revenue of France in Time of Peace.

| | |
|---|---|
| The necessary charge of the Governm.t requires...................... | 7 Mill.s Sterlg. |
| The Incident charge of the Government............................... | 1½ Mill.s |
| The Yearly Surplus applicable to the Increase of shipp.g & to Navall and Military stores, or to lay up in mony .................. | 2 Millions. |
| | 10½ Mill.s |

Which yearly Surplus of 2 Mill.s is capable of raiseing a Bank in Ships of Warr; in Naval and Military Stores, & in ready Mony to the value of 20 Mill.s Sterlg. upon the Enjoyment of 10 Years Peace.
Supposing then that the Present Warr has in 7 years cost France 70 Millions, or Com.s annis 10 Mill.s ℘ annum

| | |
|---|---|
| They had at the begining thereof in ships of Warr Extry & in stores & mony at Least .................................................... | 10 Mill.s Sterlg. |
| They have Spar'd out of the Incident charges of the Governm.t ⅔.d parts, or one Mill.n ℘ ann. in all .......................................... | 7 Mill.s Sterlg. |
| They have rais'd extry Taxes 7 Mill.s ℘ ann. or........................... | 49 Mill.s |
| They have got by Prizes at Sea, & Advantages at Land................. | 4 Mill.s |
| In all........... | 70 Mill.s |

And the whole Taxes & Revenue of the crown ordinary & Extry has been 17½ Mill.s ℘ an. or 25.s ℘ head ℘ ann.

As to the State of France An.o 1695.

| | |
|---|---|
| It may well be presum'd, That by the Interruption of Trade and the Desertion of the Refugees, The Income of France is Lessend 10 Mill.s ℘ ann. & is now But..... | 74 Mill.s Sterlg. |
| That the People of France are Less-en'd ½ of a Million, & being now but 13,500,000 Souls have redue'd their expences about 9g. ℘ Head ℘ ann. viz.t from 5£ .. .. To 4£ 11.s ... d whereby the Present yearly consumption is................................................. | 61½ Mill.s |
| That the Yearly charge of the Warr is now Increas'd To .. | 11 Mill.s |
| That the Necessary charge of the Government, is still..... | 7 Mill.s |
| The Incident charges............................................. | ½ Mill.s |
| In all....... | 80 Mill.s |

| | |
|---|---|
| Soe that France does now actually decrease near a 12.$^{th}$ part of it's annual Income, or ........ | 6 Mill.$^{s}$ ℘ ann. |

As to the State of Holland Anno. 1688.

| | |
|---|---|
| That Holland contains ........ | 8 Mill.$^{s}$ of acres. |
| That the Number of People is ........ | 2,200,000 Souls. |
| That to each Soul there is in Land ........ | 3⅔ Acres. |
| That the Rents of the Land Houses & Hereditam.$^{ts}$ is 10.$^{s}$ ℘ Acre, or. ........ | 4 Mill.$^{s}$ Sterlg. ℘ ann. |
| That the Trade & business of Holland is ........ | 13¾ Mill.$^{a}$ Sterlg. ℘ ann. |
| So that the whole Income of Holland is ........ | 17¾ Mill.$^{s}$ ℘ annum |

| | | | £ | s | d | |
|---|---|---|---|---|---|---|
| That the General Income of Holland Being ........ | 17¾ | Mill.$^{s}$ Sterlg. is | 8 | 1 | 4 | ℘ Head. |
| Whereof the Taxes or Publick Revenue... | 4¾ | d.$^{o}$ or | 2 | 3 | 2 | ℘ head. |
| Consumption in Dyet apparell & Incident Charges over & above the Taxes ........ | 11 | d.$^{o}$ or | 5 | .. | .. | ℘ head. |
| Yearly Increase ........ | 2 | d.$^{o}$ or | .. | 18 | 2 | ℘ head. |
| | 17¾ | d.$^{o}$ or | 8 | 1 | 4 | ℘ head. |

As to the 4¾ Mill.$^{s}$ Sterl. Publick Revenue

| | | |
|---|---|---|
| The ordinary charge of the Governm.$^{t}$ is ........ | 2,750,000£ | |
| Interest mony for 25 Mill.$^{s}$ at 4 ℘ Cent ........ | 1,000,000 | 3,750,000£ Sterlg. |
| The Incident or Discretionary Expences ........ | | 500,000 Sterlg. |
| The Yearly Surplus applicable to the Increase of Shipping & to Naval & Military Stores, or to Lay up in mony ........ | | 500,000 Sterlg. |
| | | 4,750,000£ Sterlg. |

Supposing then, That the Present Warr has in 7 Years cost Holland 22 Millions, or 3,150,000 Sterlg. ℘ ann.

| | |
|---|---|
| They had An.$^{o}$ 1688 in Ships of Warr Extry & in Stores & publick mony at Least ........ | 5 Mill.$^{s}$ Sterlg. |
| They have apply'd out of their ord.$^{ry}$ Revenue the Discretionary Expences & surplus 1 Mill. ℘ ann ........ | 7 Mill.$^{s}$ |
| They have rais'd Extry Taxes 1½ Mill. ℘ Ann. or ........ | 10½ Mill.$^{s}$ |
| | In all 22½ Mill.$^{s}$ |

As to the State of Holland 1695.

Supposing that the Governm.$^{t}$ is decreas'd 4½ Mill.$^{s}$ Sterlg. Since the beginning of the Warr to the Year 1695.

Yet considering that by a more than ordinary Frugality in Dyet, apparel, & such other Incid.$^{t}$ charges as relate to the Consumption of things w.$^{ch}$ amounts to about 13 Mill.$^{s}$ ℘ ann The People may well have Saved a 26.$^{th}$ Part, or Half a Mill.$^{n}$ ℘ Ann of their ord.$^{ry}$ Expence, In all for 7 Years ........ 3,500,000£ Sterlg.

| | |
|---|---|
| And that by a more than ordinary Industry & application to Trade during the Warr, & the great benefitt they have made thereof by the High price of all Forreign Commodities Especially those from India (occasion'd in great measure by the Losse of so many English East India Ships, and the difficulties which the English E.[t] Ind.[a] Comp.[a] hath lain under of late years) they may well have advanced their Proffitt by Trade Half a Million ⅌ ann. more In all for 7 Years............. | 3,500,000[£] Sterlg. |
| And that out of the 2 Mill.[s] Yearly Increase in times of Peace the Additional Taxes this Warr, haveing been but 1½ Mill. ⅌ Ann there remains an Increase of ½ a M. ⅌ ann. In all for 7 Y.[s]..... | 3,500,000[£] Sterlg. |
| It follows that tho' the Governm.[t] is Decreas'd....................... | 4½ Millions |
| Yet the People have Increas'd .......................................... | 0½ Mill.[s] |
| So that Holl.[d] in gen.[ll] is Richer than at the begin.[g] of the Warr by.......................................................................... | 6 Mill.[s] |
| Allowing then the Present Income of Holl.[d] to be Half a Million ⅌ ann. more than in times of Peace viz.[t]............................ | 18,250,000[£] Sterlg. |
| The ordinary Charge of the Government............................ | 2,750,000 Sterlg. |
| Interest Mony for 25 Mill.[s] Sterlg...................................... | 1,000,000 |
| The Extry. Charge of the Warr at a medium ........................ | 3,150,000 |
| The Yearly consumption ½ a Mill.[n] Lesse than in times of Peace ................................................................... | 10,500,000 |
| In all........... | 17,400,000[£] Sterlg. |
| It follows That there is yet an annual Increase In general of ...... | 850,000[£] |
| That is to say, The Publick Revenue has decreas'd annually....... | 650,000 |
| But the People have Increas'd com. annis............................. | 1,500,000[£] |

12. The State & Condition of the three Nations of England, France, & Holland Compar'd one with another, with Respect to the Years 1688 & 1695.

The Expence of the 3 Nations in Dyet I thus Estimate Anno. 1695.

| | England £ | France £ | Holland £ | In all. £ |
|---|---|---|---|---|
| 1. In Bread, Bread corn Cakes, Biscuit, Pastry Puddings, & all things made of Meal or Flower ...................... | 4,300,000 | 10,600,000 | 1,400,000 | 16,300,000 |
| 2. In Beef Mutton, veal, Lamb, Piggs, Pork, Bacon, Kids, venson, conies ....................... | 3,300,000 | 5,600,000 | 800,000 | 10,000,000 |
| 3. In Butter Cheese & Milk ......................... | 2,300,000 | 4,200,000 | 600,000 | 7,100,000 |
| 4. In Malt Drink or Beer & Ale only..................... | 5,800,000 | 100,000 | 1,200,000 | 7,100,000 |

| | | | | |
|---|---|---|---|---|
| 5. In Wine Brandy Spirits, & Strong Liquors, Cider, Perry, Mum, Mead, Metheglin, & made Wines........................ | 1,300,000 | 9,000,000 | 400,000 | 10,600,000 |
| 6. In Fish, Fowle & Eggs.... | 1,700,000 | 3,900,000 | 1,100,000 | 6,500,000 |
| 7. In Fruit Roots & Garden Stuff.......................... | 1,200,000 | 3,600,000 | 400,000 | 5,200,000 |
| 8. In salt, oyl, Pickles, Spices Glocay & confectionary Ware Jellyes, Sweets meets & c.$^{a}$................. | 1,100,000 | 3,000,000 | 300,000 | 4,400,000 |
| | 21,000,000 | 38,000,000 | 6,200,000 | 65,200,000$^{£}$ |

Hence We may observe.

That if England Contain 5,500,000 Souls, France 13½ Mill.$^{a}$ and Holland 2,200,000 Then each Head Spends in Diet one with another 3$^{£}$ 1.$^{s}$ 4.$^{d}$ ℘ Ann. viz.$^{t}$ Each Head in Eng.$^{d}$ 3$^{£}$ 16.$^{s}$ 5.$^{d}$ In France 2$^{£}$ 16.$^{s}$ 2.$^{d}$ In Holland 2$^{£}$ 16.$^{s}$ 5.$^{d}$

According to the Following Scheme.

| | England. | | | France. | | | Holland. | | |
|---|---|---|---|---|---|---|---|---|---|
| | £ | s | d | £ | s | d | £ | s | d |
| 1. Bread, Bread corn &c.$^{a}$...................... | .. | 15 | 8 | .. | 15 | 1 | .. | 12 | 9 |
| 2. Flesh meat .................................... | .. | 12 | .. | .. | 8 | .. | .. | 7 | 3 |
| 3. Butter cheese & Milk........................ | .. | 8 | 5 | .. | 6 | .. | .. | 5 | 6 |
| 4. Ale & Beer.................................... | 1 | 1 | 1 | .. | .. | 2 | .. | 10 | 11 |
| 5. Wine Spirits & Strong Liqu.$^{rs}$............ | .. | 4 | 8 | .. | 12 | 11 | .. | 3 | 8 |
| 6. Fish, Fowle & Eggs.......................... | .. | 6 | 2 | .. | 5 | 7 | .. | 10 | .. |
| 7. Fruit, roots, & Garden stuff................ | .. | 4 | 4 | .. | 5 | 2 | .. | 3 | 8 |
| 8. Salt, oyl, Pickles, Grocery &c.$^{a}$........... | .. | 4 | .. | .. | 4 | 3 | .. | 2 | 8 |
| | 3 | 16 | 5 | 2 | 16 | 2 | 2 | 16 | 5 |

[The table on p. 155 comes here in the MS.]

Hence it follows, That from the year 1688 To 1695 England has decreas'd in People 50,000 France 500,000 And Holland is Increased 40,000.

That England is Decreas'd in its Income a Million, France 10 Millions, But Holland is Increasd Half a Million.

That England has rais'd Extry Taxes com. annis about 4½ Mill.$^{s}$ ℘ ann. France 7 Millions ℘ ann; Holland about a Million & a Half ℘ ann.

That Engalnd has Lessen'd it's ordinary Expence 700,000$^{£}$ ℘ ann France 8 Millions. Holland ½ a Million.

Lastly That if England Decreases annually 3 Mill.$^{s}$ Sterlg. or a 14.$^{th}$ part of its annual Income, and France 6 Mill.$^{s}$ or near a 12.$^{th}$ part of 74 Mill.$^{s}$ The Decrease of England is in Proportion to the Decrease of France but as 6 to 7 Whereas Holland Increases a 21.$^{th}$ Part.

That the Expence of the 3 Nations may be thus proportion'd for the years 1988 & 1695.

| | | Dyet. | Apparell. | Incident Charges. | Generall Expence. | Generall Income. | Increase. | |
|---|---|---|---|---|---|---|---|---|
| 1688 | Engl.[d] | 21,300,000£ | 10,400,000£ | 10,000,000£ | 41,700,000£ | 43,500,000£ | 1,800,000£ | |
| | France | 41,000,000 | 18,500,000 | 21,000,000 | 80,500,000 | 84,000,000 | 3,500,000 | |
| | Holl.[d] | 6,400,000 | 3,000,000 | 6,350,000 | 15,750,000 | 17,750,000 | 2,000,000 | |
| | | 68,700,000 | 32,400,000 | 37,350,000 | 138,450,000 | 147,250,000 | 8,800,000 | |
| 1695 | Engl.[d] | 21,000,000 | 10,200,000 | 14,300,000 | 45,500,000 | 42,500,000 | 3,000,000 | Decrease |
| | France | 38,000,000 | 16,000,000 | 26,000,000 | 80,000,000 | 74,000,000 | 6,000,000 | Decrease |
| | Holl.[d] | 6,200,000 | 2,800,000 | 8,400,000 | 17,400,000 | 18,250,000 | 850,000 | Increase |
| | | 65,200,000 | 31,000,000 | 49,700,000 | 147,900,000 | 141,750,000 | 6,150,000 | Decrease |

Lastly as to the General Account of Eng.[d] France, & Holl.[d] for the years 1688 & 1695 I have added this further Scheme.

| | | Number of People | Yearly Income ℘ Head £ | s | d | Publick Revenue & Taxes £ | Taxes ℘ head £ | s | d | Annunall Consumption besides Taxes £ | Consumpt.[n] ℘ Head £ | s | d | | Annall Increase In all £ | Increase ℘ Head £ | s | d | |
|---|---|---|---|---|---|---|---|---|---|---|---|---|---|---|---|---|---|---|---|
| 1688 | Engl.[d] | 5,500,000 | 7 | 18 | .. | 2,000,000 | .. | 7 | 3 | 39,700,000 | 7 | 4 | .. | | 1,800,000 | .. | 6 | 8 | |
| | France | 14,000,000 | 6 | 3 | .. | 10,500,000 | .. | 15 | .. | 70,500,000 | 5 | .. | 9 | | 5,000,000 | .. | 7 | .. | |
| | Holl.[d] | 2,200,000 | 8 | 1 | 4 | 4,750,000 | 2 | 3 | 2 | 11,000,000 | 5 | .. | .. | | 2,000,000 | .. | 18 | 4 | |
| | | 21,700,000 | 6 | 15 | 9 | 17,250,000 | .. | 15 | 10 | 121,200,000 | 5 | 11 | 9 | | 8,800,000 | .. | 8 | 1 | |
| | | | £ | s | d | | £ | s | d | | £ | s | d | | | £ | s | d | |
| 1695 | Eng.[ld] | 5,450,000 | 7 | 16 | .. | 6,500,000 | 1 | 4 | .. | 39,000,000 | 7 | 3 | .. | D. | 3,000,000 | .. | 11 | .. | Decr. |
| | France | 13,500,000 | 5 | 18 | .. | 17,500,000 | 1 | 5 | .. | 62,500,000 | 4 | 18 | 2 | D. | 6,000,000 | .. | 8 | 10 | Decr. |
| | Holl.[d] | 2,240,000 | 8 | 2 | 9 | 6,900,000 | 3 | 1 | 7 | 15,500,000 | 4 | 13 | 9 | In. | 850,000 | .. | 7 | 7 | Incr. |
| | | 21,440,000 | 6 | 12 | .. | 30,900,000 | 1 | 8 | 10 | 117,000,000 | 5 | 9 | 4 | D. | 6,150,000 | .. | 5 | 9 | Decr. |

# Appendix 4

# Gregory King's Letter about Queen Anne's Bounty

## PAGE ONE.

Some Observations upon the Schemes of the number & Value of Spiritual Livings in England with relation to their Augmentation

I find it is justly Suspected That the Valuation of the smaller Livings thô upon oath are understated—

Which manifestly appears to me by the differences between those under 10£ p. añ. to those under 80£ p añ—

For those of 30£ p añ and upwards and under 40£ being returned to be 921 in Number, and those under 50£ 60£ and 70£ gradually decrease in Number (thô not as they ought to do) still those between 70 and 80 p añ are Returned but 211 in Number; The decrease afterwards in proportion should not be for those between 80 and 90£ p añ. above Number of 150 and those between 90 and 100£ p añ not above 100 in Number, making in all but 5332 Livings under 100£ p añ. which is too fast a decrease of the Numbers after 40£ p añ—

And I dare say were the Numbers rightly Returned, those under 30£ per añ would in the whole be fewer by about 600 and those under 80£ p añ fewer by 200 or upwards.—

according to the following scheme

| By the Returns as far as to 80£ p anñ | | | By my comparisoñ | |
|---|---|---|---|---|
| | single numbers | numbers added | single numbers | numbers added |
| | {under 10£ p anñ 471 | | under 10£—400—400 | |
| {by | {under 20£———745 | 1216 | under 20£—620—1020 | |
| the | {under 30£———906 | 2122 | under 30£—760—1780 | |
| returns | {under 40£———921 | 3043 | under 40£—750—2530 | |
| | {under 50£———783 | 3826 | under 50£—680—3210 | |
| | {under 60£———620 | 4446 | under 60£—600—3810 | |
| {by | {under 70£———425 | 4871 | under 70£—550—4360 | |
| compari- | {under 80£———211 | 5082 | under 80£—500—4860 | |
| son in | {under 90£———150 | 5232 | under 90£—470—5330 | |
| propor- | {under100£———100 | 5332 | under100£—440—5770 | |
| tion to | above100£———3848 | 9180 | above100£-3410—9180 | |
| ye returns | | | | |

However since the Numbers and Values Returned are to be the Foundation for augmenting the Smaller Livings. the Inequality or Defect of the Returns is of little importance. As to the Observation That the Tythes since H.8 time are Sunk from a Tenth to less than a 40th part of the present Real Value, the meaning of that Observation wants Explaining—

For if it be in Rectories Consisting of Glebe and Tythes, Suppose the Living was actually worth in H.8 time 100£ p anñ. and was rated for Tenths—£10—

And Supposing the Increase of money since that time be quadruple and consequently the value of the Land and its produce quadruple also; The Value of such a Living in H.8 time would be now 400£ p anñ and yet the Tenths remain but 10£ p anñ which is to the advantage of the Incumbent— °vide page 3—

## PAGE TWO.

I agree that a true Valuation of the Greater Benefices from 100£ to 110£, 120£ ve and so to 200£ ve would be of use, especially the Impropriations; But from the Returns already made, I do not See but my scheme carried on to 200£ p anñ. may furnish the Ingenious observer with a foundation for further Inferences, For whose sake I here continue it—

Continuation of Mr Kings Scheme or Computation of the Number and value of the Spiritual Livings above 100£ p anñ. to 200£ p anñ.

p anñ.

above 89£ ve under 100£—440—5770 as before
110—400—5770
120—360—6540
130—350—6890
140—320—7210
150—290—7500
160—250—7750
170—220—7970
180—200—8770
190—180—8500
200—150—8500
above 200—680—9180

I agree with the Observation that the Reducing all the greater and lesser Livings to a Certainty or Medium (as a Competency for the Clergy) is not a sufficient Competency as being but about 64£ p anñ. on an equality; and I doubt not but it is generally agreed that 100£ p anñ. would but be a Competency for the Inferior Clergy of Engld.

The Land Tax of 4d. p Pound on Rents in England, Exclusive of Money and Stock, comes to near 1,800,000£. So the Rents of the Land as Taxed is about 9 millions; There is no doubt but if fully Taxed, the Rents or yearly value would be 12 millions, The produce thereof in Corn Land is generally Treble to the Rent, in Pasture double; So that taking the produce to be equal to 2 Rents and a half it amounts to 30 Millions p anñ.

If the 9180 Livings were augmented from 64£ p anñ. (on an Equality as they seem to stand at present by the Returns) to 100£ p anñ. The yearly Value of the Livings after being so Augmented would be but 918,000£ which would be but a 32th part of the yearly produce __ or about 7d. p £ whereas had the Clergy their full Tenths of the 30 Millions it would amount to 3 Millions p anñ. or almost 327£ p anñ each living on Equality—| -

That the Small Livings want augmentation is generally agreed.

The Clergy as well as the poor are our Proletarys, for furnishing us with people, and—would be much more so, when the means of subsisting are Increased, for they might sooner quit their Celibacy in the Universities, would marry sooner and into better families with some tolerable Portions, which would lessen the Number of Maidens and Widows capable of Breeding which now lye so heavy on Our Hands: The Contempt of the Clergy would be much Lessend or taken away for among all the Reasons for that Contempt the want of full Subsistence I am sure is the Principal, They would apply more to their studies, being then Enabled to buy Books, would be persons of brighter parts fitter Conversation for the Gentry, who would think it now below a young son; and their doctrine would have a greater Influence on those under their Care—

A Reducing all Livings to an Equality I think Impolitic, the Dignitaries of ye Church not being enow to Encite Spritely and Generous minds to diligence, and besides many of our Prebendaries want as much augmenting as the Parochial Cures; Tis true by my scheme there should be 680 Livings above 200£ p anñ but that's no great Number—in comparison with the 8500 Livings under 200£ p anñ—

## PAGE THREE.

If the Value of the Impropriations (as they are commonly called) were Enquired into, perhaps It will appear that they are Greater in Value than the Rectories, number for number; They are not properly the Estates of Laymen, neither are they all in Lay hands. But if a Fund could be raised for buying in some of these by allowing 2 or 3 years purchase at present for the Reversion (after a Term of 60 years, which by that time would sink almost all settlemn. joyntures &c Such a provision for the future seems to me a good Expedient The Clergy being like a Corporacoñ with perpetual succession. But this is not my Province) Thô I should be glad to know how a sum under—£50 000 would bring the Lesser Livings Immediately to 50£ p anñ each and put them under a Foot of considerable future Improvement? But my thoughts carrying me much forwarder than the present advantage I should prefer the purchasing Reversionary Interests in Impropriacoñs which generally speaking would come Cheaper than other Estates to which they are Estimated Inferior by one or two years purchase in 20—

There is no end of Conceptions on such Topics So that among so many Great and Good men as are the Governors of Her Mâties Bounty to the Clergy there is no Room to doubt but Her Mâties Pious Intention for augmenting the Livings of the Smaller Clergy will meet with its desired success—

GK

## 15 NOVR 1710

°But this is different where there is a modus, for in such Case the modus does not Increase thô the Value of the Land Tythes or Houses or Hereditamts. for which such Modus is taken Increases daily—

So that all Modus's will be to the Detrimnt of the Incumbent in time to come. And the case is the same where any annual Stipend is allowed which will always decrease in Value as the Species of money and the value of Lands Increases

Care therefore ought to be taken in augmenting Small Livings to bring them up to a full Competency or else what is now augmented if it be by stipends will in 200 years more want a further augmentation, and so on Infinitum—

# Appendix 5

# The Life of Gregory King by George Chalmers

[9]

## NOTICES OF *THE LIFE* OF GREGORY KING.

THIS ingenious, and modest man, was born on the 15th of December 1648, in the parish of Stow, at Litchfield; which was also the birth-place of Ashmole, and of the father of Camden. This curious computer was the son of Gregory King, and Elizabeth, his first wife, who was the daughter of Mr. J. Andrews of Sandwich, in Kent. This family of Kings were originally of Leicester, where they had lived for generations, and long remained.*

The father of our *political arithmetician* was himself a studier of the mathematics; and practised surveying of land, and dyalling, as a profession; but with more attention to *good fellowship*, than mathematical studies generally allow: and, the care of the family devolved of course on the mother, who, if she had been less obscure, had emulated the most eminent of the Roman matrons. The father, however, with all his laxity of *company-keeping*, was extremely attentive to the education of his children.*

With this parental ardour for literature, the father "packt away to school, at two years of age," his little Gregory to some *matron old*, who is "lost in the dreary shades

* Nichols's Leicest. vol. iii. pref. v.

* Gregory King, the Herald, seems to have foreseen, with heraldic prescience, the danger of oblivion. And, he left behind him "Miscellaneous notes of his birth, education, and "advancement," which have been published by Mr. W. Dallaway, in his Inquiries into the science of Heraldry, from a manuscript in the Bodleian Library. These Notes, which I have abridged, unfortunately end in 1694. I have tried to glean some additional notices, which continue the subsequent incidents of the useful life of Gregory King.

of dull obscurity." Instructed by her, who "knew unruly brats with birch to tame," he read the psalter, when three years old, and the bible at four, when he could scarcely speak. While thus employed, he was seized with a paralytic complaint, which so affected his person, though not his intellect, that his father, fearing a perpetual deformity, often prayed, that God would take his son to himself. He recovered, however, and while he was not six years old, he was sent to the Free School, to learn his accidence. Mr. Thomas Bevans had the satisfaction of teaching this little genius Latin, Hebrew, and Greek. In his eleventh year, he learned rhetoric, while he himself taught children "to write, and cast accounts." In his thirteenth year, he read Hesiod, and Homer; and while he was engaged in making Greek verses, he taught himself "to survey land," while his father was more agreeably occupied with *his good fellowship*: yet, ought it not to be forgotten, that the father taught his son, as much at home, as the boy learned at school. At this period of his life, he gained money, and applause, by acting, in the Free School, the fool's part of *Ropeny*, in the pastoral comedy of Amyntas. He distinguished himself so much, *in playing the fool*, that this circumstance introduced him into life, while his more solid accomplishments of learning, as they were less seen, were passed over in neglect, and seem never to have contributed any thing to his fortune, or his fame.

In December 1662, at the age of fourteen, our actor, who had attracted the notice of Dr. Hunter of Litchfield, was recommended, by him, as a clerk to DUGDALE, whose labours have insured his immortality. In his service, and school, Gregory King was initiated in the knowledge of Heraldry, and Drawing;—and he taught himself French. He now attended this great antiquary, and herald, upon his respective *visitations*, during several years. It was, on those journeys, that he acquired the local knowledge, and the accuracy of mind, which enabled him, in after-times, to become one of the greatest masters of *political arithmetic*, during the intelligent age of Davenant, and Petty.

But, Dugdale's visitations being ended in 1667, this circumstance brought to a conclusion the services, and instructions of King. Dugdale, however, recommended him to Lord Hatton, who, as an antiquary, wished for the assistance of an Archaiological Secretary. In this situation, King continued to the year 1669, when Lord Hatton's passion, or pursuits, failing, he civilly dismissed his helper. King now returned to his native place, where he found his father married to a second wife. Here he continued a twelvemonth; teaching the youth to write, and cast accounts; and employing himself in painting, and in instructing inquisitive persons to read ancient writings. While he was thus occupied, he was still under age. King was now invited by Mr. Chetwynd, of Injestry, a gentleman of curious learning, to peruse his charters, to draw his seals, and to form his genealogy.* King was at length known, as a person of various knowledge, and useful accomplishments: and he was invited by the dowager lady Gerard, to be her Steward, auditor, and secretary. With her ladyship, he remained at Sandon, in Staffordshire, acting in those several characters, and helping her ladyship, in drawing, and painting, till August 1672.

He at this epoch removed from Sandon to London, the proper scene, for genius to exert its powers, and talents to employ their faculties. He was, naturally, welcomed by

* In the 6th vol. of Leland's Itin. p, 96, there is a letter to Hern, dated the 16th May, 1711, which mentions this connection; but mistakes the name; calling King, *Charles*, instead of Gregory.

his old master, Dugdale, who introduced him to the heralds, and to HOLLAR, the engraver. But, King was still to be employed, in some profitable service, which might be analogous to his studies, and contributive to his livelihood. Such a person was wanted, by OGILBY, who was then occupied, under *a patent*, as Royal Cosmographer, in book-making and printing, in map-making and engraving, in road measuring and etching. To him, was King now recommended by Hollar; and, during some time, was our ingenions calculator employed, with Ogilby, in writing notes, in engraving seals, and in reducing *sculps*. A new Britannia was at length projected, by that noted projector: and, roads were now to be measured, towns to be *ichnographied*, and shires to be surveyed. King attended Falgate, in making a survey of his native county of Essex, in 1672; collecting notes out of churches, and copying records, for the historical department. King was the first, who made a survey of London upon a scale of a hundred feet to an inch, which expressed the ground-plot of every house and garden: this curious map of the metropolis was engraved by Hollar.

But, such undertakings required more capital, than Ogilby could command, and, in this distress, he projected a *lottery of books*, which King ingeniously contrived, and honestly managed, for him: he also framed a lesser *lottery of books*, for Bristol fair, at St. James's tide, 1673, which turned to *the good advantage* of Ogilby, under the management of King.

For all those helps, the Royal Cosmographer was grateful, although he was poor, and old. And Ogilby proposed to King to make, on his own account, a survey of Westminster, upon the same scale, as that of London. This great work, he undertook, in 1674, and performed, with the help of Falgate, in less than a twelvemonth. He was thus induced to fix his lodging in St. James's-street, Covent-garden, at the house of Mrs. Ann Powel, *a maiden gentlewoman*, the daughter of Mr. J. Powel, of Tirley, Gloucestershire, who was of the Powels of Denbigh: and her he married, on the 20th of July, 1674, in the 26th year of his age.

Westminster was at length surveyed; and King now occupied himself with engraving maps of various countries, and geographical cards, which were composed by Sir Peter Wych, and first published by Broome, the bookseller; and which were the prototypes of all the subsequent cards of that nature. King full continued, on different occasions, his original business of surveying land, and copying chartularies. He now surveyed *Soho-fields*, projected *Soho-Square*, and the adjacent streets, and drew up the articles, for erecting the buildings. In 1681, he copied, for the President of the Council, perhaps, the Privy Council Registers, during the interesting region of Edward VI.* He assisted Sandford, in drawing up his well-known genealogical history; compiling a part of the text, and preparing the whole for the press.

These occupations enabled King to renew his acquaintance with Lee, the Chester herald, who introduced him to Mr. Andrew Hay, the secretary to the Earl of Norwich, who then acted as Deputy Earl Marshal. In the dispute, which, at that time existed, between the jurisdiction of Walker, the garter king, and the authority of the Earl Marshal, King made himself useful to the higher power, and this usefulness made him *Rouge Dragon*, in 1677, upon the deaths of Walker, and Lee; being created on the 24th

* I have in my library this copy, in three folio volumes, finely written by King, with his name inscribed, as copyist, and splendidly bound, and ornamented, with an earl's coronet.

of June, in that year, at the College of Arms, by the Earl of Peterborough, the Deputy Earl Marshal. The death of Walker brought to the head of the College of Arms, DUGDALE, who renewed his kindness to his old clerk, while he was yet inconsiderable, from the late loss of his friend Lee, and poor, from the smallness of his official emoluments. At Lady Day, 1680, King removed into the college, where he was nearer his proper affairs, and was better able to attend to the interests of himself, and his friends.

In 1681, 1682, and 1683, King was, chiefly, occupied, in making heraldic surveys of several shires, whereby he gained some money, but lost the kindness of Sir Henry St. George, the *Clarenceux*. This misfortune, however, as it was not owing to his fault, did not prevent his advancement. The death of the Duke of Norfolk brought his son the Earl of Arundel into the high office of Earl Marshal. King's usefulness, and modesty, which had been noticed, by this eminent person, were now rewarded by him: and, King was on this occasion appointed registrar of the College of Arms, notwithstanding the objections of Sir Henry St. George; an office, that he had for some time executed, for the emoluments of Devenish, his predecessor. The enmity of Clarenceux did not prevent him, from asking King's company, and assistance, when he made his *visitation* of Cambridge, and Huntingdon, in 1684.

But, the time was at length come, when our *Rouge Dragon* was to be engaged in greater events. The demise of Charles II. penetrated the heart of King, who had been struck with the good humour, and accustomed grace of a prince, who had acquired those captivating arts in the school of instructive adversity. He bore a considerable part, in the funeral solemnity of that lamented sovereign; as he prepared the *escocheons*, by direction of Dugdale. And, he attended the proclaiming of James II., with *sad dismay*, and *after thoughts disturbed, submitting to what seemed remediless*. Our Rouge Dragon now prepared, by Dugdale's order, no doubt, "the ceremonials, and schemes," for the subsequent coronation. And, king James, declaring, that he would have the account of his coronation printed, Sandford, and Grégory King, were allowed by the Earl Marshal to execute the king's wish. The management, and execution, of this undertaking fell chiefly upon our *Rouge Dragon*; yet, he allowed Sandford's name to stand in the title-page; and reserved only one-third of the profits to himself, without any of the honours. His prudence foresaw, that detraction would fasten on a work, which could not be made perfect. The two undertakers, merely, saved the expence of the book, amounting to £. 600: for, the *sculps;* being many, and tedious, the necessary time carried the hour of publication forward to the eye of another coronation. In 1687, our *Rouge Dragon* attended the *visitation* of London by desire of the *Clarenceux*, as he had before attended him on the visitations of Cambridge, and Huntingdon. King had long struggled with fortune. His bounty to his relations had absorbed all his savings, before his marriage. Ogilby had died indebted to him £. 200, in 1676. His marriage, however, laid a good foundation of future competence, though fruition was somewhat retarded by his liberal manner of living. In 1687, he began, however, to lend money on houses. In 1683, he purchased land, in the parish of Holy Cross, Essex, of the value of £. 21. 1 s. a year. He soon after laid out £. 1,260, in purchasing a three-and-thirty years lease of sixty houses, in St. Catharines, the rental whereof amounted to £. 220 a year: yet, to accomplish this great adventure, he was obliged to borrow more than half the purchase money. And the taxes of king William's time running very high, and the rents falling, these two unlooked for circumstances reduced a good bargain to little value. In 1688, his old associate Sandford, who smarted from the suspension of the Earl Marshall, resigned to him his place of Lancaster Herald, which cost him a hundred and sixty pounds.

But, uncommon prospects again opened on his intelligent eyes. When he heard of the imprisonment of the seven bishops, he cried out: "Then farewell to popeny in England;" foreseeing, that such violence much destroy itself. And, upon reading the Prince of Orange's *declaration,* he equally foretold, "that the prince came not without an expectation of the crown." Our herald pitied the misfortunes of king James, the more, as he was attached, with so many greater persons, in that age, to the hereditary descent of the crown. These sentiments, however, did not prevent him, from obeying the Earl Marshal's order, founded on the authority of the House of Lords, for proclaiming king William, and queen Mary. He afterwards proclaimed the order for the Court of Claims; assisted at several fittings of a committee of bishops, for drawing up the coronation service; and prepared four books for that ceremony; one for the king, one for the queen, one for the princess Anne, and one for the bishop of London, as he had recently done before the coronation of king James: and, he gave extraordinary assistance, in forming the ceremonial of that extraordinary solemnity; and, upon the coronation day, he undertook the fatiguing task of calling into order the peers, and peeresses, in the House of Lords, their majesties being present. Such were the parts, which our herald was destined to act in that uncommon scene, wherein great knowledge of ceremony, and greater fortitude of mind, were requisite to just performance.

Our herald was at length to distinguish himself as the interpreter of the wishes, and civilities of kings, and princes, to each other. The Elector of Brandenburgh was chosen knight of the garter, in January, 1689. And, Sir Thomas St. George, the garter-king, declining, from his great age, the splendid task of carrying the order, our herald was prevailed on to accept that office, having Latin, and French, and other qualities sufficient. His coadjutor, in this commission, was the nephew of Burnet, the bishop of Salisbury, Johnston, who was afterwards secretary of state in Scotland. The commission, the credential letter, the instructions were all drawn, and engrossed by our herald, and approved of by the chancellor of the order. The commissioners set out, in February; arrived at Berlin, in May; and after a distinguished reception, they invested the elector with the order of the garter, accompanied by the accustomed splendour of such ceremonies; and they were rewarded with adequate munificence. Returning by Hamburgh, our herald was entertained, nobly, by Sir Paul Rycaut, and by the English merchants, who, in doing honour to the king's heraldic representative, on a splendid embassage, tried to do honour also to the nation. And, returning to London, in August, our herald concluded his negociation, by making the compliments of the electoral family to the queen, and delivering to her majesty an amber cabinet from the electress.

The Duke of Zell was elected a knight of the garter, in the beginning of 1691: and the king, declaring that he would invest the Duke with his own hands, at the Hague, Sir Thomas St. George thought himself obliged to carry the ensigns; and was induced to invite our herald to accompany him, on an errand so profitable, and splendid. They arrived at the Hague, the day after king William had departed to endeavour to raise the siege of Mons. The magnificent ceremony of investing the Duke took place, on the 8th of May, in the presence of several English nobles of the highest rank. Rewarded, and gratified, the heralds returned to London, in June, when they concluded an extraordinary scene of illustrious action.

From this elevation, our herald descended into his youthful walks of land surveying. In July and August 1691, he performed what he had long promised to Jesus College,

Cambridge, by surveying their lands in Oxford, Gloucester, and Glamorganshire. The wet, which he received, in performing this trust, brought on a sciatic, which greatly distressed him. This did not, however, hinder him from drawing up the claim of lady Essex Griffin to the barony of Audley of Waldon, as he had successfully supported the claim of Lord Thanet to the barony of Clifford, in the year before. He soon after conducted the installation of the Earl of Dorset at Windsor. And owing to whatever cause, his sciatic returned with such violence, as to deprive him, for a time, of the use of his limbs, and of his speech and memory. This was the more distressful, as the king sent orders, for carrying the garter to the Elector of Saxony. Sir Thomas St. George was then occupied with love, and marriage, at the ripe age of seventy-eight: and, he entreated our herald, while he was yet in a state of convalescence, to undertake that splendid, but fatiguing embassage. Their majesties resident at the courts of Lunenburgh, Sir William Colt, was joined in the commission with our herald, who drew up the commission, the credential letter, and instructions. Yet, the dispatch of these authorities was attended, with great delay, and the payment of the requisite money, with still greater. These envoys, at length, arrived at Dresden, where they had been long expected, on the 9th of January, 1693. It was now resolved to outdo the Elector of Brandenburgh, in magnificent expence, and munificent rewards. The grand ceremony was performed, on the 26th of January, with extraordinary splendour. Such carousals, as were on this occasion, displayed, had seldom been seen. The two commissioners, as the custom was, dined with the Elector. And our herald, departing from Dresden, the scene of so many festivities, arrived at the Hague, where he delivered the Elector's compliments to the king, who allowed him to return to England, pleased with his journey, and enriched with presents.

Our herald was again occupied with his usual affairs, till the 5th of June, 1694, when he conducted the instalment of several princes, and peers, at Windsor, with the gorgeous ceremonies of that unusual scene.

In the mean time, Sir John Dugdale proposed to resign his office of *norroy* to Mr. King: but, the Earl Marshal, owing to whatever cause, refused his consent to every importunity. The demise of Mary, on the 28th of December, 1694, giving rise to a contest between the master of the wardrobe and the Earl Marshal, our herald was involved in the contest of those mighty potentates. And, as the disgust of the Earl Marshal was, at length, raised to resentment, he soon after transferred the pen of registrar from Mr. King to Doctor Plott, who had been recently nominated Moubray herald extraordinary.

Our herald was, at length, destined, to act, in a very different sphere. The tendency of his genius led him to *political arithmetic*, in an age, when this science of statesmen was brought into repute by men of extraordinary powers. And, Gregory King produced his *Political Conclusions*, in 1696, though his modesty did not publish those curious efforts of art, and sagacity. He allowed Doctor Davenant, a well known writer of those times, to peruse, and to garble his *political conclusions*. This writer, when treating "of the use of political arithmetic," praises Gregory King, for his *general knowledge* of this science, and speaks of his "scheme of the inhabitants of England, as more distinct, than was ever made, concerning the people of any other country." He avows his obligations to that "wonderful genious," for many lights, and informations. He, indeed, made great use of those observations, by publishing mutilated extracts from a consistent whole. The observations, and conclusions, of Gregory King, are now published, at length, for the first time. His original genius, his local knowledge, his scientific practice, qualified him, in a high degree, to carry this practical science of public business far beyond. Sir William Petty, the original inventor of the art.*

From the publications of Davenant, if had been apparent, is there were not other evidence, that Gregory King was a very communicative disposition. By means of STEPNEY, who is still remembered, as a negociator, and a poet, he laid before the *Board of Trade*, in September, 1696, "a scheme of the inhabitants of the city of Gloucester." This *scheme* is now subjoined to the political conclusions of Gregory King as a proper supplement. To this paper, I have added, for the useful purpose of contrast, the numbers of houses, of the males and females, and of the souls in the same city, at present.

We may easily suppose, that King became acquainted with Stepney, while they were both so frequently employed, as *envoys* to foreign courts; the one for matters of ceremony, the other, for points of business. While the Board of Trade were occupied with the difficult, and important, concerns of *the* POOR, Stepney communicated to them, King's *computation* of the endowed hospitals, and alms-houses, in England. This was received, on the 27th of September, 1697, by the Board, who "ordered it to be copied for use, as occasion may serve*." This paper, I have now subjoined, as a second supplement to King's political conclusions: while *the poor* continue to be objects of our care, this *computation* of such an arithmetician will always have its value. Thus useful was Gregory King, in his life; and thus usefully are his labours brought into political consideration, at present.

The gratitude of Davenant spoke of Gregory King, as *a jewel*, which was fit, for any *statesman's cabinet*. This friendly intimation seems not to have been quite disregarded. The expenditure of the wars of William, and of Anne, required, that the public accounts should be stated. An annual act seems to have passed, during the first reign, for that important end, from 1692.† This salutary measure was continued, at the commencement of the second of those hostile reigns.* Gregory King acted, as secretary to the comptrollers of army accounts; he continued, as the secretary of the commissioners for stating the public accounts, to the hour of his death.† From the tendency of his genius, employments; we may perceive how qualified he was to estimate the state of the nation.

In the midst of all those employments, Gregory King had often reason to think that, "the world is full of rubs." The weight of Sir John Vanburgh rubbed against his feelings, in 1709. It was then in contemplation to bring Sir John into the patent of Clarenceux, though he was a stranger, in the college of heralds. On the 10th of January, 1710, King wrote to Mr. Harley, to whom he was known; remonstrating against a measure, which was ruinous to the college, and injurious to himself: he stated to the minister, his "being bred up from a youth under Sir William Dugdale;" his employ-

* Dav. Discourses on the Pub. Rev. and Trade, 1698, p. 17.

* The Board's Journal, B. 279.

† 4–5. W. and M. ch. 11.; 5–6, W. and M. ch. 23.; 6–7. W. and M. ch. 23.; 6–7. W. ch. 7; 7–8. W. ch. 8. for stating the public accounts of the kingdom.

* 1 An. ch. 10.

† His Epitaph, on the 17th of March, 1711-12, Gregory King, from the commissioners for stating the public accounts, laid before the House of Lords, the receipts and issues of the exchequer, from Michaelmas 1710, to do, 1711. Lord's Journ. of that date.

ment, for twenty years under the garter king, whose sworn deputy he long had been: he urged "the disservice to the public, to have the heads of a society ignorant in its faculty, and a coadjutor himself to want a coadjutor*." Vanburgh's wit, I fear, prevailed over King's arithmetick.

Gregory King did not long survive that mortification, which sacrificed propriety to influence, and substituted ignorance for knowledge. He died, on the 29th of August, 1712, when he had passed his grand climacteric; and was buried in the chancel of St. Bennet's, Paul's Wharf, on the 3d of September, by the side of the wife of his youth.† He was twice married; first, to Anne Powel, as we have seen: and secondly in February, 1701, to Frances Graham, the sister of William Graham. He had one son, Thomas, and two daughters, Elizabeth, and Frances, who all died, before their father, under age. He made his will, on the 30th of November, 1709; to which he added two codicils; whereby he constituted his wife his sole executrix, who raised, as she was directed by his will, a monument to his memory, which will be longer preserved by his *political conclusions*. He left her in easy circumstances; and he bequeathed many legacies to his relations, to whom he was always kind;‡ and to his friends, to whom he was ever obliging.

Gregory King was obviously an accomplished person: he wrote a beautiful hand;* and he practised drawing, skilfully. From nature, he had very vigorous faculties; quickness of apprehension, and strength of sagacity: from education, and habit, he possessed steady application to whatever employment; and dextrous facility, in whatever affairs: and he was a person of such powers, as to distinguish him, in an age, when eminent men, in his several accomplishments, abounded. He who surpassed PETTY, as a political calculator, must be allowed to have been a master of moral arithmetick. As a *Herald*, KING is ranked next, in knowledge, to GLOVER, who is deemed *the first*; and was the instructor of CAMDEN. His whole life furnishes an example how a man of talents, and address, may surmount every difficulty, and raise himself from poverty, and insignificance, to competence, and distinction.

* The original letter is in the British Museum. Harl. No. 7,525.

† Parish Register. His monumental inscription, is in Le Neve, p. 243; and in Dallaway, wherein the name of his second wife is blundered.

‡ He mentioned his brother, John King, "long since [1709] deceased," and his brother Thomas King, "of the Excise Office, London:" but, the particularity of his will does not mention any brother, or any children of any brother, of the name of *Charles* King.

* His autograph is in Dallaway's Heraldry, pl. xv. facing p. 221: but, I know not, if there be any picture of him.

# Notes

1. Charles Davenant, *Political and Commercial Works*, ed. Sir Charles Whitworth, vol. 2, (London: Horsfield, 1771), 224; also see index s.v. "famine" and "Arithmetic, Political." I cite the table and discuss it further in Chapter 6 and then discuss it again in Chapter 11. This table never actually appeared in King's published writing, but convention attributed it to him. On the attribution to King, see G. Heberton Evans, Jr., "The Law of Demand—The Roles of Gregory King and Charles Davenant," *The Quarterly Journal of Economics* 81 (1967): 483–492. See also Jinbang Kim, "Jevons versus Cairnes on Exact Economic Laws," in Ingrid H. Rima, ed., *Measurement, Quantification, and Economic Analysis: Numeracy in Economics* (London: Routledge, 1995), 140–156.

2. The beautiful new Folio edition makes reading *Domesday* a pleasure. See Ann Williams and G. H. Martin, eds., *Domesday Book: A Complete Translation* (London: Folio, 2003).

3. P. E. Jones and A. V. Judges, "London Population in the Late Seventeenth Century," *The Economic History Review* (October 1935): 45–63. David Glass, "Two Papers on Gregory King," in *Population in History*, ed. Glass and D. E. C. Eversley, (London: Arnold, 1965), pp. 158–220; and David Glass, *London Inhabitants within the Walls* (London: London Record Society, 1966).

4. See for instance Peter Laslett, "The Study of Social Structure from Listings of Inhabitants," in *English Historical Demography*, ed. E. A. Wrigley, (London: Weidenfeld & Nicoloson, 1966), pp. 160–208, especially pp. 176–177; and also Peter Laslett, "Natural and Political Observations on the Population of Late Seventeenth-Century England: Reflections on the Work of Gregory King and John Graunt," and "Addendum—Criticisms and Revisions of Gregory King's Workings and Results," in *Surveying the People*, ed. Kevin Schurer and Tom Arkell, (Oxford, EN: Leopard's Head Press, 1992), pp. 6–30.

5. G. S. Holmes, "Gregory King and the Social Structure of Pre-Industrial England," *Transactions of the Royal Historical Society*, 5th ser., 27 (1977): 41–68.

6. I am grateful to the British Library for copying for me materials with the following shelf marks: Harl. 6837, Harl. 6832, Harl. 1898, and Harl. 7022.

7. Wolfgang Lutz, Warren Sanderson, and Sergei Scherbov, "The End of World Population Growth," *Nature* 412 (August 2001) 543–545. See also Department of Economic and Social Affairs, Population Division, *Long-Range World Population Projections: Based on the 1998 Revision* (New York: United Nations, 2000).

8. Nico Keilman, "Uncertain Population Forecasts," *Nature* 412 (August 2001): 490–491.

9. David Salsburg, *The Lady Tasting Tea: How Statistics Revolutionized Science in the Twentieth Century* (New York: W. H. Freeman, 2001), pp. 293–294. See also Sir Ronald A. Fisher, "Mathematics of a Lady Tasting Tea," in *The World of Mathematics*, ed. James R. Newman, vol. 3, (New York: Simon and Schuster, 1956), pp. 1512–1523; Newman's work was an anthology whose entire Part VIII, "Statistics and the Design of Experiments," was highly relevant to this discussion because it reprints many crucial early texts including Jacob Bernoulli's "The Law of Large Numbers," Edmund Halley's discussion of the population of Breslau, and John Graunt's study of the London bills of mortality.

10. Stephen M. Stigler, *The History of Statistics: The Measurement of Uncertainty before 1900* (Cambridge, MA: Harvard University Press, 1986), p. 4.

11. Quote from Stigler, *History of Statistics*, pp. 62–66. See Bernoulli's own text, "The Law of Large Numbers," in Newman, *The World of Mathematics*, vol. 3, pp. 1452–1455.

12. This argument is based on Salsburg, *Tea*, pp. 296–301.

13. Salsburg, *Tea*, pp. 142–144.

14. Salsburg, *Tea*, p. 298.

15. Peter Stalker, *The No-Nonsense Guide to International Migration* (London: Verso, 2001), pp. 12–15.

16. For instance, Isaac Newton (1642–1727) said in the final paragraph of his *Optics*, book III, part I, 1704, that he hoped natural philosophy "shall at length be perfected," and that "the bounds of moral philosophy will also be enlarged."

17. F.M.A. Voltaire, *The Elements of Sir Isaac Newton's Philosophy*, tr. John Hanna (New York: Classics of Science, 1995); original edition 1738. "Hard" was a word in common usage in this context, meaning a true or fully scientific scientist, but the word was colloquial, and I apologize if it was unclear to the reader.

18. For up-to-date views, see F. De Gandt, *Force and Geometry in Newton's Principia*, tr. C. Wilson (Princeton, NJ: Princeton University Press, 1995); Patricia Fara, *Newton: The Making of Genius* (New York: Columbia University Press, 2002); and Michael White, *Isaac Newton: The Last Sorcerer* (Reading, MA: Helix, 1997). White stressed the importance of alchemy. An ambitious novel recently depicted Newton more or less as many historians now see him: Neal Stephenson, *Quicksilver* (New York: Morrow, 2003). Various sites on the Internet allow one to read Newton's voluminous alchemical writings and (even more relevant to King) his interpretations of Biblical chronology and prophecy, and experiences with those materials form valuable introductions to the deficiencies of Voltaire's views.

19. For an older view of the history of economics, see William Letwin, *The Origins of Scientific Economics* (Garden City, NJ: Doubleday, 1964).

20. Patrick J. Buchanan, *The Death of the West: How Dying Populations and Immigrant Invasions Imperil Our Country and Civilization* (New York: St Martin's Press, 2002).

21. See also Geoffrey Holmes, *The Making of a Great Power: Late Stuart and Early*

*Georgian Britain 1660–1772* (London: Longman, 1993), especially pp. 44–46, 69–81, and 410–412.

22. Colin Brooks, "Projecting, Political Arithmetic, and the Act of 1695," *English Historical Review*, XCVII (1982): pp. 31–53.

23. See *Encyclopaedia Britannica* (Edinburgh, GB: Bell and Macfarquhar, 1771), index s.v. "arithmetick." While published several decades after King's death, this article is very valuable for understanding his shop arithmetic. I will cite Robert Record, Thomas Everard, and other writers in shop arithmetic whom King might have read. However, this Britannica article differed in no significant way from their works, and I strongly recommend it as the clearest explanation of shop arithmetic that I have seen.

24. John Brewer, *The Sinews of Power: War, Money, and the English State 1688–1783* (Cambridge, MA: Harvard University Press, 1988).

25. http://www.college-of-arms.gov.uk/about/7.htm (accessed May 22, 2002). See *The Dictionary of National Biography on CD-Rom* (Oxford, EN: Oxford University Press, 1995), index s.v. Vanbrugh or Vanburgh, Sir John 1664–1726; and King, Gregory 1648–1712. See also Chalmers on the life of Gregory King, reprinted as a supplement to this book.

26. For instance, Charles Davenant, *Political and Commercial Works*, ed. Sir Charles Whitworth, vol. I, (London: Horsfield, 1771), pp. 125–302.

27. Peter Laslett, ed. *Works by J. Graunt and G. King* (Westmead, EN: Gregg International, 1973). As the pages of this volume are not numbered consecutively, it is difficult to cite it. The volume contains the complete text of King's *Natural and Political Observations*, reprinted from the edition by George Chalmers.

28. Margaret Spufford, "Poverty Portrayed: Gregory King and Eccleshall in Staffordshire in the 1690s," *Staffordshire Studies* 7 (1995): 11.

29. The key document for King is his autobiography, reprinted at the back of this book. See also E.G.R. Taylor, *The Mathematical Practitioners of Tudor and Stuart England* (Cambridge, EN: Cambridge University Press, 1954), pp. 212, 260.

30. Davenant, *Works*, vol. I, p. 138. Cf. Daniel Defoe, *An Essay upon Projects*, ed. Joyce D. Kennedy, Michael Seidel, and M. E. Novak. (New York: AMS, 1999). The remainder of the paragraph follows Joan Thirsk, *Economic Policy and Projects: The Development of a Consumer Society in Early Modern England* (Oxford, EN: Oxford University Press, 1988).

31. See Frances Willmoth, *Sir Jonas Moore: Practical Mathematics and Restoration Science* (Woodbridge, EN: Boydell, 1993); projectors and giddy projects, pp. 88–120.

32. Joseph M. Levine, *Dr. Woodward's Shield: History, Science, and Satire in Augustan England* (Berkeley and Los Angeles: University of California Press, 1977), pp. 16–17. For a general introduction to the late seventeenth century, with an emphasis on the importance of dueling, see Victor Stater, *Duke Hamilton Is Dead* (New York: Hill and Wang, 1999). Gresham College was named after Sir Thomas Gresham (1519–1579), wealthy London merchant, patron of natural philosophy, and founder of the bourse that became the Royal Exchange.

33. L. Stone, *The Crisis of the Aristocracy 1588–1641* (Oxford, EN: Oxford University Press, 1965).

34. Stigler, *History of Statistics*, p. 4.

35. Shichiro Matsukawa, "Origin and Significance of Political Arithmetic," *Annals of the Hitotsubashi Academy* 6 (1955): 53–79.

36. Sir William Petty, *Economic Writings*, ed. C. H. Hull, vol. 2, (Cambridge, EN:

Cambridge University Press, 1899), p. 129. Petty cited Francis Bacon's *Advancement of Learning* as another model of the empirical method.

37. Peter Buck, "People Who Counted: Political Arithmetic in the Eighteenth Century," *Isis* LXXIII (1982), is a valuable introduction to the subject. Buck has shown how much resistance there was in the countryside to government efforts to obtain accurate statistics, especially for incomes.

38. Geoffrey Clark, *Betting on Lives: The Culture of Life Insurance in England, 1695–1775* (New York: Manchester University Press, 1999). See also Peter L. Bernstein, *Against the Gods: The Remarkable Story of Risk* (New York: John Wiley, 1996).

39. Anders Hald, *A History of Probability and Statistics and Their Applications before 1750* (New York: Wiley, 1990), pp. 220–274.

40. Hald, *Probability*, p. 6; on Nicholas Bernoulli's theorem see also pp. 264–267. A binomial has one of two outcomes. On goodness of fit, see also Salsburg, *Tea*, pp. 96–97: "By the twentieth century, mathematicians could test two or more competing mathematical models for reality and use the data to reject one of them." For examples of goodness of fit, see Martin Sternstein, *Statistics* (Hauppauge, NY: Barron's, 1996), pp. 219–231; page 219 supplied the following quotation: "Suppose that a commercial is run once on television, once on radio, and once in a newspaper. The advertising agency believes that any potential customer has a 20 percent chance of seeing the ad on TV, a 20 percent chance of hearing it on the radio, and a 20 percent chance of reading it in the paper. In a telephone survey of 800 customers, the numbers claiming to have been exposed to the ad 0, 1, 2, or 3 times are. . . . "

41. Steven Shapin, *The Scientific Revolution* (Chicago: University of Chicago Press, 1996), p. 3. For a similar view, see also Peter Dear, *Revolutionizing the Sciences: European Knowledge and Its Ambitions, 1500–1700* (Princeton, NJ: Princeton University Press, 2001).

42. Ian Hacking, *The Emergence of Probability: A Philosophical Study of Early Ideas about Probability, Induction, and Statistical Inference* (New York: Cambridge University Press, 1975), p. 28. See also Douglas Lane Patey, *Probability and Literary Form: Philosophic Theory and Literary Practice in the Augustan Age* (Cambridge, EN: Cambridge University Press, 1984), pp. 266–273; Patey said that Hacking's analysis of probability had its roots in the work of Michel Foucault. For an exposition of the older view, see Herbert Butterfield, *The Origins of Modern Science* (London: Bell, 1965), esp. pp. 52–53 on Harvey and the circulation of the blood.

43. Steven Shapin, *A Social History of Truth: Civility and Science in Seventeenth-Century England* (Chicago: University of Chicago Press, 1994), p. xxvii. By the way, on pages 46 and 48 Shapin cited Gregory King's data about social structure.

44. Barbara Shapiro, *A Culture of Fact: England 1550–1720* (Ithaca, NY: Cornell University Press, 2000) and elsewhere has argued persuasively that legal practice shaped the ways that early modern people used the English words "fact" and "probability." Lorraine Daston, *Classical Probability in the Enlightenment* (Princeton, NJ: Princeton University Press, 1988) refined Shapiro's argument and applied it to mathematical probability.

45. Quoted in Hacking, *The Emergence of Probability*, p. 105.

46. Allen G. Debus, *The English Paracelsians* (New York: Watts, 1965); Charles Webster, *From Paracelsus to Newton: Magic and the Making of Modern Science* (New York: Barnes & Noble, 1996).

47. Francis Bacon, *Advancement of Learning, Novum Organum, New Atlantis*, in *Great*

*Books of the Western World* (Chicago: Encyclopaedia Britannica, 1952), p. 114. See also Hacking, *Emergence of Probability*, p. 27; and Ian Hacking, *Representing and Intervening: Introductory Topics in the Philosophy of Natural Science* (Cambridge, EN: Cambridge University Press, 1983), pp. 246–261.

48. Davenant, *Works*, vol. I, p. 130. Davenant said that Petty rather made his court than spoke his mind.

49. Julian Martin, *Francis Bacon, The State, and the Reform of Natural Philosophy* (Cambridge, EN: Cambridge University Press, 1992).

50. The London mathematical world of the 1690s was well described in the first chapter of N. Guicciardini, *The Development of the Newtonian Calculus in Britain 1700–1800* (Cambridge, EN: Cambridge University Press, 1985). Newton was very guarded about his work on fluxions, but he allowed Halley and a few others to glimpse it.

51. Nicholas Barbon, *A Discourse of Trade*, ed. Jacob H. Hollander (Baltimore, MD: Johns Hopkins University Press, 1934); p. 24. See also Andrea Finkelstein, *Harmony and the Balance: An Intellectual History of Seventeenth-Century English Economic Thought* (Ann Arbor: University of Michigan Press, 2000), especially pp. 205–218.

52. This entire discussion of Cheyne relies upon Anita Guerrini, *Obesity and Depression in the Enlightenment: The Life and Times of George Cheyne* (Norman: University of Oklahoma Press, 2000); quote about "Newtonianism" on p. 38.

53. E. Vilquin, "Vauban Inventeur des Recensements," *Annales de Démographie Historique* 1975, pp. 207–257. See also Emmanuel Le Roy Ladurie, "The Chief Defects of Gregory King," in *The Territory of the Historian*, tr. Ben and Siän Reynolds (Chicago: University of Chicago Press, 1979), pp. 180–191. Marco Polo did describe a system of local registers. The Japanese shogun or national governor also collected similar data, as visitors can see in an excellent exhibit at the Edo-Tokyo Museum, Tokyo.

54. Davenant, *Works*, vol. II, p. 175.

55. Thomas Burnet, *The Sacred Theory of the Earth*, introduction by Basil Willey (Carbondale: Southern Illinois University Press, 1965).

56. Levine, *Dr. Woodward's Shield*, p. 26

57. Alan Cutler, *The Seashell on the Mountaintop: A Story of the Humble Genius Who Discovered a New History of the Earth* (Frederick, MD: Recorded Books, 2003).

58. For instance, Peter Dear, *Discipline and Experience: The Mathematical Way in the Scientific Revolution* (Chicago: University of Chicago Press, 1985). p. 9.

59. James Ussher, *The Annals of the World* (London: E. Tyler, 1658) and, by the same author, *The Later Part of the Annals* (London: E. Tyler, 1658). All quotations here are from the unpaged "epistle to the reader" at the beginning of the first volume. For comment on Ussher, see Graham Parry, *The Trophies of Time: English Antiquarians of the Seventeenth Century* (Oxford, EN: Oxford University Press, 1995), pp. 130–156.

60. E. G. Richards, *Mapping Time: The Calendar and Its History* (Oxford, EN: Oxford University Press, 1998), p. 225.

61. James Evans, *The History and Practice of Ancient Astronomy* (New York: Oxford University Press, 1998), pp. 205–207, 245–287. See also F.M.A. Voltaire, *Philosophical Letters*, tr. Ernest Dilworth, (New York: Dover, 2003), pp. 79–85.

62. See Anthony T. Grafton, "Joseph Scaliger and Historical Chronology: The Rise and Fall of a Discipline," *History and Theory*, 14, 2 (1975): 158–185. For a more general introduction, see Charles Webster, *The Great Instauration: Science, Medicine, and Reform 1626–1660* (London: Duckworth, 1975), esp. pp. 25, 119, 120, 246–323. See also

Richard H. Popkin, *The History of Scepticism from Erasmus to Spinoza* (Berkeley and Los Angeles: University of California Press, 1979), esp. pp. 214–228. Cf. Giambattista Vico, *The New Science*, trans. and ed. T. G. Bergin and M. H. Fisch (Ithaca, NY: Cornell University Press, 1968), paragraphs 736–740, pp. 281–284.

63. Michael Hunter, *John Aubrey and the Realm of Learning* (London: Duckworth, 1975), p. 71.

64. Vincent Foster Hopper, *Medieval Number Symbolism: Its Sources, Meaning, and Influence on Thought and Expression* (Mineola, NY: Dover, 2000). This book was first published in 1938.

65. The phrase is from Alfred W. Crosby, *The Measure of Reality: Quantification and Western Society, 1250–1600* (New York: Cambridge University Press, 1997), p. 66.

66. Jacob Klein, *Greek Mathematical Thought and the Origin of Algebra*, trans. Eva Brann (New York: Dover, 1992); see Eva Brann's Translator's Note, pp. vii–ix, for discussion of *quantum* in Latin and *posón* in Greek, words that tell *how many*.

67. Nichomachus of Gerasa, *Introduction to Arithmetic*, in *Great Books of the Western World*, tr. Martin L. Ooge (Chicago: Encyclopaedia Britannica, 1971), see esp. pp. 811–812. On Nichomachus, see Sir Thomas Little Heath, *A Manual of Greek Mathematics* (New York: Dover, 1963), pp. 61–70; Giorgio de Santillana and Walter Pitts, "Philolaos in Limbo, or What Happened to the Pythagoreans?" in *Reflections on Men and Ideas*, ed. Giorgio de Santillana, (Cambridge, MA: M.I.T. Press, 1968), p. 193, quotes from an ancient writer the telling phrase that Pythagorean mathematics was "the theory of proportion and the construction of cosmic figures." See also Allen G. Debus, "Mathematics and Nature in the Chemical Texts of the Renaissance," *Ambix* 13, 1 (February 1968): 1–28; and Ian Mueller, "Mathematics, Earlier Greek," in *Encyclopedia of Classical Philosophy*, ed. Donald J. Zeyl, Daniel T. Devereux and Philip Mitsis. (Westport, CT: Greenwood Press, 1997), pp. 315–322; and Edna Kramer, *The Nature and Growth of Modern Mathematics* (Princeton, NJ: Princeton University Press, 1981), esp. chapters one and two. The distinction between substance and accident is of course Aristotelian.

68. Gerolamo Cardano, *Ars Magna or the Rules of Algebra*, tr. T. Richard Witmer (New York: Dover, 1968), p. 1.

69. Gerolamo Cardano, *The Book on Games of Chance: "Liber de Ludo Aleae,"* tr. Sydney Henry Gould, foreword by Samuel S. Wilks (New York: Holt, Rinehart and Winston, 1961). See Kramer, *Modern Mathematics*, p. 292; Oystein Ore, *Cardano: The Gambling Scholar* (Princeton, NJ: Princeton University Press, 1953).

70. Frank J. Swetz, *Capitalism and Arithmetic: The New Math of the Fifteenth Century* (La Salle, IL: Open Court, 1989). This book contains the full text of the *Treviso Arithmetic* translated by David Eugene Smith. Permit a personal note. A visitor from Singapore, who identified himself as "an overseas Chinese," pointed out that abacus-based trading math continued in wide Asian use. He produced a copy of *The Fundamental Operations in Bead Arithmetic: How to Use the Chinese Abacus* (printed in Hong Kong without mention of author, publisher, or date, but clearly very recent). It gave both a valuable summary of the method and also a brief history. This little book, in effect, was an Asian version of the *Treviso Arithmetic*.

71. Kenneth Charlton and Margaret Spufford, "Literacy, Society, and Education," in *The Cambridge History of Early Modern Literature*, ed. David Loewenstein and Janel Mueller, (Cambridge, EN: Cambridge University Press, 2002), pp. 15–54. I am grateful to Professor Spufford for sending me an advance copy of this valuable essay.

72. In a giant work, Robert Record also used Arabic numbers for magical purposes. See Record, *The Castle of Knowledge* (Amsterdam: Theatrum Orbis Terrarum, 1975). This is a reprint of the London edition of 1556. Record said in his preface that human reason could capture the heavens. He published this book in the reign of Queen Mary I. During that reign, Dee also found employment as a royal astrologer and then subsequently was thrown into prison upon accusations of necromancy.

73. Peter J. French, *John Dee: The World of an Elizabethan Magus* (New York: Ark, 1987), esp. pp. 160–207. French was a student of the great scholar Frances A. Yates, a pioneer in the study of the combination of mathematics and magic. See for instance Frances A. Yates, *Theatre of the World* (Chicago: University of Chicago Press, 1969). However, recent scholars have persuasively cast Dee in a new light, making him less a magician than French or Yates. See for instance William H. Sherman, *John Dee: The Politics of Reading and Writing in the English Renaissance* (Amherst: University of Massachusetts Press, 1995). Whether or not Dee was a full-time magician, he was certainly a mystic. His mathematics were mystical. These questions relate directly to King. Because of the popularity of Record's work, and because of Dee's introduction to it, we may presume that King had some knowledge of Dee. Yet nothing of this mysticism was to be found in King's demographic calculations. I think that absence was a mark of King's mastery and skill in shop arithmetic.

74. John Dee, *The Mathematica Preface to the Elements of Geometrie of Euclid of Megara (1570)*, ed. with an introduction by Allen G. Debus (New York: Science History Publications, 1975). See also John Dee, *On Astronomy*, tr. Wayne Shumaker, with an introduction by J. L. Heilbron (Berkeley and Los Angeles: University of California Press, 1978).

75. Robert Record, *Records Arithmetic or, The Ground of Arts*, ed. and enlarged by John Dee (London: Fletcher, 1668). I am grateful to my university library for finding this rare book but also regret that no earlier edition was available to us. The *Dictionary of National Biography* spelled the name with a final *e*, but his printed books spelled it *Record*.

76. Francis B. Johnson and Sanford V. Larkey, "Robert Record's Mathematical Teaching and the Anti-Aristotelian Movement," *The Huntington Library Bulletin* 7 (1935): 59–87.

77. D. R. Woolf, *The Idea of History in Early Stuart England* (Toronto: University of Toronto Press, 1990), p. 242; see also Woolf's discussion of Bacon's influence on antiquarians, pp. 146–158.

78. John Prideaux, *An Easy and Compendious Introduction for Reading All Sorts of Histories* (Oxford, EN: Lichfield, 1682). This book states itself to be the sixth edition.

79. Randall Collins, *The Sociology of Philosophies: A Global Theory of Intellectual Change* (Cambridge, MA: Harvard University Press, 1998).

80. Margery Purver, *The Royal Society: Concept and Creation* (Cambridge, MA: MIT Press, 1965).

81. Brian W. Hill, *Robert Harley: Speaker, Secretary of State, and Prime Minister* (New Haven, CT: Yale University Press, 1988).

82. Betty A. Schellenberg, *The Conversational Circle: Re-reading the English Novel 1770–1775* (Lexington: University Press of Kentucky, 1996). This book was very helpful. Professor Schellenberg also kindly took the time to reply to questions that I sent her, and I am very grateful.

83. Quoted in Schellenberg, *Circle*, p. 18.

84. Sociologist Norbert Elias wrote about the influence on intellectuals from royal courts. See Johan Goudsblom and Stephen Mennell, eds., *The Norbert Elias Reader* (Oxford, EN: Blackwell, 1998).

85. Quoted in Schellenberg, *Circle*, p. 1.

86. Anne Goldgar, *Impolite Learning: Conduct and Community in the Republic of Letters 1680–1750* (New Haven, CT: Yale University Press, 1995).

87. Davenant, *Works*, vol. I, p. 135.

88. See Sir William Petty, *Economic Writings*, ed. Charles Henry Hull, vol. 1, (Cambridge, EN: Cambridge University Press, 1899), p. 249.

89. J.G.A. Pocock, *The Machiavellian Moment: Florentine Political Thought and the Atlantic Republican Tradition* (Princeton, NJ: Princeton University Press, 1975), see the index s.v. Davenant. See also J.G.A. Pocock, *Virtue, Commerce, and History* (Cambridge, EN: Cambridge University Press, 1985), p. 231

90. See Davenant, *Works*, vol. II, p. 216. See also Davenant, *Works*, vol. I, p. 287.

91. Charles Davenant, *Political and Commercial Works*, ed. Sir Charles Whitworth, vol. IV, (London: Horsfield, 1771), p. 169.

92. Thomas Everard, *Stereometry, or, the Art of Gauging Made Easie, by the Help of a Sliding-Rule Which Shews the Area's [sic] of Circles in Gallon, and the Square and Cube-Root of Any Number under 100000, by Inspection, with an Appendix of Conick Sections* (London: R. Clavel, 1703).

93. See Michael Baxandall, *Painting and Experience in Fifteenth-Century Italy* (Oxford, EN: Oxford University Press, 1988).

94. See John Blagrave, *Baculum Familiare* (New York: Da Capo Press, 1970), original edition 1590; and William Leybourn, *The Compleat Surveyor* (London: G. Sawbridge, 1657); see also F.M.L. Thompson, *Chartered Surveyors: The Growth of a Profession* (London: Routledge & Kegan Paul, 1968).

95. Baxandall, *Painting and Experience in Fifteenth-Century Italy*, pp. 81–108.

96. Quoted in *Goldgar*, *Republic*, p. 28.

97. John Chamberlayne, *Magna Britannia Notitia: or, the Present State of Great Britain with Divers Remarks upon the Ancient State Thereof* (London: Timothy Goodwin, 1710), p. 27. I am grateful to the Thomas Jefferson Library of the University of Missouri Saint Louis for the extended loan of a copy of this rare book. King's letter to Chamberlayne is in the collection of King's papers at the Dr. Johnson Museum, Lichfield, mentioned in the next chapter. I am grateful to the Dr. Johnson Museum for Xerox copies of the Gregory King materials in their collection, and my citations are from those copies.

98. I have tried to track this firm, and I presume that it is Meyers and Company, 80 New Bond Street, Mayfair W1.

99. See L. M. Beattie, *John Arbuthnot* (New York: Russell, 1967), esp. pp. 326–346. See also G. A. Aitken, *The Life and Works of John Arbuthnot* (New York: Russell, 1968), pp. 421–422.

100. G.F.A. Best, *Temporal Pillars, Queen Anne's Bounty, the Ecclesiastical Commissioners, and the Church of England* (Cambridge, EN: Cambridge University Press, 1964), p. 525.

101. For a history of these matters, the reader should consult Alan Savidge, *The Foundation and Early Years of Queen Anne's Bounty* (London: SPCK, 1955). Seen also Ian Green, "The First Five Years of Queen Anne's Bounty," in *Princes and Paupers in*

*the English Church, 1500–1800*, ed. R. O'Day and F. Heal, (Towata, NJ: Barnes & Noble, 1981), pp. 231–254.

102. Cf. Donald E. Ginter, *A Measure of Wealth: The English Land Tax in Historical Analysis* (Montreal and Kingston: McGill-Queen's, 1992), see esp. "major problems," pp. 30–51.

103. John Ecton, *Liber Valorum and Decimarum, Being an Account of Such Ecclesiastical Benefices in England and Wales As Now Stand Charged with or Lately were Discharged from the Payment of First Fruits and Tenths* (London: R. Gosling, 1723). See also John Bacon, *Liber Regis Thesaurus Ecclesiasticarum* (London: Bacon, 1736).

104. David Ogg, *England in the Reigns of James II and William III* (Oxford, EN: Oxford University Press, 1969), pp. 30–6. In the paragraph that follows, I echo Ogg's summary of Glass. See Chapter 11 for a discussion of Jones and Judges upon whose prior research Glass constructed much of his analysis of King.

105. Margaret Spufford, *The Potential of the Hearth Tax Returns* (London: British Association for Local History, 2000). This pamphlet republished an edited text of the 2000 Phillimore Lecture, and the same material appeared in *The Local Historian* 30, 4 (November 2000); see discussion of Gregory King, p. 5. Having studied hearth tax records throughout her career, Professor Spufford skillfully established their value for historians, and she recently established an ongoing project for the collection and publication of hearth data.

106. Jones and Judges, "London Population in the Late Seventeenth Century," pp. 45–63.

107. Quoted in Kevin Schurer, "Variations in Household Structure in the Seventeenth Century: Toward a Regional Analysis," in *Surveying the People*, ed. Schurer and Arkell p. 253; see also Peter Laslett and Richard Wall, eds., *Household and Family in Past Time* (Cambridge, EN: Cambridge University Press, 1972), the seminal work.

108. See Chris Husbands, "Hearths, Wealth and Occupations: An Exploration of the Hearth Tax in the later Seventeenth Century," in *Surveying the People*, ed. Schurer and Arkell, pp. 65–77.

109. Elona Cuthbertson, *Gregory King's Harefield: An English Village in the 1690's* (Uxbridge, EN: Hillingdon Borough Libraries, 1992).

110. Richard Wall, "England: Mean Household Size from Printed Sources," in *Household and Family in Past Time*, ed. Laslett and Wall, p.164.

111. This appears in the margin of manuscript page 89 of King's "Burns Journal," printed in Laslett, *The Earliest Classics*, Westmead, EN: Gregg International, 1973. The formula would be $x + 2y + y/20$.

112. John Napier, *The Construction of the Wonderful Canon of Logarithms* (New York: Gryphon Editions, 1997), pp. 12–13. James Ussher had a better cause to know logarithms than did King because the mathematician Henry Briggs was an intermediary between Napier and James Ussher's younger brother, Ambrose Ussher.

113. John A. Taylor, *British Monarchy, English Church Establishment, and Civil Liberty* (Westport, CT: Greenwood Press, 1996), esp. pp. 91–105.

114. Collins, *Sociology of Philosophies*, see index s.v. "Law of Small Numbers," echoed Fisher's predecessor, Jacob Bernoulli, who spoke of the Law of Large Numbers. Bernoulli meant that, as one increased the number of trials, one saw more clearly the probabilities involved in a process on trial. If one increased the number of trials of a particular medical intervention, for instance, one saw more clearly the probability that it was (or was not) beneficial. Borrowing the phrase from Bernoulli and inverting it,

Collins spoke instead of the Law of Small Numbers. He thought that was a identifiable general process with rules. Schools of philosophy reduced themselves from many to few.

115. Remember that seventeenth-century mathematical probability presumed a determined material universe. Chapter 1 dealt with that point.

116. Nieves Mathews, *Francis Bacon: The History of a Character Assassination* (New Haven, CT: Yale University Press, 1996).

117. Robert Schware, *Quantification in the History of Political Thought: Toward a Qualitative Approach* (Westport, CT: Greenwood Press, 1981), pp. 55–82.

118. Francis Bacon, *Essays*, ed. J. Pitcher (New York: Penguin, 1992), p. 148. See also Markku Peltonen, "Politics and Science: Frances Bacon and the True Greatness of States," *The Historical Journal* 35, 2 (1992): 279–305. Peltonen argued that the essay on the true greatness of states was not a part of Bacon's larger scientific program. Instead, the true greatness essay related to ancient republican theory.

119. Philip Kreager, "New Light on Graunt," *Population Studies*, 42 (1988): 129–140.

120. Quentin Skinner, *Reason and Rhetoric in the Philosophy of Thomas Hobbes* (Cambridge, EN: Cambridge University Press, 1996).

121. John Aubrey, *Brief Lives*, ed. Oliver Lawson Dick (London: Secker & Warburg, 1968), p. 150.

122. Ezio Vailati and Paolo Mancosu, "Torricelli's Infinitely Long Solid and Its Reception in the Seventeenth Century," *Isis* 82 (1991): 50–70.

123. Helen M. Pycior, "Mathematics and Philosophy: Wallis, Hobbes, Barrow, and Berkeley" *Journal of the History of Ideas* (1987): 265–286.

124. Douglas M. Jesseph, *Berkeley's Philosophy of Mathematics* (Chicago: University of Chicago Press, 1993). See also Theodore Messenger, "Berkeley and Tymoczko on Mystery in Mathematics," in *Berkeley: Critical and Interpretive Essays*, ed. Colin M. Turbayne,(Manchester, EN: Manchester University Press, 1982), pp. 83–94.

125. Mark Balaguer, *Platonism and Anti-Platonism in Mathematics* (New York: Oxford University Press, 1998).

126. Richard Courant and Herbert Robbins, revised Ian Stewart, *What Is Mathematics?* (New York: Oxford University Press, 1996); original edition 1941; see also Reuben Hersh, *What Is Mathematics, Really?* (New York: Oxford University Press, 1997).

127. Julian Hoppit, "Political Arithmetic in Eighteenth-Century England," *Economic History Review* 49, 3 (1996): 516–540, quote from p. 516.

128. A. M. Endres, "The Functions of Numerical Data in the Writings of Graunt, Petty, and Davenant," *History of Political Economy* 17, 2, (1985): 245–264.

129. Adam Smith, *Correspondence*, ed. E. C. Mossner and I. Ross (Oxford, EN: Oxford University Press, 1987), p. 288.

130. See Dumas Malone, *The Public Life of Thomas Cooper 1783–1839* (New Haven, CT: Yale University Press, 1926).

131. Karin Johannisson, "Society in Numbers: The Debate over Quantification in Eighteenth-Century Political Economy," in *The Quantifying Spirit in the Eighteenth Century*, ed. Tore Frangsmyr, J. L. Heilbron, and Robin E. Rider, (Berkeley: University of California Press, 1990), pp. 343–361. See also Theodore M. Porter, *The Rise of Statistical Thinking 1820–1900* (Princeton, NJ: Princeton University Press, 1986), pp. 18–39.

132. This account follows Grace Amelia Cockroft, *The Public Life of George Chalmers* (New York: Columbia University Press, 1939).

133. Ingrid H. Rima, introduction to *Measurement, Quantification, and Economic Analysis*, "nefarious" on p. 10; see also R. W. Dimand, "'I Have no Great Faith in Political Arithmetic,' Adam Smith and Quantitative Political Economy," in *Measurement, Quantification, and Economic Analysis*, ed., Rima, pp. 22–30.

134. George Chalmers, *Considerations on Commerce, Bullion, and Coins* (New York: Kelley, 1969). The original edition appeared in 1811.

135. For an interesting comment from the perspective of 1875, see W. S. Lindsay, *History of Merchant Shipping and Ancient Commerce*, vol. II (New York: AMS Press, 1965), p. 256. Lindsay remarked that American diplomats in London pleaded for free trade as a principle while their own government at home strictly regulated British shipping in practice.

136. This account follows Rosalind Mitchison, *Agricultural Sir John: The Life of Sir John Sinclair of Ulbster* (London: Geoffrey Bles, 1962).

137. J. G. Lockhart, *Memoirs of Sir Walter Scott*, vol. II, (London: Macmillan, 1914), p. 197.

138. The same quote appeared, together with a discussion of Sinclair, in Ian Hacking, *The Taming of Chance* (Cambridge, EN: Cambridge University Press, 1990), pp. 16–26. The quotation was from Sir J. Sinclair, *Statistical Account of Scotland*, vol. XX, App. p. xiii, 1798.

139. Roy Porter, *English Society in the Eighteenth Century* (London: Penguin, 1990), pp. 12, 14, 48, 68, 70–71, 82, 143, 204; the quotations below are from pp. 14 and 48.

140. Stephen M. Stigler, "Jevons on the King-Davenant Law of Demand: A Simple Resolution of a Historical Puzzle" *History of Political Economy* 26, 2 (Summer 1994): 185–191. See also Victor Rouguet La Garrigue, *Les Problèmes de la Corrélation et de l'Élasticité Étude Théorique autour de la Loi de King* (Paris: Hermann & Cie., 1948).

141. Cf. Joseph C. Pitt, "Galilei, Galileo," in *Encyclopedia of Empiricism*, ed. Don Garrett and Edward Barbanell, (Westport, CT: Greenwood Press, 1997), pp. 112–113. Pitt remarked that Galileo did not know the term *empirical* and therefore could not have applied it to his work. If we apply it, we do so without his blessing. However, we are justified in thinking that Galileo used a "fairly basic" empiricism based, first, on a preference for observation over dogmatic assertion, a preference that led, second, to his rejection of occult causes. He also strongly favored mathematics as a method of analysis in natural philosophy. His rejection of Aristotle's notions of causation was no doubt influential for Bacon and others.

142. J. L. Heilbron, *Geometry Civilized: History, Culture, and Technique* (New York: Oxford University Press, 1998); see also Michael Sharratt, *Galileo: Decisive Innovator* (Cambridge, EN: Cambridge University Press, 1994).

# Select Bibliography

* Denotes materials especially suited for someone who is new to reading Gregory King's contributions to political economy.

Aitken, G. A. *The Life and Works of John Arbuthnot.* New York: Russell, 1968.

Bacon, Francis. *Works*, ed. Brian Vickers. Oxford, EN: Oxford University Press, 1996.

Bacon, John. *Liber Regis Thesaurus Ecclesiasticarum.* London: Bacon, 1736.

Balaguer, Mark. *Platonism and Anti-Platonism in Mathematics.* New York: Oxford University Press, 1998.

Barbon, Nicholas. *A Discourse of Trade*, ed. Jacob H. Hollander. Baltimore, MD: Johns Hopkins University Press, 1934.

Baxandall, Michael. *Painting and Experience in Fifteenth-Century Italy.* Oxford, EN: Oxford University Press, 1988.

Bernstein, Peter L. *Against the Gods: The Remarkable Story of Risk.* New York: John Wiley, 1996.

Best, G.F.A. *Temporal Pillars, Queen Anne's Bounty, the Ecclesiastical Commissioners, and the Church of England.* Cambridge, EN: Cambridge University Press, 1964.

Biagioli, Mario. *Galileo Courtier: The Practice of Science in the Culture of Absolutism.* Chicago: University of Chicago Press, 1993.

Blagrave, John. *Baculum Familiare.* New York: Da Capo Press, 1970.

*Buck, Peter. "People Who Counted: Political Arithmetic in the Eighteenth Century." *Isis* LXXIII (1982).

Burnet, Thomas. *The Sacred Theory of the Earth*, introduction by Basil Willey. Carbondale: Southern Illinois University Press, 1965.

Butterfield, Herbert. *The Origins of Modern Science.* London: Bell, 1965.

*Brewer, John. *The Sinews of Power: War, Money, and the English State 1688–1783.* Cambridge, MA: Harvard University Press, 1988.

*Brooks, Colin. "Projecting, Political Arithmetic, and the Act of 1695." *English Historical Review* XCVII (1982): 31–53.

Cardano, Gerolamo. *Ars Magna or the Rules of Algebra*, tr. T. Richard Witmer. New York: Dover, 1968.

———. *The Book on Games of Chance: "Liber de Ludo Aleae,"* tr. Sydney Henry Gould, foreword by Samuel S. Wilks. New York: Holt, Rinehart and Winston, 1961.

Chalmers, George. *Considerations on Commerce, Bullion, and Coins*. New York: Kelley, 1969.

Chamberlayne, John. *Magna Britannia Notitia: or, the Present State of Great Britain with Divers Remarks upon the Ancient State Thereof*. London: Timothy Goodwin, 1710.

*Charlton, Kenneth, and Margaret Spufford. "Literacy, Society, and Education." In *The Cambridge History of Early Modern Literature*, ed. David Loewenstein and Janel Mueller. Cambridge, EN: Cambridge University Press, 2002, pp. 15–54.

Clark, Geoffrey. *Betting on Lives: The Culture of Life Insurance in England, 1695–1775*. New York: Manchester University Press, 1999.

Cockroft, Grace Amelia. *The Public Life of George Chalmers*. New York: Columbia University Press, 1939.

Cohen, I. B. *Introduction to Isaac Newton's Principia*. Cambridge, MA: Harvard University Press, 1971.

*Collins, Randall. *The Sociology of Philosophies: A Global Theory of Intellectual Change*. Cambridge, MA: Harvard University Press, 1998.

Coster, Will. *Family and Kingship in England 1450–1800*. New York: Longman, 2001.

Courant, Richard, and Herbert Robbins, revised Ian Stewart. *What Is Mathematics?* New York: Oxford University Press, 1996.

Crosby, Alfred W. *The Measure of Reality: Quantification and Western Society 1250–1600*. New York: Cambridge University Press, 1997.

*Cuthbertson, E. *Gregory King's Harefield: An English Village in the 1690's*. Uxbridge, EN: Hillingdon Borough Libraries, 1992.

Cutler, Alan. *The Seashell on the Mountaintop: A Story of the Humble Genius Who Discovered a New History of the Earth*. Frederick, MD: Recorded Books, 2003.

*Darcy, R., and Richard C. Rohrs. *A Guide to Quantitative History*. Westport, CT: Praeger Press, 1995.

Daston, Lorraine. *Classical Probability in the Enlightenment*. Princeton, NJ: Princeton University Press, 1988.

*Davenant, Charles. *Political and Commercial Works*, ed. Sir Charles Whitworth. London: Horsfield, 1771.

De Gandt, F. *Force and Geometry in Newton's Principia*, tr. C. Wilson. Princeton, NJ: Princeton University Press, 1995.

Dear, Peter. *Discipline and Experience: The Mathematical Way in the Scientific Revolution*. Chicago: University of Chicago Press, 1985.

———. *Revolutionizing the Sciences: European Knowledge and Its Ambitions, 1500–1700*. Princeton, NJ: Princeton University Press, 2001.

Debus, Allen G. *The English Paracelsians*. New York: Watts, 1965.

———. "Mathematics and Nature in the Chemical Texts of the Renaissance." *Ambix* 13, 1 (February 1968): 1–28.

Dee, John. *The Mathematica Preface to the Elements of Geometrie of Euclid of Megara (1570)*, ed. with an introduction by Allen G. Debus. New York: Science History Publications, 1975.

———. *On Astronomy*, tr. Wayne Shumaker, with an introduction by J. L. Heilbron. Berkeley and Los Angeles: University of California Press, 1978.

Dunn, John, J. O. Urmson, and A. J. Ayer. *The British Empiricists*. New York: Oxford University Press, 1992.

Ecton, John. *Liber Valorum and Decimarum, Being an Account of Such Ecclesiastical Benefices in England and Wales As Now Stand Charged with or Lately Were Discharged from the Payment of First Fruits and Tenths*. London: R. Gosling, 1723.

*Endres, A. M. "The Functions of Numerical Data in the Writings of Graunt, Petty, and Davenant." *History of Political Economy* 17, 2 (1985): 245–264.

*Evans, G. Heberton, Jr. "The Law of Demand—The Roles of Gregory King and Charles Davenant." *The Quarterly Journal of Economics* 81 (1967): 483–492.

Evans, James. *The History and Practice of Ancient Astronomy*. New York: Oxford University Press, 1998.

Everard, Thomas. *Stereometry, or, the Art of Gauging Made Easie, by the Help of a Sliding-Rule Which Shews the Area's [sic] of Circles in Gallon, and the Square and Cube-Root of Any Number under 100000, by Inspection, with an Appendix of Conick Sections*. London: R. Clavel, 1703.

Fara, Patricia. *Newton: The Making of Genius*. New York: Columbia University Press, 2002.

Field, J. V. *The Invention of Infinity: Mathematics and Art in the Renaissance*. New York: Oxford University Press, 1997.

*Finkelstein, Andrea. *Harmony and the Balance: An Intellectual History of Seventeenth-Century English Economic Thought*. Ann Arbor: University of Michigan Press, 2000.

Frangsmyr, Tore, J. L. Heilbron, and Robin E. Rider, eds. *The Quantifying Spirit in the Eighteenth Century*. Berkeley: University of California Press, 1990.

French, Peter J. *John Dee: The World of an Elizabethan Magus*. New York: Ark, 1987.

Garrett, Don, and Edward Barbanell, eds. *Encyclopedia of Empiricism*. Westport, CT: Greenwood Press, 1997.

Ginter, Donald E. *A Measure of Wealth: The English Land Tax in Historical Analysis*. Montreal and Kingston: McGill-Queen's, 1992.

*Glass, David. *London Inhabitants within the Walls*. London: London Record Society, 1966.

*Glass, David, and D.E.C. Eversley, eds. *Population in History*. London: Arnold, 1965, pp. 158–220.

Glendinning, Victoria. *Jonathan Swift: A Portrait*. New York: Holt, 1998.

Goldgar, Anne. *Impolite Learning: Conduct and Community in the Republic of Letters 1680–1750*. New Haven, CT: Yale University Press, 1995.

Grafton, Anthony T. "Joseph Scaliger and Historical Chronology: The Rise and Fall of a Discipline." *History and Theory* 14, 2 (1975): 158–185.

Guerrini, Anita. *Obesity and Depression in the Enlightenment: The Life and Times of George Cheyne*. Norman: University of Oklahoma Press, 2000.

Guicciardini, N. *The Development of the Newtonian Calculus in Britain 1700–1800*. Cambridge, EN: Cambridge University Press, 1985.

*Hacking, Ian. *The Emergence of Probability: A Philosophical Study of Early Ideas about Probability, Induction, and Statistical Inference*. New York: Cambridge University Press, 1975.

———. *Representing and Intervening: Introductory Topics in the Philosophy of Natural Science.* Cambridge, EN: Cambridge University Press, 1983.

*———. *The Taming of Chance.* Cambridge, EN: Cambridge University Press, 1990.

*Hald, Anders. *A History of Probability and Statistics and their Applications before 1750.* New York: Wiley, 1990.

Heath, Sir Thomas Little. *A Manual of Greek Mathematics.* New York: Dover, 1963.

Heilbron, J. L. *Geometry Civilized: History, Culture, and Technique.* New York: Oxford University Press, 1998.

Hersh, Reuben. *What Is Mathematics, Really?* New York: Oxford University Press, 1997.

*Hill, Brian W. *Robert Harley: Speaker, Secretary of State, and Prime Minister.* New Haven, CT: Yale University Press, 1988.

Hobbes, Thomas. *Correspondence*, ed. Noel Malcolm. Oxford, EN: Oxford University Press, 1994.

Holmes, G. S. "Gregory King and the Social Structure of Pre-Industrial England." *Transactions of the Royal Historical Society*, 5th ser., 27 (1977): 41–68.

———. *The Making of a Great Power: Late Stuart and Early Georgian Britain 1660–1772.* London: Longman, 1993.

Hopper, Vincent Foster. *Medieval Number Symbolism: Its Sources, Meaning, and Influence on Thought and Expression.* Mineola, NY: Dover, 2000.

*Hoppit, Julian. "Political Arithmetic in Eighteenth-Century England." *Economic History Review* 49, 3 (1996): 516–540.

Hunter, Michael. *John Aubrey and the Realm of Learning.* London: Duckworth, 1975.

———. *Science and Society in Restoration England.* Cambridge, EN: Cambridge University Press, 1981.

Jesseph, Douglas M. *Berkeley's Philosophy of Mathematics.* Chicago: University of Chicago Press, 1993.

*Johnson, Francis B., and Sanford V. Larkey, "Robert Record's Mathematical Teaching and the Anti-Aristotelian Movement." *The Huntington Library Bulletin* 7 (1935): 59–87.

*Jones, P. E., and A. V. Judges. "London Population in the Late Seventeenth Century." *The Economic History Review* (October 1935): 45–63.

Keilman, Nico. "Uncertain Population Forecasts." *Nature* 412 (August 2001): 490–491.

Klein, Jacob. *Greek Mathematical Thought and the Origin of Algebra*, trans. Eva Brann. New York: Dover, 1992.

Koyré, A. *The Astronomical Revolution*, tr. R. Maddison. New York: Dover, 1973.

*Kramer, Edna. *The Nature and Growth of Modern Mathematics.* Princeton, NJ: Princeton University Press, 1981.

*Kreager, Philip. "New Light on Graunt." *Population Studies* 42 (1988): 129–140.

Ladurie, Emmanuel Le Roy. "The Chief Defects of Gregory King." In *The Territory of the Historian*, tr. Ben Reynolds and Siän Reynolds. Chicago: University of Chicago Press, 1979.

La Garrigue, Victor Rouguet. *Les Problèmes de la Corrélation et de l'Élasticité Étude Théorique autour de la Loi de King.* Paris: Hermann & Cie., 1948.

*Laslett, Peter. *The Earliest Classics.* Westmead, EN: Gregg International, 1973.

———. *The World We Have Lost.* London: Methuen, 1971.

*Laslett, Peter, and Richard Wall, eds. *Household and Family in Past Time*. Cambridge, EN: Cambridge University Press, 1972.

Letwin, William. *The Origins of Scientific Economics*. Garden City, NJ: Doubleday, 1964.

Levine, Joseph M. *Dr. Woodward's Shield: History, Science, and Satire in Augustan England*. Berkeley and Los Angeles: University of California Press, 1977.

Leybourn, William. *The Compleat Surveyor*. London: G. Sawbridge, 1657.

Lindsay, W. S. *History of Merchant Shipping and Ancient Commerce*. New York: AMS Press, 1965.

Lutz, Wolfgang, Warren Sanderson, and Sergei Scherbov. "The End of World Population Growth." *Nature* 412 (August 2001): 543–545.

Malone, Dumas. *The Public Life of Thomas Cooper 1783–1839*. New Haven, CT: Yale University Press, 1926.

Mancosu, Paolo. *Philosophy of Mathematics and Mathematical Practice in the Seventeenth Century*. Oxford, EN: Oxford University Press, 1996.

Mancosu, Paolo, and Vailati, Ezio. "Torricelli's Infinitely Long Solid and Its Philosophical Reception in the Seventeenth Century." *Isis* 82 (1991): 50–70.

*Martin, Julian. *Francis Bacon, The State, and the Reform of Natural Philosophy*. Cambridge, EN: Cambridge University Press, 1992.

Mathias, Peter, ed. *Science and Society 1600–1900*. Cambridge, EN: Cambridge University Press, 1972.

*Matsukawa, Shichiro. "Origin and Significance of Political Arithmetic." *Annals of the Hitotsubashi Academy* 6 (1955): 53–79.

Merton, Robert K. *Science, Technology and Society in Seventeenth Century England*. New York: Fertig, 1970.

Mitchison, Rosalind. *Agricultural Sir John: The Life of Sir John Sinclair of Ulbster*. London: Geoffrey Bles, 1962.

Mueller, Ian. "Mathematics, Earlier Greek." In *Encyclopedia of Classical Philosophy*, ed. Donald J. Zeyl, Daniel T. Devereux, and Philip Mitsis. Westport, CT: Greenwood Press, 1997, pp. 315–322.

Napier, John. *The Construction of the Wonderful Canon of Logarithms*. New York: Gryphon Editions, 1997.

*Newman, James R. *The World of Mathematics*. New York: Simon and Schuster, 1956.

Nichomachus of Gerasa, "Introduction to Arithmetic." In *Great Books of the Western World*, tr. Martin L. Ooge. Chicago: Encyclopaedia Britannica, 1971.

O'Day, R., and F. Heal, eds. *Princes and Paupers in the English Church, 1500–1800*. Towata, NJ: Barnes & Noble, 1981.

Ogg, David. *England in the Reigns of James II and William III*. Oxford, EN: Oxford University Press, 1969.

Ore, Oystein. *Cardano: The Gambling Scholar*. Princeton, NJ: Princeton University Press, 1953.

Osler, Margaret J., ed. *Rethinking the Scientific Revolution*. Cambridge, EN: Cambridge University Press, 2000.

*Parry, Graham. *The Trophies of Time: English Antiquarians of the Seventeenth Century*. Oxford, EN: Oxford University Press, 1995.

Patey, Douglas Lane. *Probability and Literary Form: Philosophic Theory and Literary Practice in the Augustan Age*. Cambridge, EN: Cambridge University Press, 1984.

Peltonen, Markku. *Classical Humanism and Republicanism in English Political Thought 1570–1640*. Cambridge, EN: Cambridge University Press, 1995.

———. "Politics and Science: Frances Bacon and the True Greatness of States." *The Historical Journal* 35, 2 (1992): 279–305.
———, ed. *The Cambridge Companion to Bacon*. Cambridge, EN: Cambridge University Press, 1996.
*Petty, Sir William. *Economic Writings*, ed. C. H. Hull. Cambridge, EN: Cambridge University Press, 1899.
Poovey, Mary. *A History of the Modern Fact: Problems of Knowledge in the Sciences of Wealth and Society*. Chicago: University of Chicago Press, 1998.
Popkin, Richard H. *The History of Scepticism from Erasmus to Spinoza*. Berkeley and Los Angeles: University of California Press, 1979.
*Porter, Roy. *English Society in the Eighteenth Century*. London: Penguin, 1990.
Porter, Theodore M. *The Rise of Statistical Thinking 1820–1900*. Princeton, NJ: Princeton University Press, 1986.
Prideaux, John. *An Easy and Compendious Introduction for Reading all sorts of Histories*. Oxford, EN: Lichfield, 1682.
Purver, Margery. *The Royal Society: Concept and Creation*. Cambridge, MA: MIT Press, 1965.
Pycior, Helen M. "Mathematics and Philosophy: Wallis, Hobbes, Barrow, and Berkeley." *Journal of the History of Ideas* (1987): 265–286.
Record, Robert. *The Castle of Knowledge*. Amsterdam: Theatrum Orbis Terrarum, 1975.
*———. *Records Arithmetic or, The Ground of Arts*, ed. and enlarged by John Dee. London: Fletcher, 1668.
Richards, E. G. *Mapping Time: The Calendar and Its History*. Oxford, EN: Oxford University Press, 1998.
*Rima, Ingrid H., ed. *Measurement, Quantification, and Economic Analysis: Numeracy in Economics*. London: Routledge, 1995.
*Salsburg, David. *The Lady Tasting Tea: How Statistics Revolutionized Science in the Twentieth Century*. New York: W. H. Freeman, 2001.
*Santillana, Giorgio de. *Reflections on Men and Ideas*. Cambridge, MA: M.I.T. Press. 1968.
Savidge, Alan. *The Foundation and Early Years of Queen Anne's Bounty*. London: SPCK, 1955.
Schellenberg, Betty A. *The Conversational Circle: Re-reading the English Novel 1770–1775*. Lexington: University Press of Kentucky, 1996.
*Schurer, Kevin, and Arkell, Tom, eds. *Surveying the People*. Oxford, EN: Leopard's Head Press, 1992.
*Schware, Robert. *Quantification in the History of Political Thought: Toward a Qualitative Approach*. Westport, CT: Greenwood Press, 1981.
Seife, Charles. *Zero: The Biography of a Dangerous Idea*. New York: Viking, 2000.
*Shapin, Steven. *The Scientific Revolution*. Chicago: University of Chicago Press, 1996, p. 3.
*———. *A Social History of Truth: Civility and Science in Seventeenth-Century England*. Chicago: University of Chicago Press, 1994.
Shapiro, Barbara. "The Concept of 'Fact': Legal Origins and Cultural Diffusion." *Albion* 6 (1994): 227–252.
*———. *A Culture of Fact: England 1550–1720*. Ithaca, NY: Cornell University Press, 2000.

Sharratt, Michael. *Galileo: Decisive Innovator.* Cambridge, EN: Cambridge University Press, 1994.
Sherman, William H. *John Dee: The Politics of Reading and Writing in the English Renaissance.* Amherst: University of Massachusetts Press, 1995.
Siraisi, Nancy. *The Clock and the Mirror: Girolamo Cardano and Renaissance Medicine.* Princeton, NJ: Princeton University Press, 1997.
Skinner, Q. *Reason and Rhetoric in the Philosophy of Hobbes.* Cambridge, EN: Cambridge University Press, 1996.
Smith, Adam. *Correspondence,* ed. E. C. Mossner and I. Ross. Oxford, EN: Oxford University Press, 1987.
Sorell, Tom, ed. *The Cambridge Companion to Hobbes.* Cambridge, EN: Cambridge University Press, 1996.
*Spufford, Margaret. *The Potential of the Hearth Tax Returns.* London: British Association for Local History, 2000.
*———. "Poverty Portrayed: Gregory King and Eccleshall in Staffordshire in the 1690s." *Staffordshire Studies* 7 (1995).
Stalker, Peter. *The No-Nonsense Guide to International Migration.* London: Verso, 2001.
Stater, Victor. *Duke Hamilton Is Dead.* New York: Hill and Wang, 1999.
*Stigler, Stephen M. *The History of Statistics: The Measurement of Uncertainty before 1900.* Cambridge, MA: Harvard University Press, 1986.
*———. "Jevons on the King-Davenant Law of Demand: A Simple Resolution of a Historical Puzzle." *History of Political Economy* 26, 2 (Summer 1994): 185–191.
Stone, L. *The Crisis of the Aristocracy 1588–1641.* Oxford, EN: Oxford University Press, 1965.
*Swetz, Frank J. *Capitalism and Arithmetic: The New Math of the Fifteenth Century.* La Salle, IL: Open Court, 1989.
Taylor, E.G.R. *The Mathematical Practitioners of Tudor and Stuart England.* Cambridge, EN: Cambridge University Press, 1954.
*Thirsk, Joan. *Economic Policy and Projects: The Development of a Consumer Society in Early Modern England.* Oxford, EN: Oxford University Press, 1988.
Thompson, F.M.L. *Chartered Surveyors: The Growth of a Profession.* London: Routledge & Kegan Paul, 1968.
Turbayne, Colin M., ed. *Berkeley: Critical and Interpretive Essays.* Manchester, EN: Manchester University Press, 1982.
Urbach, Peter. *Sir Francis Bacon's Philosophy of Science.* La Salle, IL: Open Court, 1987.
Ussher, James. *The Annals of the World.* London: E. Tyler, 1658.
———. *The Later Part of the Annals.* London: E. Tyler, 1658.
*Vilquin, E. "Vauban Inventeur des Recensements." *Annales de Démographie Historique* (1975): 207–257.
Voltaire, F.M.A. *The Elements of Sir Isaac Newton's Philosophy,* tr. John Hanna. New York: Classics of Science, 1995; original edition 1738.
———. *Philosophical Letters,* tr. Ernest Dilworth. New York: Dover, 2003.
Wagner, Anthony Richard, Richmond Herald. *The Records and Collections of the College of Arms.* London: Burkes Peerage, 1952.
Webster, Charles. *From Paracelsus to Newton: Magic and the Making of Modern Science.* New York: Barnes & Noble, 1996.
*———. *The Great Instauration: Science Medicine and Reform 1626–1660.* London: Duckworth, 1975.

*Whatman, Susanna. *The Housekeeping Book.* London: National Trust, 2000.
White, Michael. *Isaac Newton: The Last Sorcerer.* Reading, MA: Helix, 1997.
Willmoth, Frances. *Sir Jonas Moore: Practical Mathematics and Restoration Science.* Woodbridge, EN: Boydell, 1993.
Woolf, D. R. *The Idea of History in Early Stuart England.* Toronto: University of Toronto Press, 1990.
*Wrigley, E. A., ed. *English Historical Demography.* London: Weidenfeld & Nicoloson, 1966.
*Wrigley, E. A., R. S. Davies, J. E. Oeppen, and R. S. Schofield. *English Population History from Family Reconstitution 1590–1837.* Cambridge, EN: Cambridge University Press, 1997.

# Index


Abacus, 42, 43, 45, 69
Addison, Joseph, 38
Algebra, 80–81; King and, 70
*The Ambassadors* (Holbein), 43–44
Annuities, statistics and, 24–25
Arabic numerals, 42, 45, 46
Arbuthnot, John, 23–24, 60, 61, 62, 65
*Arithmetic for Merchants*, 44
*Ars Conjectandi* (Bernoulli), 25
Ashburnham, Sir Denny, 56
Aubrey, John, 41, 80–81
Autobiography of King, 15, 20; change of loyalty and, 18; text of, 97–111

Bacon, Francis, 22, 29, 35, 53, 78–79; common law and, 31–32; controversy about, 76–77; conversational circles and, 49–50; empiricism and, 30–32; probability and, 75–76
Bacon, Sir Nicholas, 32
Barbon, Nicholas, 33
Barrow, Isaac, 43
Baxandall, Michael, 57
Berkeley, Bishop George, 81–82, 94
Bernoulli, Jacob, 7–8, 25, 28, 81, 94
Bernoulli, Johann (Jean), 25, 81, 94
Bernoulli, Nicholas, 25, 81, 94
Biagioli, Mario, 3
*Bibliothèque Angloise*, 59
Bills of mortality, 24, 32, 78
Biography of King (Chalmers), text of, 161–68
Bounty. *See* Queen Anne's Bounty
Brewer, John, 12
*Britannia* (Camden), 87
Brooks, Colin, 11
Buchanan, Pat, 9–10
Burnet, Thomas, 38–39, 41

Calculus, 43
*Caledonia* (Chalmers), 87–88
Calverd, Felix, 56
Camden, William, 87
Cardano, Gerolamo, 42–43
Catholicism, declarations of indulgence and, 15–16
Cauchy, Louis-Augustin, 81
Chalmers, George, 2, 19, 20, 26, 57, 75; as antiquarian, 87–88; biography of King, 161–68; political arithmetic and, 83–90
Chalmers' *Estimate*, 88
Chamberlayne, John, 59–60, 61–66, 73
Chance. *See* Probability

Cheyne, George, 33–34
Churchill, John, 51
Church of England: declarations of indulgence and, 15–16; Queen Anne's Bounty and, 61–66
Cocker, Edward, 44
College of Arms, 16–17, 18, 19, 20, 52
Collins, Randall, 49–50, 51, 52
Common law: equity and, 29, 31–32; probability and, 27, 58
Convention: higher mathematics as, 6; mathematical constructs as, 82; shop arithmetic as, 12–13, 26, 41–42
Conversation, as term, 51
Conversible (Hume), 52–53, 57, 59, 65, 89
Cooper, Thomas, 84
Copernicus, 77
Cromwell, Thomas, 32
Cuthbertson, Elona, 73

Danby, Lord, 19
Davenant, Charles, 2, 9, 19, 22, 31, 45, 46–47, 62, 63; conversational circle and, 53–55; death of, 83; on King, 21, 37; King's Law and, 1, 59, 95
D'Avenant, Sir William, 53, 55
*Death of the West* (Buchanan), 9–10
Decimal fractions, King and, 56, 72–73
Declarations of indulgence (James II), 15–16
Dedekind, Richard, 81
Dee, John, 44, 46
*De Humani Corporis Fabrica* (Vesalius), 30
Demographic prediction: difficulty of, 5–6, 8–9, 10, 13; limitations of, 5–6
Demography, King's change from heraldry to, 13, 18–19, 21–22
Descartes, Réne, 43, 81
Determinism, 8, 10, 76, 11-12; collapse of, 8; Hobbes and, 79–80; laws of nature and, 7; statistics and, 7
"Difference of the difference," 72
*Discourses on the Publick Revenues and of the Trade of England* (Davenant), 53
*Domesday Book*, 1
Doubling (population), 71–72, 74, 95
Dr. Johnson Birthplace Museum, 61, 65
Dugdale, Sir William, 22; as antiquarian, 46, 87; King's heraldry and, 18, 19, 20

Edgeworth, F. Y., 75, 76
*Elements of Geometry* (Euclid), 41, 44
Elton, G. R., 31–32
Empiricism: Galileo and, 93; Hobbes and, 80; King and, 34, 38, 45, 71, 95, 96; medicine and, 29, 30–31; statistics and, 23–24
Epistemology, 79, 81
Equity, common law and, 29, 31–32
*Essay on the East India Trade* (Davenant), 54
*Essay upon Ways and Means of Supplying the War* (Davenant), 54
*Essays upon the Ballance of Power* (Davenant), 53–54
*An Estimate of the Comparative Strength of Great Britain* (Chalmers), 88
Euclid, 41, 44, 80
Euler, Leonhard, 81
Everard, Thomas, 56–57

Fermat, Pierre de, 7, 43
Fielding, Henry, 49, 51, 53
Fisher, Sir Ronald, 8, 75, 76, 79
Flood (Biblical account), population chronology and, 37–41, 45, 65, 70–71
Free trade, 85–86
Friend, John, 56

Galen of Pergamum, 28–30, 39
Galileo, 12, 77, 78; algebra and, 81; empiricism and, 93–94; geometry and, 43
*Galileo Courtier* (Biagioli), 3
Gambling. *See* Probability
Games of chance. *See* Probability
George III, 85
Gilbert, William, 78
Glass, David V., 2, 3–4, 11, 58, 67–68, 69, 73, 74, 92, 95
Godolphin, Sidney, 51
Graunt, John, 28, 35, 94; bills of

mortality and, 24, 32, 83; empiricism and, 23–24; influence of, 25; probability and, 76; shop arithmetic and, 12–13, 25–26

Hacking, Ian, 12, 27, 28, 30, 35
Halley, Edmund: life insurance and, 25
Hamper, William, 20
Harley, Robert, 19, 22, 50–51, 52, 58, 69, 70; fall of, 85; Queen Anne's Bounty and, 62, 63, 65–66; shop arithmetic and, 32–33
Harrington, James, 35–36
Harvey, William, 30, 78
Hearth data, 67–68
Heraldry, King's change to demography from, 13, 18–19, 21–22
Higher mathematics, 12, 41–42; as convention, 6; mysticism and, 34, 38, 40, 43, 70, 93
*History of the Coronation of James II and of His Royal Consort Queen Mary*, 17, 20
Hobbes, Thomas, 12, 41, 57, 76, 79–81
Holbein, Hans (the younger), 43–44
Holmes, Geoffrey, 2–3, 10–11, 13, 66, 92
Hooke, Robert, 41
Horneby, Nathaniel, 56
Hoskins (Hoskyns), Sir John, 41
Hume, David, 49, 51, 52–53, 83, 89
Huntington, Robert, 56
Husbands, Chris, 68
Huygens, Christiaan, annuities and, 25

*Introduction to Arithmetic* (Nichomachus), 42
*Itinerary in England and Wales* (Leland), 87

James II, 20; declarations of indulgence and, 15–16; King's change of loyalty and, 13, 15, 17, 18; King's heraldry and, 16–17
Jenkinson, Charles, 85, 86
Jevons, W. S., 9, 75, 76, 84, 92
Jones, P. E., 2, 3–4, 11, 67–68, 69, 74, 92, 95
*Journal to Stella* (Swift), 51
Judges, A. V., 2, 3–4, 11, 67–68, 69, 74, 92, 95

"Kashnor" manuscript, 57–58
Keilman, Nico, 5–6
Kepler, Johannes, 12, 43, 93
King-Davenant Law. *See* King's Law
King's 1696 estimates: political influence on King and, 3–4; scholarly debate about, 2–4, 10–11; value of, 95
King's Law, 1, 49, 54, 58–59, 75, 84, 92–93, 94–96
Kolmogorov, A. N., 8

Lagrange, Joseph-Louis, 81
Laplace, Marquis de, 81
Laslett, Peter, 2–3, 11, 49, 69, 92
Law of Demand. *See* King's Law
Law of King (Law of Demand). *See* King's Law
Law of Large Numbers, 7
Laws of nature, attempts to systemetize, 9. *See also* Determinism
Learned (Hume), 52–53, 57, 59, 65, 89
Leibniz, G. W., 25, 43, 81
Leland, John, 87
*Leviathan* (Hobbes), 81
Life insurance, statistics and, 24–25
Lutz, Wolfgang, 5, 6
Lyell, Sir Charles, 41

Martin, Julian, 31
Marx, Karl, 54
Mary II, 16, 38, 62; King's change of loyalty and, 15, 17, 18
Massie, Joseph, 84
Mathematical probability. *See* Probability
Mead, Richard, 23, 28, 29, 30, 39
Medicine, statistics and, 28–32
Mercantilism, 85–86
Monmouth's rebellion, 18
Mysticism: higher mathematics and, 34, 38, 40, 43, 70, 93; shop arithmetic and, 44–46

Napier, John, 72–73
*Natural and Political Observations and Conclusions on the State and Condition of England* (King), 10, 19, 61; text of, 125–55. *See also* King's 1696 estimates
*Nature* (journal), population predictions and, 5–6, 9, 91–92
Naval trade: King on, 113–24
*New Atlantis* (Bacon), 53, 79
Newton, Sir Isaac, 9, 11, 33–34, 39–40, 43, 81
Newtonianism, 33–34
Nichomachus of Gerasa, 42
*Novum Organum* (Bacon), 31

*Oceana* (Harrington), 34–35
Ogilby, John, 41
Old Whigs, 54
*Opticks* (Leibniz), 43

Paracelsus, 29, 30
Parry, Francis, 56
Pascal, Blaise, 7, 43, 79, 81
Pearson, Karl, 8
Petty, Sir William, 10, 22, 35, 53, 94; political anatomy and, 24; political arithmetic and, 31; probability and, 76; shop arithmetic and, 12–13, 25–26, 28
Physics, laws of nature and, 9
Polemic, demographic prediction and, 9–10, 11, 13
Political anatomy (Petty), 24
Political arithmetic, 8, 53, 62, 75; decline of, 83–90; Petty and, 24, 31; as term, 24, 82, 84, 89
Political influence: of King, 32; King's 1696 estimates and, 3, 10–11, 19
Political motivation, of King, 16, 17–18
Politics, demographic prediction and, 6
Polo, Marco, 34, 41
Popkin, Richard, 45
Population estimates (King). *See* King's 1696 estimates
Porter, Roy, 2, 91–92, 95
Price, Richard, 84
Prideaux, John, 46
*Principia Mathematica* (Leibniz), 43
Probability, 1–2, 75–76; common law and, 27, 58; as a discipline, 90; empiricism and, 24; games of chance and, 7; history of, 8, 11–12; human behavior and, 8–9; improved system of, 8; limitations of, 6, 11, 90, 93
Projects: conversational circles and, 49, 50, 51; Dugdale's influence on King and, 20–21; as term, 21

Queen Anne's Bounty, 2, 19, 59, 60, 61–66, 73, 89; King's letter about, 157–60
*Queries in Order to the Description of Britannia*, 41

Rank and status: as criteria for truth, 27–28
Record, Robert, 44–45, 46, 53, 70
Revolution of 1688, 16, 18
Royal Society, 41, 49–50, 59
*The Royal Tenth* (Vauban), 34

*Sacred Theory of the Earth* (Burnet), 38–39
Salsburg, David, 6–8, 9, 10, 11
Sampling, 73, 94
Sanderson, Warren, 5
Sandford, Francis, 17
Scaliger, Joseph, 45, 69
Scherbov, Sergei, 5
Scientific Revolution, 27
Shapin, Steven, 12, 27–28, 96
Shapiro, Barbara, 27–28
Shop arithmetic, 31; abacus and, 42, 43, 45; approximate accuracy and, 55–56, 58; Arabic numerals and, 42, 46; as convention, 12–13, 26, 41–42; exclusivity and, 53; King's upbringing and, 19, 22; King's use of, 34, 38, 95; mysticism and, 44–46; Queen Anne's Bounty and, 56; social analysis and, 32–33, 78
Sinclair, Sir John, 26, 75, 84, 88–89
Slide rule, 56–57, 73
Smith, Adam, 83, 84, 86

Social status, as criterion for truth, 27–28
Spufford, Margaret, 13, 19
Stalker, Peter, 8–9
*The Starry Messenger* (Galileo), 78, 93, 95
Statistics, as term, 1, 26, 88–89
Status and rank, as criteria for truth, 27–28
*Stereometry* (Everard), 56, 57
Stigler, Stephen M., 6–7, 10, 11, 23–24
Stone, Lawrence, 51
Strong, William, 56
Supply and demand, 1, 93. *See also* King's Law
Surveying, 58; King's upbringing and, 19, 33; Vauban and, 34
Swift, Jonathan, 21, 51–52, 60

Telesio, Bernadino, 77, 78
Torricelli, Evangelista, 81
*Treviso Arithmetic*, 43
*True Picture of a Modern Whig* (Davenant), 55
*Two New Sciences* (Galileo), 78

Ussher, Archbishop James, 34, 37–41, 45, 46, 65, 69–72, 76

Vanbrugh, Sir John, 16
Vauban, Sébastien de, 33, 34, 58
Vesalius, Andreas, 30, 77, 78
Voltaire, 9

Wall, Richard, 68–69, 73
Wealth estimates (King). *See* King's 1696 estimates
Weierstrass, Karl, 81
Willey, Basil, 38, 40
William (prince of Orange). *See* William III
William III, 16, 20, 38, 62; King's change of loyalty and, 13, 15, 17, 18
Witt, Richard, 44
Woodward, John, 23, 28, 29, 30; the Flood and, 35, 39
Wren, Christopher, 41

Young, Arthur, 84
Young, G. M., 49, 57
Yung, K. K., 61

Zero, 42, 43, 46

**About the Author**

JOHN A. TAYLOR is Professor of History at Southern Illinois University, Edwardsville. He has also taught in Japan and Russia as a Fulbright scholar. Among his other books are *British Monarchy, English Church Establishment, and Civil Liberty* (Greenwood, 1996) and *Diana, Self-Interest, and British National Identity* (Praeger, 2000).

## Recent Titles in Contributions to the Study of World History

One King, One Law, Three Faiths: Religion and the Rise of Absolutism and Seventeenth-Century Metz
*Patricia Behre Miskimin*

South Sea Maidens: Western Fantasy and Sexual Politics in the South Pacific
*Michael Sturma*

A History of the French Anarchist Movement, 1917–1045
*David Berry*

Security and Progress: Lord Salisbury at the India Office
*Paul R. Brumpton*

Exploring Nationalisms of China: Themes and Conflicts
*C. X. George Wei and Xiaoyuan Liu, editors*

Tolerance, Suspicion, and Hostility: Changing U.S. Attitudes Towards the Japanese Communist Movement, 1944–1947
*Henry Oinas-Kukkonen*

Churchill's Guests: Britain and the Belgian Exiles during World War II
*Robert W. Allen*

Securing American Independence: John Jay and the French Alliance
*Frank W. Brecher*

The Oder-Neisse Line: The United States, Poland, and Germany in the Cold War
*Debra J. Allen*

The Last Word? Essays on Official History in the United States and British Commonwealth
*Jeffrey Grey, editor*

Defending the West: The Truman-Churchill Correspondence, 1945–1960
*Edited with an Introduction by G. W. Sand*

U.S. Development Aid: Achievements in and Failures in the Twentieth Century
*Samuel Hale Butterfield*

www.ingramcontent.com/pod-product-compliance
Ingram Content Group UK Ltd.
Pitfield, Milton Keynes, MK11 3LW, UK
UKHW020817290926
15470UKWH00003B/1205

9 780313 313066